access to history

Politics, Presidency and Society in the USA 1968–2001

Vivienne Sanders

This high-quality material is endorsed by Edexcel and has been through a rigorous quality assurance programme to ensure that it is a suitable companion to the specification for both learners and teachers. This does not mean that its contents will be used verbatim when setting examinations nor is it to be read as being the official specification – a copy of which is available at www.edexcel.org.uk.

Study guides revised and updated, 2008, by Angela Leonard (Edexcel).

The Publishers would like to thank the following for permission to reproduce copyright illustrations: AP Photo/PA Photo, page 182; Associated Press, pages 165, 168, 169, 203, 216, 218, 220; © Bettman/CORBIS, pages 6, 16, 37, 51, 97, 98; © Corbis, pages 22, 44, 56; FilmMagic, page 219; George Bush Presidential Library and Museum, page 148 (bottom); Getty Images, pages 41, 121; © David Hume Kennerly/Gerald R. Ford Library/Corbis, page 67; © Wally McNamee/CORBIS, pages 78, 139, 159; © The New Yorker Collection 2004 Mick Stevens from cartoonbank.com. All Rights Reserved, page 209 (top); © Reuters/CORBIS, page 175; © Soqui Ted/CORBIS SYGMA, page 212; Time & Life Pictures/Getty Images, pages 4, 12, 63, 134, 148 (top).

The Publishers would like to acknowledge use of the following extracts: Oxford University Press Inc, USA for an extract from *Restless Giant: The United States from Watergate to Bush Vs. Gore* by James T. Patterson, 2005.

Every effort has been made to trace all copyright holders, but if any have been inadvertently overlooked the Publishers will be pleased to make the necessary arrangements at the first opportunity.

Although every effort has been made to ensure that website addresses are correct at time of going to press, Hodder Education cannot be held responsible for the content of any website mentioned in this book. It is sometimes possible to find a relocated web page by typing in the address of the home page for a website in the URL window of your browser.

Hachette Livre UK's policy is to use papers that are natural, renewable and recyclable products and made from wood grown in sustainable forests. The logging and manufacturing processes are expected to conform to the environmental regulations of the country of origin.

Orders: please contact Bookpoint Ltd, 130 Milton Park, Abingdon, Oxon OX14 4SB. Telephone: (44) 01235 827720. Fax: (44) 01235 400454. Lines are open 9.00–5.00, Monday to Saturday, with a 24-hour message answering service. Visit our website at www.hoddereducation.co.uk

Cover photo © Wally McNamee/Corbis
Typeset in 10/12pt Baskerville by Gray Publishing, Tunbridge Wells, Kent
Printed in Malta

A catalogue record for this title is available from the British Library.

ISBN: 978 0340 965 986

Contents

Dedication   v

Chapter 1 The State of the Union in 1968   1
  1 The Significance of 1968   1
  2 The Tet Offensive and the Vietnam War (January–February 1968)   2
  3 Martin Luther King and Black Americans, April 1968   3
  4 Bobby Kennedy and America's Poor, May–June 1968   5
  5 The Democratic National Convention in Chicago and Students, August 1968   9
  6 The Miss America Pageant and Women, September 1968   13
  7 The November 1968 Presidential Election and Middle America   15

Chapter 2 President Nixon 1969–74   20
  1 Richard Nixon's Background   21
  2 Nixon's Election as President in 1968   25
  3 Getting Re-elected in 1972   34
  4 The Watergate Scandal   47
  5 The Results and Significance of Watergate   57
  Study Guide   65

Chapter 3 Presidents Ford (1974–7) and Carter (1977–81)   66
  1 Gerald Ford – Background   66
  2 Gerald Ford – The Half-a-Term President   69
  3 Jimmy Carter – Background   77
  4 Why did President Carter Fail to Get Re-elected?   80
  5 The New Right   93
  Study Guide   95

Chapter 4 President Reagan 1981–9   96
  1 Preparation for the Presidency   96
  2 The 'Imperilled Presidency'?   104
  3 Reagan's First Term: Aims, Methods and Achievements   106
  4 Reagan's Re-election in 1984   113
  5 Reagan's Second Term   114
  6 An 'Amiable Dunce'?   123
  7 The Reagan Legacy   126
  Study Guide   137

Chapter 5 President George H.W. Bush 1989–93   138

1 Background   138
2 Comparing Bush with Reagan   141
3 'The Vision Thing' – Education and the Environment   143
4 Bush vs Congress   145
5 Social Themes: The New Right, The Supreme Court, Sex, Drugs and Race   146
6 Foreign Policy   150
7 The 1992 Election   152
8 Bush – The Verdict   155
9 American Society in the 1980s   156
Study Guide   157

Chapter 6 President Clinton 1993–2001   158

1 Bill Clinton – Background   159
2 The 1992 Presidential Election   161
3 President Clinton's First Term   163
4 Republican Opposition and Extremism   171
5 The 1996 Presidential Election   180
6 The Monica Lewinsky Affair   181
7 Foreign Policy   188
8 Clinton's Presidency – Conclusions   189
Study Guide   195

Chapter 7 Sport and American Society   196

1 Sport Reflecting the 'American Way'   196
2 Sport and Race Relations   199
3 Women and Sport   202
4 What Affects Sport? The Olympics and the Cold War   205
5 AIDS and the Gay Community   206
Study Guide   207

Chapter 8 The State of the Union in 2000   208

1 Multicultural America in 2000   208
2 Women in 2000   214
3 'One Nation, Two Cultures'?   215
4 The US Economy in 2000   220
5 Politics in 2000   221
6 The Thematic Approach to 1968–2001   222
Study Guide   223

Glossary   224

Index   232

Dedication

Keith Randell (1943–2002)

The *Access to History* series was conceived and developed by Keith, who created a series to 'cater for students as they are, not as we might wish them to be'. He leaves a living legacy of a series that for over 20 years has provided a trusted, stimulating and well-loved accompaniment to post-16 study. Our aim with these new editions is to continue to offer students the best possible support for their studies.

1

The State of the Union in 1968

POINTS TO CONSIDER

This introductory chapter aims to show the preoccupations and characteristics of the United States in 1968 through studying the significance of several events in that year:

- The Tet Offensive demonstrates the impact of the Vietnam War on US politics
- The presidential election campaign and the assassinations of Martin Luther King and Bobby Kennedy show concern about race, poverty and disorder
- The Miss America Pageant illustrates feminism

Key dates

1968	January–February	Communists' Tet Offensive in Vietnam
	March	President Johnson said he would not stand for re-election
	April	Martin Luther King assassinated
	June	Bobby Kennedy assassinated
	August	Democratic National Convention in Chicago
	September	Miss America Pageant disrupted
	November	Nixon beat Humphrey in the presidential election

Key question
How and why was the year 1968 significant?

1 | The Significance of 1968

Rarely in American history does a presidential election year [1968] coincide with the cresting of such powerful social forces. In a bewildering array of successive crises, each magnified by the overwhelming power of the mass media ... all of the conflicts that had emerged out of the postwar years surfaced and came before the American people for a decision. The ultimate consequence was defeat for those who sought a new society based on peace, equality and social justice; victory for those who rallied in defence of the **status quo**.

Key term

Status quo
The current state of affairs.

Thus did historian William Chafe sum up the significance of the year 1968 in American history. Chafe depicted a society that contemporaries thought was coming apart. What were the 'successive crises' and what 'tensions' do they illuminate?

- The Tet Offensive (January–February 1968) illuminated the tensions relating to the Vietnam War.
- The death of Martin Luther King (April 1968) reflected racial tensions.
- The triumph and tragedy of Robert Kennedy (May–June 1968) highlighted the tensions between rich and poor and the use of violence as a form of political discourse.
- The Democratic National Convention at Chicago (August 1968) demonstrated the tensions between students, politicians and Middle America.
- The disruption of the Miss America Pageant (September 1968) illustrated the tensions between **feminists** and traditionalists.
- The presidential election triumph of Richard Nixon (November 1968) reflected the tensions between 'those who rallied in defence of the status quo' and those who protested against it and sought change.

Key terms

Feminists
Advocates of equal political, social, economic and legal rights for women.

Cold War
The struggle between the capitalist USA and the Communist Soviet Union, c1947–89.

Summary diagram: The significance of 1968

Crises in 1968
- Tet Offensive
- Death of King
- Death of Bobby Kennedy
- Democrats in Chicago
- Miss America
- Election of Nixon

Tensions illuminated
- Vietnam War issues
- Racial tensions
- Class and political tensions
- Young vs old
- Feminists vs traditionalists
- Conservation vs change

---

2 | The Tet Offensive and the Vietnam War (January–February 1968)

(a) The main event – the Tet Offensive

The year began calmly enough, until on 30 January 1968 the Vietnamese Communists launched a great offensive in South Vietnam. Sixty million Americans watching TV in the evenings saw US troops and their South Vietnamese allies struggle to clear Communists out of the South Vietnamese capital, Saigon, and even out of the US embassy itself.

(b) The background to the Tet Offensive

The **Cold War** had led Presidents Truman (1945–53), Eisenhower (1953–61), Kennedy (1961–3) and Johnson (1963–9) to try to prevent **Ho Chi Minh**'s Communists from taking over the whole of Vietnam. Eisenhower had established an anti-Communist South Vietnamese state, to which Kennedy and Johnson had given ever-increasing aid. In 1965 Johnson sent in American ground troops. By January 1968, half a million

Key question
What was the significance of the Tet Offensive?

Key date
Communists' Tet Offensive in Vietnam: January–February 1968

Key figure
Ho Chi Minh (1890–1965)
Vietnamese Communist who led the successful struggle against France (1945–56) and the USA (1956–69).

Key date

President Johnson said he would not stand for re-election: March 1968

Key terms

NLF
Vietnamese Communist National Liberation Front.

Primary
Before a presidential election, the Democrats and Republicans hold a kind of competition or mini-election in every state. In this competition, which is mostly called a primary, they decide which candidate they would like to represent their party in the election.

US soldiers in Vietnam were trying, but failing, to stop Communist North Vietnam and its many supporters in South Vietnam from destroying that unpopular South Vietnamese state.

(c) The significance of the Tet Offensive

When the US media showed Communists in the grounds of the US embassy in South Vietnam's capital, Saigon, many Americans believed that it exposed the American failure in Vietnam, demonstrating the 'credibility gap' between the Johnson administration's claim that the USA was winning the war in Vietnam and what was actually happening there.

On 31 March, Johnson declared that he would not seek the Democratic Party's nomination for the presidential election in November 1968, but would seek peace instead. Tet had made it clear that the United States would have to de-escalate in Vietnam, and had taken President Johnson out of the 1968 presidential election race.

Johnson's exit from the race opened the way for a struggle within the Democratic Party. Hundreds of college students stopped chanting 'Ho, Ho, Ho Chi Minh, the **NLF** is gonna win'. Instead, they said 'be clean for Gene', shaved off their beards, swapped their jeans for suits and ties, and campaigned for Minnesota Senator Eugene McCarthy's anti-war bid for the Democratic nomination. McCarthy won a resounding victory in the New Hampshire **primary**.

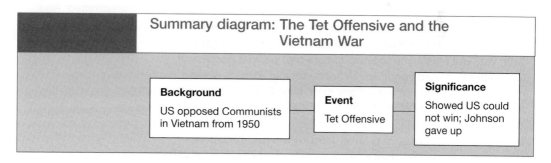

Summary diagram: The Tet Offensive and the Vietnam War

Background
US opposed Communists in Vietnam from 1950

Event
Tet Offensive

Significance
Showed US could not win; Johnson gave up

Key question
What was the significance of the assassination of Martin Luther King?

Key term

Civil rights movement
The predominantly black movement for equal rights for African Americans, c1956–c68.

3 | Martin Luther King and Black Americans, April 1968

(a) The main event – the assassination of Martin Luther King

In March 1968 black garbage workers who were on strike had invited civil rights leader Martin Luther King to Memphis, Tennessee, to help them in their campaign for equal pay. In Memphis for several days, King was disturbed by the black violence there. In a speech on the evening of 3 April, he reviewed the triumphs of the **civil rights movement**, then prophetically said:

Martin Luther King lies dying on the balcony of the Lorraine Motel, Memphis, Tennessee. The people are pointing to the direction of the shot. What reasons might Martin Luther King have had for choosing to stay in this cheap motel while in Memphis?

Like anybody, I would like to live a long life. Longevity has its place. But I'm not concerned about that now. I just wanted to do God's will. And he's allowed me to go up to the mountain top. And I've looked over. And I've seen the Promised Land. I may not get there with you. But I want you to know tonight that we as a people will get to the Promised Land. So I'm happy tonight. I'm not worried about anything. I'm not fearing any man. Mine Eyes Have Seen the Glory of the Coming of the Lord!

> **Key date**
>
> Martin Luther King assassinated: April 1968

The next morning King was shot dead by a white racist. His assassination provoked major black riots in 100 cities, in which 46 people died, 3000 were injured and 27,000 were arrested. It took 21,000 federal troops and 34,000 National Guardsmen to restore order after $45 million worth of damage to property.

(b) The background to King's assassination and the riots

(i) What had King achieved before 1968?

Martin Luther King was the generally acknowledged leader of the civil rights movement, which had helped bring about the demise of *de jure* **segregation** in the South through the 1964 Civil Rights Act and the 1965 Voting Rights Act. After he had helped bring about this revolutionary legislation, he had turned his attention to the problems in the Northern black ghettos. King's Chicago ghetto campaign in 1966 demonstrated that *de facto* **segregation**

> **Key terms**
>
> *De jure* **segregation**
> The segregation of blacks and whites in public places by law.
>
> *De facto* **segregation**
> The segregation of blacks and whites in residential areas and some other public places in practice if not in law.

in the North, which helped keep ghettos dwellers in poor housing, poor schools and poverty, was going to be even harder to end than the legal segregation in the South.

(ii) Black divisions in 1968

By 1968, blacks were divided between those (mostly middle class and Southerners) who still followed King and his dream of integration into white America and those (mostly Northern ghetto dwellers or rural poor) who were disillusioned with white America and keen to remain separate from it. Most of the separatists were advocates of ill-defined '**black power**'. Both pro- and anti-integrationist blacks talked of black power in terms of greater economic, political and social equality, but separatists also dreamed of an international working-class revolution, or a separate state for blacks in the United States. Separatists sometimes deemed violence to be the most effective way to demonstrate their discontent. After all, as black radical H. Rap Brown claimed, 'Violence is as American as apple pie'. America's black ghettos first erupted in 1964. By 1968, summer ghetto riots were an annual occurrence.

Key term

Black power
A vaguely defined black movement with aims including separatism, and greater economic, political, social and legal equality for African Americans.

(c) The significance of the assassination of King and the riots

The events in Memphis demonstrated black divisions and white racism, while the assassination itself and the subsequent riots suggested that the United States was a racially divided society in which political dialogue had been replaced by acts of violence.

Summary diagram: Martin Luther King and black Americans

Background	Events	Significance
King led high-profile campaigns for racial equality from 1956	King's assassination (by a white racist) led to black urban riots	Showed racial hatred and violent nature of US society

---

Key question
What was the significance of the assassination of Bobby Kennedy?

4 | Bobby Kennedy and America's Poor, May–June 1968

(a) The main event – the assassination of Bobby Kennedy

In spring 1968, with the incumbent President out of the race, the two leading candidates for the Democratic Party's nomination for the presidency were Eugene McCarthy and Robert (Bobby) Kennedy. Kennedy narrowly won the crucial California primary, but was then assassinated by a loner who did not agree with Kennedy's position on the Middle East. On the airplane that carried Kennedy's coffin back East, there were three women widowed by an assassin's bullet in 1960s America: Bobby

Key date

Bobby Kennedy assassinated: June 1968

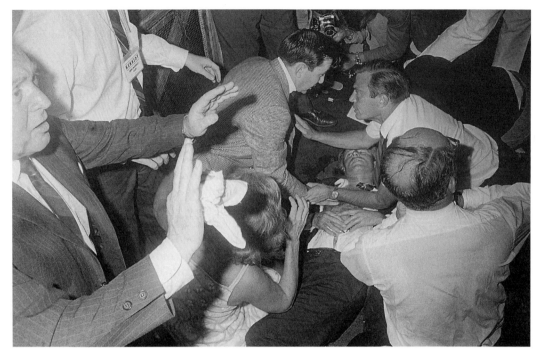

Bobby Kennedy lies dying on the floor of a Los Angeles hotel after winning the California primary. What do the assassinations of Bobby Kennedy and Martin Luther King suggest about American society and politics in 1968?

Kennedy's widow Ethel Kennedy, his brother John's widow Jackie Kennedy, and Martin Luther King's widow Coretta Scott King.

(b) Background to the triumph and tragedy of Bobby Kennedy
(i) The Kennedy family
Bobby Kennedy came from a wealthy Boston Irish American family. When Bobby's elder brother John was elected President, Bobby was given a post in his cabinet. After President John Kennedy was assassinated in November 1963, Bobby stood for election to the Senate.

(ii) Bobby Kennedy's empathy for the less privileged
Bobby Kennedy was changed by his brother's death. After the assassination he developed what the less privileged perceived to be a unique empathy with them and their suffering. 'You know', said Kenneth Clark, a black leader, 'it is possible for human beings to grow. This man had grown.' People tried to explain why they liked him. After Kennedy's support of the striking **Chicano** farmworkers in California, their leader, Cesar Chavez, was impressed:

> Robert didn't come to us and tell us what was good for us. He came to us and asked two questions ... 'What do you want? And how can I help?' That's why we loved him ... He was able to see things through the eyes of the poor ... It was like he was ours.

Chicano
Chicanos (also known as Latinos or Hispanic Americans) were citizens or residents of the USA. Usually Spanish speaking, they (or their ancestors) were immigrants from Latin American countries such as Mexico.

Key term

Key terms

Native American reservations
Native Americans were residents of the USA whose ancestors had inhabited the continent before the arrival of white Europeans. Whites had confined Native Americans to lands called reservations.

'Great Society'
President Johnson said he wanted to create a US society free from the racism and poverty which were particularly prevalent in the urban ghettos.

When Kennedy investigated the appalling poverty on **Native American reservations** in Oklahoma and New York State, Native Americans were similarly impressed:

> Loving a public official for an Indian is almost unheard of, but we trusted him ... We had faith in him ... Spiritually he was an Indian!

A black activist echoed that:

> He did things that I wouldn't do. He went into the dirtiest, filthiest, poorest black homes ... and he would sit with the baby who had wet open sores and whose belly was bloated from malnutrition, and he would sit and touch and hold those babies ... I wouldn't do that! I didn't do that! But he did ... That's why I am for him.

Kennedy declared that 'today in America we are two worlds', the prosperous white world and the 'dark and hopeless place' in which the non-whites lived. He felt that Johnson was so preoccupied with the Vietnam War that he had forgotten his dreams of building a **'Great Society'** in America and was 'through with the domestic problems, with the cities'.

(iii) Bobby Kennedy running for the presidency

In November 1967 a friend urged Kennedy to run for the presidency because of the 'moral imperative of stopping the war by dislodging Johnson'. Despite having turned publicly against the Vietnam War in May 1965, Kennedy refused, fearing that it would split the Democratic Party and that he would be accused of conducting a personal vendetta against President Johnson:

> I would have a problem if I ran first against Johnson. People would say that I was splitting the party out of ambition and envy. No one would believe I was doing it because of how I felt about Vietnam and the poor people ... I think someone else would have to be the first to run.

The *New York Post* publisher advised him against it: 'Who is for you? ... The young, the minorities, the Negroes, the Puerto Ricans.' This did not seem enough, until Tet and McCarthy's victory in New Hampshire showed how vulnerable President Johnson was. Kennedy's friend, Arthur Schlesinger Jr, said if Bobby ran he would be criticised as 'a Johnny-come-lately trying to cash in after brave Eugene McCarthy had done the real fighting'. Schlesinger advised him to endorse McCarthy instead, but Bobby said, 'I can't do that. It would be too humiliating ... Kennedys don't act that way.' On 16 March 1968, Bobby Kennedy declared his candidacy:

> I run to seek new policies, policies to end the bloodshed in Vietnam and in our cities, policies to close the gap that now exists between black and white, between rich and poor, between young and old in this country.

Two weeks later, President Johnson announced that he was 'taking the first step to de-escalate the conflict in Vietnam' and that he would not stand for re-election. Johnson said later, his 'biggest worry' was not Vietnam but 'divisiveness and pessimism' in the USA.

(iv) Bobby Kennedy and the 'sickness' in America's soul

So, by the end of March 1968, there were three American figures who seemed likely to make the USA a more equal and caring society: presidential candidates Eugene McCarthy and Bobby Kennedy, and black leader Martin Luther King. However, on 4 April, Bobby Kennedy had to announce to a black ghetto audience that King had been assassinated. In a moving speech, Kennedy reminded them that he too had lost someone that he loved, that his brother had been killed – by a white man. He asked them not to blame all whites, and the next day he spoke about what was wrong with American society:

> We calmly accept newspaper reports of civilians slaughtered in far off lands. We glorify killing on movie and TV screens and call it entertainment … [But even that violence is not as bad as] the violence that afflicts the poor, that poisons relations between men because their skin has different colours. This is the slow destruction of a child by hunger … Violence breeds violence … only a cleansing of our whole society can remove this sickness from our soul.

(v) Kennedy vs McCarthy in the primaries

While Kennedy appealed more to the poor of all colours, his rival for the Democratic nomination, Eugene McCarthy, appealed more to the middle class. Kennedy won the Indiana primary, in a state full of factory workers and ghettos. He then took Nebraska, but white, middle-class Oregon went to McCarthy. 'There is nothing for me to get hold of' in affluent Oregon, said Kennedy. 'Let's face it, I appeal best to people who have problems.' By now the press, once sceptical, was increasingly pro-Kennedy. 'Quite frankly', said the *New York Times*, Bobby Kennedy was 'an easy man to fall in love with'.

(c) The significance of Bobby Kennedy in 1968

The richest nation in the world contained many poor people. Out of a population of around 200 million, 33 million lived below the **poverty line**. As a Democrat, President Johnson had hoped to establish a 'Great Society', in which inequality would be banished, but he was distracted by the Vietnam War. In spring 1968, both Democratic candidates, McCarthy and Kennedy, tried to keep poverty and inequality on the agenda.

Columnist Robert Scheer believed Bobby Kennedy really 'gave a shit about Indians … gave a shit about what was happening to black people', but nevertheless represented 'the illusion of dissent without its substance'. Scheer thought Bobby would have sold out for power. Columnist Joseph Alsop disagreed: 'They think he is

Key figure

Hubert Humphrey (1911–78)
Vice President Humphrey had long been one of the most liberal members of the Democratic Party, but by 1968 he was tainted by his association with the Johnson administration, which had escalated the Vietnam War.

Key term

Poverty line
An amount set by the US government; those whose annual family income is below this are legally defined as 'poor', which is important for federal aid entitlements.

Youth International Party

A radical student group that wanted to show contempt for the political system during the Democratic Party Convention at Chicago in 1968.

cold, calculating, ruthless. Actually he is hot-blooded, romantic, compassionate.' Whoever was right, with Kennedy gone, it was easier for President Johnson to reassert control over the Democratic Party, and to get it to nominate his Vice President **Hubert Humphrey** as the Democratic presidential candidate. Humphrey was too much 'Johnson's boy' to be able to defeat the Republican candidate Richard Nixon.

Bobby Kennedy's death demonstrated the violence that bedevilled American society in politics, probably ended the hopes of the 'Great Society' and helped give the presidency to Nixon.

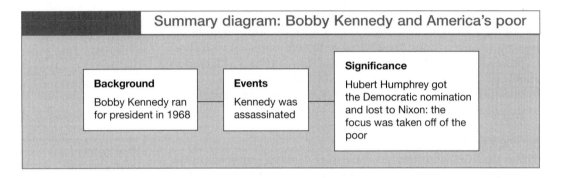

Summary diagram: Bobby Kennedy and America's poor

Background

Bobby Kennedy ran for president in 1968

Events

Kennedy was assassinated

Significance

Hubert Humphrey got the Democratic nomination and lost to Nixon: the focus was taken off of the poor

Key question
What was the significance of the Democratic National Convention in Chicago?

Key date

Democratic National Convention in Chicago: August 1968

Key terms

National Convention
A few weeks before the presidential election the Republicans and Democrats both hold National Conventions in which each party selects or confirms its candidate for the presidency.

Billies
Clubs used by American police.

5 | The Democratic National Convention in Chicago and Students, August 1968

(a) The main event – student riots in Chicago

'I won't vote. Every good man we get they kill', said one New Yorker after the deaths of King and Kennedy. The **Youth International Party** (Yippies) wanted a more ostentatious show of contempt for the American political process. They called on young people to come to Chicago to disrupt the Democratic **National Convention**. They spread rumours that they were going to put the psychedelic drug LSD in the city's water supply.

Chicago's Mayor Daley mobilised around 12,000 police, and banned marches. The Yippies produced a candidate for President, 'Pigasus', a squealing, rotund young pig. Some threw bags of urine at the police, who in turn removed their badges and nameplates and retaliated. 'The cops had one thing on their minds. Club and then gas, club and then gas', said one journalist. A British reporter recorded that:

> The kids screamed and were beaten to the ground by cops who had completely lost their cool ... They were rapped in the genitals by cops swinging **billies**.

Inside the Convention Hall, some thought the Convention should be cancelled. One congressman accused radicals of wanting 'pot instead of patriotism' and 'riots instead of reason'.

(b) Background to the student unrest in Chicago
(i) College unrest

By 1968 nearly half of American youth attended college: a degree was considered essential for a decent job. Student radicalism had first become evident at Berkeley, part of the University of California, in the winter of 1964–5, after the college authorities had tried to restrict the distribution of political literature on campus. The Berkeley protests triggered national student protests against the curriculum, college governments, and college relationships with the **federal government** (especially the Defence Department, and thereby the Vietnam War). With the escalation of the Vietnam War, the students had a single cause upon which to fix their dissatisfaction with their parents' generation and with the ruling élite. One student wrote, 'I have the awful feeling of being a stranger in the land', unable to communicate with those in power without 'immediately' being 'characterised as a confused extremist'.

Students adopted an alternative lifestyle (the **counterculture**) to that of the dominant culture.

(ii) The counterculture

Those students who rejected American society's emphasis upon individualism, competitiveness and materialism, emphasised communal living, harmony and the uniform of faded blue jeans. They listened to music that reaffirmed their beliefs, singing 'We Shall Overcome' with Joan Baez, 'All You Need is Love' with the Beatles, and anti-war songs. While their parents drank alcohol, which was socially acceptable, the students smoked marijuana, which was not. The more extreme exponents of the counterculture, **hippies** graduated from marijuana to stronger drugs such as LSD.

How to spot a hippie
Long hair (male and female)
Colourful, flowery shirts (male)
Beads (male and female)
Bell-bottom trousers (male) or long skirts (female)
No make-up (female)
Burning candles and incense
Eastern religious symbols decorating living quarters
Shopping at army surplus and Salvation Army stores for fatigues (male)
Sandals (male and female)
Peace symbols
Flowers in their hair (female)
Tie-dyed psychedelic T-shirt (female) (bright dyes splashed on knotted white T-shirts, in patterns described as psychedelic)

Key term

Federal government
The USA is a federated state. Individual states such as California and Texas have considerable power (e.g. over transport and education). The national or federal government, based in Washington DC, consists of the President, Congress (which makes laws) and the Supreme Court (which interprets laws).

Key question
What was the counterculture?

Key terms

Counterculture
An alternative lifestyle to the dominant culture; in the case of 1960s' America, the 'drop-out' mentality, as compared to the dominant, materialistic, hard-working culture of the students' parents.

Hippies
Young people (often students) who, in the 1960s, rejected the beliefs and fashions of the older generation, and favoured free love and drugs.

(iii) Hippies

In the mid-1960s, the group of alienated young people moved into the Haight-Ashbury area of San Francisco, where they wore 'alternative' clothes (British 'mod' fashions, granny gowns, Indian kaftans), attended 'happenings', smoked and sold pot, adopted new names (Blue Flash, Coyote, Apache) and grew their hair. In spring 1967, they announced a 'Summer of Love'. Around 75,000 hippies visited Haight-Ashbury.

In autumn 1967, *Time* magazine reported that 'hippie enclaves' had blossomed in every major US city. New York's East Village had poetry readings, experimental theatre and underground publications such as *Fuck You: A Magazine of the Arts*. *Time* magazine estimated that there might be 300,000 hippies, and even found some in conservative Austin, Texas.

(iv) Was it all 'sex and drugs'?

Republican **gubernatorial** candidate Ronald Reagan told reporters that student protesters' activities 'can be summed up in three words: Sex, Drugs and Treason'. The common contemporary consensus was that hippies enjoyed premarital and extramarital sex more often and more openly than previous generations. Greater female sexual freedom was facilitated by new contraceptives, such as the oral contraceptive nicknamed 'the pill'. Flouting conventional sexual mores was partly a political statement, but apolitical students also joined in the sexual revolution – it was fun.

The hippies' favourite drug was marijuana (pot), which made them feel relaxed and happy. LSD was a synthetic drug that produced colourful hallucinations and inspired much psychedelic art and some rock music. Many musicians preferred heroin, which was far more addictive and physically damaging. Some liked to combine several addictive substances, such as alcohol, cocaine and barbiturates. A Harvard professor, Dr Timothy Leary, discovered hallucinogenic mushrooms on a visit to Mexico. His *Psychedelic Review* openly advocated the use of drugs: 'Tune in, turn on and drop out' was his advice to students (Harvard University fired him).

(v) Protests in spring 1968

In spring 1968 campus protests started at Columbia University, which received federal funding for work that assisted the government in Vietnam. One student wrote to Columbia's president that 'society is sick and you and your capitalism are the sickness'. When Columbia tried to build a new gym adjacent to **Harlem**, with a separate backdoor entrance for Harlem residents, students protested against racism as well as the war, and a small group occupied the college buildings. The university called in hundreds of New York City police with billy-clubs who hit innocent spectators as well as the student occupiers. Most Columbia students went on a protest strike and the university shut down for that term.

Key terms

Gubernatorial
Pertaining to being a state governor in the United States.

Harlem
New York City's African American ghetto.

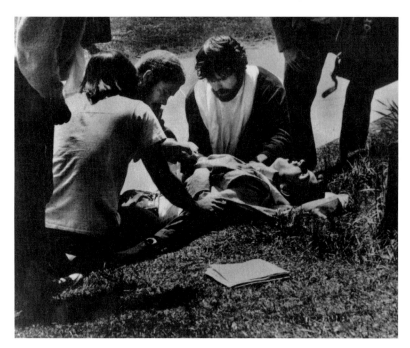

Kent State University students gather around a wounded student who was shot by the National Guard during a riot. Why do you suppose students constituted the majority of the protesters during the 1960s?

(vi) The New Left

In 1960 Tom Hayden and other students at the University of Michigan, inspired by 1930s' working-class radicals, and left-wing 1950s' writers, and by student participation in the civil rights movement, established the **Students for a Democratic Society (SDS)**. Hayden wrote the Port Huron statement, which called upon college students to change the political and social system, to liberate the poor, the non-whites and all enslaved by conformity. Hayden and his followers called themselves the **New Left** (as opposed to the Communist Old Left of the 1930s).

SDS became increasingly politically active, attacking racism, the Vietnam War and the **military–industrial complex**. However, by 1968, the New Left was increasingly divided. Different groups, such as the hippies, seemed to be trying to outdo each other in a radicalism that only served to antagonise most Americans.

(c) The significance of the students in Chicago, August 1968

Many Americans were tired of students, tired of protests and tired of violence. After the disorder at Chicago they listened when Republican presidential candidate Richard Nixon bemoaned the situation:

> As we look at America, we see cities enveloped in smoke and flame. We hear sirens in the night. We are Americans hating each other; killing each other at home.

In the minds of many Americans the events at Chicago summed up what was wrong with America. They would vote for the candidate who emphasised law and order: Richard Nixon.

Key terms

Students for a Democratic Society (SDS)
Student society established in 1960, aiming for a greater political and social freedom and equality.

New Left
Student group of the early 1960s, who wanted greater racial and economic equality and an end to social conformity.

Military–industrial complex
Influential figures in the armed forces and defence industry, who profited from war.

	Summary diagram: The Democratic National Convention in Chicago

Background	Event	Significance
1960s characterised by student protest	Democratic National Convention (Chicago) disrupted by radical students	Chaos in Chicago contributed to Nixon's triumph

Key question
What was the significance of the 1968 Miss America Pageant?

Key date

The Miss America Pageant disrupted: September 1968

6 | The Miss America Pageant and Women, September 1968

(a) The main event – the Miss America Pageant disrupted

September 1968 saw an apparent diversion from all the bitter divisions. A group of women objected to the swim-suited parade of beauties at the Miss America Pageant in Atlantic City, disrupted the proceedings and crowned a live sheep 'Miss America'.

(b) Background to the disruption of the Miss America Pageant

(i) Betty Friedan

Betty Friedan's *The Feminine Mystique* was published in 1963. In it she averred that women were imprisoned in a 'comfortable concentration camp', taught that 'they could desire no greater destiny than to glory in their own femininity'.

(ii) The impact of the civil rights movement on feminism

Along with Friedan's book, the civil rights movement provided the catalyst for feminism, in several ways:

Key terms

Title VII
The anti-sex discrimination section of the 1964 Civil Rights Act.

National Organisation for Women (NOW)
A pressure group for equal rights for women established in 1966.

Women's lib
The women's liberation movement developed in the 1960s, aiming for gender equality.

- It publicised that groups could be discriminated against on grounds of culture and physical characteristics.
- It showed successful methods of gaining legislative reform. Indeed, **Title VII** of the 1964 Civil Rights Act contained a ban on discrimination in employment on the basis of gender as well as race.
- It showed the power of pressure groups. When the government was slow to respond to Title VII, activists formed the **National Organisation for Women (NOW)** in 1966 to mobilise a pressure group on behalf of women. NOW, like the National Association for the Advancement for Colored People, aimed to work through the law and on the law.
- The black campaign for racial equality inspired women to campaign for sexual equality. Ironically, the sexism of black male activists further inspired women.

The women's movement that sought equal rights became known as known as women's liberation or '**women's lib**'. It spread quickly across campuses and cities, through 'consciousness-raising' grass-roots meetings.

(iii) SDS and women

Even the radical student organisation SDS was sexist. 'Women made peanut butter, waited on table, cleaned up and got laid. That was their role', confessed one SDS male. Although 33 per cent of SDS members were female, only 6 per cent of the executive were in 1964. The anti-war slogan 'Girls say yes to guys who say no' said it all. Whenever women in SDS tried to raise the issue of gender inequality, they got nowhere. Although SDS approved a pro-women's rights resolution, the accompanying debate was characterised by ridicule and contempt.

Daniel Patrick Moynahan, a leading figure in the Nixon administration, admitted that 'male dominance is so deeply a part of American life the males don't even notice it'.

(iv) Equal economic opportunities

By 1968, the wife went out to work in around 60 per cent of all families with an income of over $10,000. However, the women's jobs were usually menial, such as shop assistant or secretary. They were the supporting act to the main breadwinner. The employment statistics were telling: women constituted 80 per cent of teachers, but only 10 per cent of principals; 40 per cent of university students, but only 10 per cent of the faculty; two-thirds of the federal workforce, but only 2 per cent of the top jobs; 7 per cent of doctors and 3 per cent of lawyers. Articulate middle-class women began to agitate for equal pay, equal opportunities and equal respect.

(c) The significance of the disruption of 'Miss America'

Although the crowning of a sheep as 'Miss America' seems trivial compared to events in Chicago or the political assassinations, there were a considerable number of sympathetic women who believed that their struggle for equality was no laughing matter. Their conservative critics blamed 'women's lib' for America's falling birth rate, and the increased number of divorces and abortions.

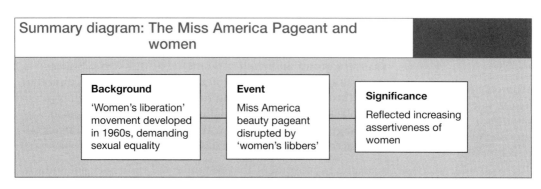

Summary diagram: The Miss America Pageant and women

Background

'Women's liberation' movement developed in 1960s, demanding sexual equality

Event

Miss America beauty pageant disrupted by 'women's libbers'

Significance

Reflected increasing assertiveness of women

Key question
What was the significance of the 1968 presidential election?

Key date

Nixon beat Humphrey in the presidential election: November 1968

Key terms

Segregationist
Someone who believed in the separation of African Americans and white people, on the grounds of black inferiority.

Middle America
A term invented by the media to describe ordinary, patriotic, middle-income Americans.

7 | The November 1968 Presidential Election and Middle America

(a) The main event – the presidential election
(i) The candidates in 1968
In November 1968 Americans elected a new President. The candidates were Hubert Humphrey (Democrat), Richard Nixon (Republican) and Alabama's **segregationist** Governor George Wallace (Independent). Wallace attacked the anti-war movement ('if any demonstrator ever lays down in front of my car it'll be the last car he will ever lay down in front of') and welfare mothers ('breeding children as a cash crop').

(ii) Nixon and the forgotten majority
Nixon said he was the one who spoke:

> for another voice … a quiet voice … It is the voice of the great majority of Americans, the forgotten Americans, the non-shouters, the non-demonstrators … those who do not break the law, people who pay their taxes and go to work, who send their kids to school, who go to their churches … people who love this country [and] cry out … 'that is enough, let's get some new leadership'.

(iii) Nixon's defeat of Humphrey
Initially, Vice President Hubert Humphrey was uninspired, tainted by his association with Johnson and the Vietnam War. Although Humphrey surged when he broke away from Johnson and the Vietnam War, urging a halt to the bombing, Nixon won a narrow victory, with 43.4 per cent of the votes. Humphrey had 42.7 per cent, Wallace 13.5 per cent.

(b) Background to the 1968 presidential election
(i) Middle America and law and order
While blacks, 'women's libbers' and many students complained about the state of society, those who had grown up abiding by the rules felt equal resentment. '**Middle America**' felt they had worked hard and patiently to get a decent home, while black power rioters wanted it as a right and at once. 'We build the city, not burn it down', said one white worker. In 1964, only 34 per cent of whites felt blacks wanted too much, too fast, but by 1968, it was 85 per cent. Congressman and future President Gerald Ford, himself the product of a broken home, asked:

> How long are we going to abdicate law and order – the backbone of civilisation – in favour of a soft social theory that the man who heaves a brick through a window or tosses a fire bomb into your car is simply the misunderstood and underprivileged product of a broken home?

(ii) Middle America's income

Middle America earned between $5000 and $15,000 per annum* and constituted around 55% of the population. Most were **blue-collar workers**, low-level bureaucrats, schoolteachers and white-collar workers. Not poor, they nevertheless existed precariously near to the poverty line. From 1956 to 1966, the amount they borrowed rose by 113 per cent, while their income increased by only 86 per cent. Inflation (4.7 per cent) made it hard for them to maintain their standard of living.

(iii) Middle America and living by the rules

Middle America felt it had lived by the rules, and now rioters and protesters wanted to change those rules. Night after night Middle America watched the ghetto riots on TV and lost patience with blacks and with the federal government. Middle America perceived the government to be taxing them heavily in order to give the money away to these undeserving poor. 'We just seem to be headed towards a collapse of everything', said one smalltown Californian newspaper. Middle America's children were drafted and in Vietnam, while student protesters lived comfortably and avoided the **draft**. 'I'm fighting for those candyasses because I don't have an old man to support me', said one soldier. Middle America asked why these college kids from wealthy families and these black rioters should not abide by the old rules.

Blue-collar workers
Manual labourers.

Draft
The US equivalent of British conscription; compulsory service in the nation's armed forces.

Key terms

* Most Britons earned under £3000 per annum at this time.

National Guardsmen standing guard in the rubble of Detroit, which was devastated by the race riots of 1967. Why do you suppose African Americans destroyed parts of their own ghetto, rather than white areas?

(iv) Archie Bunker

Middle America's favourite TV character was Archie Bunker in *All in the Family*, which was based on a BBC comedy series, *Till Death Do Us Part*. Outraged by 1960s' excess, Archie ranted at blacks, feminists, homosexuals and hippies. Created by liberal writers, the character was meant to be a ridiculous, loathsome bigot, but Middle America loved and agreed with him!

(c) The significance of the 1968 presidential election

With quite a low turnout (under 60 per cent), Nixon had won the support of fewer than 27 per cent of American voters. However, his election signalled that there would be no great changes in American society, despite the promise of early April 1968. This was, said historian William Chafe, a '**watershed**'. Traditional American values had now been reasserted. As malcontents on the left had become increasingly extreme, reaction had set in on the right.

The election had shown the increasing importance of the so-called **Sun Belt** states. Since the foundation of the USA, the nation's intellectual, economic and political powerhouse had been located in the Northeast, in the predominantly coastal area that stretched from Boston in the North, through New York City, Philadelphia and Baltimore to the nation's capital, Washington DC. In 1968 this coastal area of almost unbroken urban sprawl was known as the megalopolis. However, one of the reasons Richard Nixon was elected President in 1968 was because of his Southern Strategy, his recognition that the balance of power was changing, that the future probably lay in the Sun Belt states, where population and technology were booming.

The Sun Belt states were the states of the old **Confederacy** (North Carolina, South Carolina, Florida, Georgia, Louisiana, Mississippi, Alabama, Texas) and the dynamic new states, California, New Mexico, Oklahoma and Arizona. From 1945 to 1968, these states had doubled in population: Phoenix's population rose from 65,000 to 755,000; Houston's from 385,000 to 1.4 million. Why?

- Increased use of air-conditioning made these hotter regions more habitable.
- The federal government had made these areas far more accessible when it had financed a massive expansion of the interstate highway system.
- The federal government had awarded many defence and space contracts to the region.
- New high-tech industries such as aerospace, plastics, chemicals and electronics also flooded into the area, where labour costs were lower. Scientists flocked to industrial research zones in North Carolina, Florida, Texas and Louisiana. *Fortune* magazine noticed that around Santa Clara, California, was 'the densest concentration of innovative industry that exists anywhere in the world'. Agribusiness, defence contracts, real estate, oil and

Key terms

Watershed
In this political and social context, a turning point.

Sun Belt
States in the South, Southeast and Southwest USA, with warm climates, ranging from North Carolina in the East to California in the West.

Confederacy
Pro-slavery states in the American Civil War, 1861–5.

US POLITICAL PARTIES

Democrats	Republicans
On domestic issues, the more left-wing party that wanted to help, and therefore appealed to, less wealthy Americans. Since the Democratic President Roosevelt's New Deal in the 1930s, the party had favoured large-scale federal government intervention to help the poor	On domestic issues, the more right-wing party, that represented business (big and small) and other more affluent Americans. The Republicans had strong reservations about large-scale federal government programmes to help the poor

THE US CONSTITUTION

In 1787, the Founding Fathers drew up a constitution that set out the rules by which the USA would be governed. The constitution has not changed much since then.

The three branches of the federal government
(the people elect the President and Congress)

1. THE PRESIDENT (the executive branch)

- Elected every four years
- Cannot serve more than two terms (eight years)
- Is head of state and Commander-in-Chief of the armed forces
- Can suggest laws to Congress
- Can veto bills (proposed laws) in Congress
- Appoints a cabinet (these secretaries of state cannot sit in Congress)
- Makes proposals for the federal budget to Congress

3. THE SUPREME COURT (the judicial branch)

- The highest court in the land, it decides whether laws are constitutional
- The nine Supreme Court judges are nominated by the President then approved by Congress

2. CONGRESS (the legislative branch)

Consists of two Houses: the *Senate* and the *House of Representatives*.

Senate
- Two senators represent every state
- Senators serve six-year terms
- One-third of the senators come up for re-election every two years
- Congress makes the laws (both houses must agree)
- Congress can override a presidential veto
- Congress can impeach then remove a President from office

- Congress votes the money to finance government, after agreeing the budget with the President

House of Representatives
- Each state elects a number of representatives (congressmen) proportional to its population
- The House is elected every two years

But ...
State governments have considerable powers – they tax, make laws (e.g. over crime and punishment), etc.

Figure 1.1: The Sun Belt states of the USA.

leisure industries all contributed to the booming Sun Belt economy.

The psychology of the Sun Belt was different from that of the Northeast, which Nixon usually referred to as the home of the 'establishment' or the 'élite'. The Sun Belt contained the centre of **evangelical Protestantism** and conservatism. Most inhabitants of these sunshine states resented liberal intellectuals from the Northeast who wanted to give away their hard-earned taxes to the idle poor. They resented rich kids in Harvard and Yale and hippies who flouted authority, cushioned by daddy's wealth and influence. Significantly, the newly elected President's two homes were both in the Sun Belt: Key Biscayne, Florida, and San Clemente, California.

Key terms

Evangelical Protestantism
Some would say a more fanatical and/or enthusiastic kind of Protestantism, which tended to be socially conservative, often taking the Bible very literally.

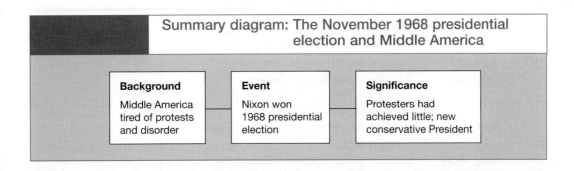

Summary diagram: The November 1968 presidential election and Middle America

Background	Event	Significance
Middle America tired of protests and disorder	Nixon won 1968 presidential election	Protesters had achieved little; new conservative President

2 President Nixon 1969–74

POINTS TO CONSIDER

Richard Nixon was never really popular with the American people and is generally considered to have been one of the USA's most unsuccessful presidents, mostly because of the Watergate scandal. Only narrowly elected in 1968, he was re-elected in a landslide victory in 1972. This chapter concentrates upon explaining:

- The significance of Nixon's pre-presidential career
- How and why he won the presidential election in 1968
- How and why he was re-elected in 1972
- The Watergate scandal
- The results and significance of Watergate

Key dates

1969	January	Nixon became President
		Nixon set up the Middle America Committee
	Oct–Nov	Moratorium protests
1970	May	Kent State students killed
1971	April	Supreme Court ruled pro-busing to further desegregation in North
	August	Nixon's New Economic Policy
1972		Nixon visited Communist China
		SALT treaty with USSR
		Nixon ended draft
	June	Watergate break-in burglars apprehended; Nixon and Haldeman discussed using CIA to halt FBI investigations into break-in
	November	Kissinger announced 'peace is at hand'; Nixon re-elected, defeating McGovern in a landslide
1973	January	Watergate burglars convicted
	February	Senate established Select Committee on Presidential Campaign Activities
	April	Haldeman, Ehrlichman and Dean resigned
	May–Aug	Senate investigated Watergate

	July	Existence of White House taping system revealed
	November	Seven White House tapes surrendered
1974	March	Seven Nixon aides indicted
	July	Supreme Court said tapes must be released; tapes proved Nixon ordered cover-up
	August 9	Nixon resigned
	September	President Ford pardoned Nixon

Key question
Does Nixon's background help explain his political performance?

Key terms

Quaker
A Christian group emphasising pacifism and silent meditation.

Yale
Yale and Harvard are the most prestigious universities in the USA.

Psychobiographer
Writers of biographies who seek explanations for their subject's later actions in their youth and family background.

1 | Richard Nixon's Background

(a) Youth and family

(i) Parents

Richard Nixon's father Frank was from a very poor family, barely educated, short-tempered and argumentative. His **Quaker** mother, Hannah, was middle class, well educated and reserved. Nixon took his father's beatings and his mother's reserve in his stride, according to his lifelong testaments of affection and admiration for both.

Life was never easy. In 1925, Nixon's younger brother died from meningitis, and Hannah spent three years away from the family's California home, nursing another sick brother in the healthier Arizona climate. (Harold died in 1933 aged 23 after years of struggle against tuberculosis.)

(ii) Education and work

Those who knew Nixon said he found working in the family grocery store demeaning. Hard-working and exceptionally clever, Nixon won a place at **Yale**. His parents could not afford to send him there, so he attended a humble, local college, then later won a scholarship to the more prestigious Duke University. Nixon always emphasised how his parents encouraged him to work hard and never give up. Throughout his education, and then as a lawyer, businessman and naval officer serving the Second World War, Nixon was admired for his honesty.

Because of his subsequent disgrace as President, **psychobiographers** have sought explanations in Nixon's background for the unattractive characteristics they consider he displayed in his political career, including mendacity, paranoia and aggression. Some wonder whether he resented his humble family background, if Hannah's Quakerism and the death of two brothers made him introspective, neurotic and a loner, and if his character struggled between inherited characteristics of aggression (from Frank) and idealism (from Hannah), and from trying to please two very different parents.

Whatever the reasons, it became evident early in Nixon's political career that many found his character unattractive.

Profile: Richard Milhous Nixon 1913–94

1913	–	Born in California; his father was a grocer
1934–7	–	Graduated from Whittier College, then Duke University Law School, North Carolina; entered law practice in Whittier
1940	–	Married Patricia (Pat) Ryan
1941–5	–	Second World War: served in the navy
1947–9	–	Elected twice to the House of Representatives; served on House Un-American Activities Committee (HUAC)
1950	–	Elected to the Senate
1952	–	Running mate for successful presidential candidate Dwight D. Eisenhower; successfully defended himself against accusations of financial impropriety with a televised speech in which he said the only gift he had received was a spaniel, 'Checkers', whom his daughters Julie and Tricia adored and would never give up
1953–61	–	As Vice President, specialised in foreign visits
1960	–	Narrowly lost the presidential election to Democrat John Kennedy
1962	–	Lost the Californian gubernatorial election; 'retired' from politics; practised law; remained a loyal Republican Party fund-raiser and after-dinner speaker
1968	–	Defeated Democrat Hubert Humphrey in the presidential election
1971	–	Tried to halt inflation by cutting federal expenditure, but had record annual budget deficits; devalued the dollar to try to help the balance of trade; his New Economic Policy put unprecedented peacetime controls upon wages and prices
1972	–	First US President to visit Communist China and the USSR; SALT I treaty with the USSR limited the nuclear arms race
June	–	Committee for the Re-election of the President (CREEP) burgled and wiretapped the Democrat headquarters at the Watergate building in Washington DC; Nixon secretly authorised a cover-up of the break-in and obstructed the FBI investigation; several newspapers investigated
November–		Re-elected in landslide victory over Democrat George McGovern

Key date: Nixon re-elected, defeating McGovern in a landslide: November 1972

1973	January	– Ended US involvement in Vietnam
	February	– Special Senate Committee established to investigate Watergate; hearings televised; aides said Nixon was involved in the cover-up and illegality
	July	– Senate Committee discovered Nixon had recorded all conversations in his office; Nixon tried but failed to deny access to the tapes
		– Second devaluation of the dollar
1974		– Several of his closest aides indicted on criminal charges and convicted
	July	– Released White House audiotapes demonstrated Nixon had obstructed justice and made false/misleading public statements; House of Representatives' Committee on the Judiciary voted to impeach him
	August	– Announced his resignation; succeeded by Vice President Gerald Ford
	September	– Pardoned by President Ford; retired to California; wrote books on his career and on international relations
1974–94		– Slowly rehabilitated as elder statesman; several presidents consulted him on international relations
1992		– Pat died; Nixon went into a deep depression
1994		– Died

Richard Nixon was very important in US politics in several ways. In his early political career he contributed greatly to the paranoid Cold War atmosphere. On social issues, he was a moderate Republican who, unlike Reagan (see page 106), did not want to dismantle the federal government safety net that previous (Democrat) presidents had set up to help the poor, sick and elderly. Until his disgrace, he helped keep the Republican Party out of the hands of right-wingers who wanted minimal government intervention to help the poor and weak in US society. He helped win many ex-Democrats to the Republican Party, especially in the South. As President, he did a great deal to help the less fortunate, but struggled with the economy. In foreign policy, he (slowly) ended the Vietnam War and improved relations with the USSR and China. He is best remembered for trying to cover up the Watergate burglary in which his men broke into the Democratic Party headquarters (see page 49). Watergate became synonymous with Nixon, dishonesty and disgrace.

(b) Congressman and Senator

Nixon first campaigned for a seat in **Congress** in 1946. He publicly suggested his Democrat rival had **Communist** sympathies, but privately acknowledged this was untrue. 'I had to win', he said. 'That's the thing you don't understand. The important thing is to win.' He won.

When he ran for the Senate in 1950, he called his opponent, Helen Gahagan Douglas, a 'Pink Lady' who 'follows the Communist Party line' and was 'pink right down to her underwear'. In Nixon's defence, many Republicans used such Communist smear tactics, often with less restraint. Douglas got revenge. Her nickname for Nixon, Tricky Dick, stuck.

(c) Vice President 1953–61

After a mere six years in Congress, because of fame gained from his election campaigns and prominence in **HUAC** (1948), Nixon was selected to be Eisenhower's running mate in 1952. After Eisenhower's victory in 1952, Nixon was on the **ticket** again in 1956.

Eisenhower was frequently ambivalent about Nixon. In the 1952 campaign, Eisenhower considered dropping Nixon when it was claimed that Nixon's backers had kept a secret fund to pay his election expenses and for his private use. Secret funds to pay election expenses were common, and Nixon had one, but it was not for private use. In 1956, Eisenhower was obviously reluctant to retain Nixon ('People don't like him' said Eisenhower) and only offered him ambivalent support in 1960 when Nixon ran against John Kennedy for the presidency.

Although militantly anti-Communist in foreign policy, Nixon was very moderate on domestic issues. He had no wish to reverse the pattern of federal government intervention initiated by President Roosevelt's **New Deal**. Nixon and Eisenhower believed American prosperity depended upon private enterprise, but that some social problems required federal intervention. Conscious that his partisan Cold War rhetoric caused some to doubt his fitness for office, Nixon moderated it in the 1960 presidential election.

(d) Unsuccessful candidate
(i) Presidential candidate 1960

In 1960, Nixon was narrowly defeated by Kennedy. Perhaps the crucial factor was dubious Democrat electoral practices in Illinois and Texas. 'We won but they stole it from us', claimed Nixon. Statesmanlike, he refused to challenge the results, although Eisenhower and Pat urged it. Nixon said it would 'tear the country to pieces'. Doubtless this confirmed his belief that politics was a dirty business, that liars and cheats came out best. 'You are never going to make it in politics', Nixon told one aide. 'You just don't know how to lie.'

Key question
When and how did Richard Nixon become famous?

Key terms

Congress
US equivalent of Britain's Parliament. It consists of the House of Representatives and the Senate. Each US state selects two senators, and a number of congressmen.

Communist
In the Cold War the capitalist USA and the Communist USSR hated and feared each other. The US particularly disliked the Communist emphasis on economic equality.

HUAC
The House Un-American Committee investigated suspected Communists within the USA.

Key question
Why was Nixon's 1968 election victory so unexpected?

Ticket
Party candidates nominated for President and Vice President constitute that party's 'ticket'.

New Deal
Roosevelt's plan to get the USA out of the 1930s' Depression; an unprecedented programme of federal aid to those most in need.

(ii) Gubernatorial candidate 1962

In 1962, Nixon half-heartedly ran for governor of California and was heavily defeated. In an emotional press conference that made some, including President Kennedy, question his sanity, Nixon said he was retiring from politics and that the media would no longer have Richard Nixon to kick around. *Time* magazine said, 'Barring a miracle, Richard Nixon can never hope to be elected to any political office again.'

Nixon's early partisan electioneering, his two great defeats in 1960 and in 1962, all combined to give him an aura of unpopularity and failure. So how did he make what contemporaries called the most amazing comeback American politics had ever seen? Nixon's work for the Republican Party in the mid-1960s, his moderation and President Johnson's policies all contributed.

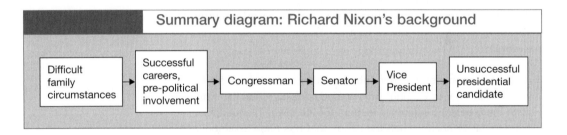

Summary diagram: Richard Nixon's background

Difficult family circumstances → Successful careers, pre-political involvement → Congressman → Senator → Vice President → Unsuccessful presidential candidate

2 | Nixon's Election as President in 1968

(a) Getting elected in 1968. Step 1 – loyal Republican

Nixon was addicted to politics, and he dreamed of a political comeback. Throughout his 'retirement', he worked tirelessly as a party fund-raiser and campaigner, contributing greatly to an impressive Republican comeback in the 1966 congressional mid-term elections. Many Republicans for whom he campaigned felt indebted to him. He was always in the news, making speeches, writing articles and giving interviews.

Nixon's loyalty and value to the party put him in a good position for a run at the Republican nomination in 1968.

(b) Getting elected in 1968. Step 2 – moderate Republican

In 1964, with the moderate Nixon's political career apparently over, the right-wing 'Old Guard' took control of the Republican Party. They gave Barry Goldwater the presidential nomination. With what Nixon called 'unforgivable folly', Goldwater declared, 'Extremism in the defence of liberty is no vice. Moderation in the pursuit of justice is no virtue.'

When Goldwater was crushingly defeated by Johnson in the 1964 presidential election, the Republican Party knew it would need a more moderate candidate in 1968. 'Old Guard' Republicans liked Richard Nixon's extreme anti-Communism.

Moderate and liberal Republicans found his position on domestic issues acceptable.

(c) Getting elected in 1968. Step 3 – 'America needs new leadership'

Key question
How did President Johnson help Nixon get elected?

After the horrors of the Depression, and what many perceived to be the success of Roosevelt's New Deal in helping the United States out of it, both Republicans and Democrats accepted the necessity of federal intervention to help ease severe social and economic problems. After his landslide victory in 1964, Johnson went way beyond the New Deal consensus, calling for the federal government to eliminate all poverty and racial inequality. In pursuit of his 'Great Society', Johnson began to lose working-class and lower-middle-class white voters who were likely to swing towards a moderate Republican in 1968. These voters were anxious about recurring ghetto riots, anti-war protesters and the Vietnam War. Nixon articulated their concerns.

In a speech in February 1968, Nixon emphasised his effective campaign slogan, 'For These Critical Years, America Needs New Leadership':

> When the strongest nation in the world can be tied down for four years in the war in Vietnam with no end in sight, when the nation with the greatest tradition of respect for the law is plagued by random lawlessness, when the nation that has been a symbol of human liberty is torn apart by racial strife, when the President of the United States cannot travel either at home or abroad without fear of a hostile demonstration, then it is time America had new leadership.

Throughout 1967 and early 1968, Nixon waged a relentlessly effective attack on President Johnson that put him in a good position to win both the Republican nomination and the presidency itself.

(d) Getting elected in 1968. Step 4 – new electioneering techniques

(i) Improved rhetoric

Key question
What was new and better in Nixon's campaigning style in 1968?

Nixon learned from Kennedy's impressive 1960 rhetoric, with its emphasis on fundamental American values. Nixon was genuinely committed to those values. When he spoke of them, his sincerity shone through.

(ii) Controlled public appearances

Nixon had also learned to limit his public appearances. He did not '**press the flesh**' in 1968. There was no need. Everyone knew him, so he did not appear in shopping malls and high school gyms. Instead he appeared statesmanlike, dignified and experienced, speaking in large auditoriums, always with audiences over 1000. Loyal aide Bob Haldeman (see page 47), told him not to exhaust himself as he had in 1960 by too many personal appearances: 'The reach of the individual campaigner

Press the flesh
The handshaking done by US political candidates.

Key term

doesn't add up to diddly-squat in votes.' Instead, Nixon reached wider audiences through TV.

Television appearances were very expensive, but the Nixon campaign raised funds brilliantly. Lessons were learned from previous TV performances, particularly Nixon's weakness before hostile, probing journalists. The Nixon campaign concentrated upon the production of edited, televised footage of question sessions with ordinary voters, whom Nixon handled with ease.

Nixon made a poor impression in the 1960 presidential election debate. He looked pale and ill, in sharp contrast to the tanned but far less healthy John Kennedy. Nixon made no such mistakes now. He kept his tan topped up in Florida.

Key question
How was glamour added to the Nixon campaign?

(e) Getting elected in 1968. Step 5 – 'sex appeal' and the Eisenhowers

Many Republicans had long dreamed of a match between Nixon's daughter Julie and Eisenhower's grandson David. Julie and David initially resisted such matchmaking efforts, but met for the first time in years on election night in 1966, and found they liked each other. When David escorted Julie to the 1966 International Debutantes Ball at the Waldorf-Astoria Hotel in New York, their photographs were front-page news and again in 1967 when they announced their marriage plans. They gave Richard Nixon's political aspirations a big boost.

Nixon lacked the glamour of potential rivals such as Bobby Kennedy and ex-film star Ronald Reagan. In early 1968, one reporter noted that in the Nixon campaign in the New Hampshire primary, 18-year-old Julie and David 'together provided most of the sex appeal – she innocent and vivacious, he innocent and unassuming. His tousled head of hair and open expression quickly won the hearts of the Republican faithful'. When David arrived at St Louis airport, a crowd of teenage girls met him. 'I touched him', squeaked a 14-year-old girl, 'I actually touched him.'

When hecklers asked Julie about her father's vagueness on Vietnam, Julie's answers were masterly:

> Daddy wants the peace talks to succeed so much he thinks he shouldn't talk about the war. When he becomes President, he'll put pressure on the Soviet Union. Remember, Daddy was in the Eisenhower Administration and they got us out of one war [Korea].

While Julie and David worked the small towns, Nixon's 22-year-old daughter Tricia and his wife Pat went to factories, schools and shopping malls. One reporter expressed amazement that Pat had survived 13 campaigning hours on two cups of coffee and a Coke. 'I don't mind', said the loyal wife. 'Creature comforts don't matter.'

David pressed his grandfather to endorse Nixon. Eisenhower, still ambivalent (see page 24), claimed that as a former President and good Republican, he had to wait until the National Convention endorsed Nixon. After his fifth heart attack

(July 1968), 77-year-old Eisenhower was emaciated and seriously ill. Nixon then successfully pressed him for a public endorsement. From hospital, in his wheelchair and bathrobe, Eisenhower announced he wanted to lay rest the persistent speculation that he had never liked Nixon: 'I just want the country to know that I have admired and respected this man and liked the man ever since I met him in 1952.' A reporter asked if David and Julie had influenced his decision. 'I think they tried to', Eisenhower said, giving the press his famous grin for the last time.

(f) Getting elected in 1968. Step 6 – gaining the Republican nomination

Key question
How did Nixon get the Republican nomination in 1968?

Journalist James Reston was convinced that it would be Nixon vs Johnson in the 1968 presidential election. It worried him:

> They just happen to be the two politicians who inspire more distrust among more people in this country than any other two men in American political life.

In March 1968 Johnson said he would not seek re-election, but Nixon went on to win the Republican nomination because:

- As an ex-Vice President he offered a great deal of governmental experience.
- He was associated with the prosperity and calm of the Eisenhower years.
- Eisenhower, who had finally enthusiastically endorsed Nixon's candidacy, had led the US Army in Europe during the Second World War and served his country again, as President, for eight years. He inspired affection in the country at large and particularly in the Republican Party. As death neared, his emotional appeal increased. Most of the audience, male and female, were in tears when, in his acceptance speech at the Republican National Convention in August 1968, Nixon said:

> General Eisenhower, as you know, lies critically ill in the Walter Reed Hospital tonight. I have talked, however, with Mrs Eisenhower on the telephone. She tells me that his heart is with us. She says that there is nothing that he lives more for, and there is nothing that would lift him more, than for us to win in November. And I say, let's win this one for Ike [Ike was Eisenhower's nickname].

- Republicans knew Nixon had done a good job in attacking the Johnson administration.
- Nixon's rivals for the Republican nomination had bad luck (Governor Reagan lost many conservative Republicans when the press reported that there were many homosexuals working for him) or made errors (Governor George Romney antagonised conservative Republicans when he lamented that he had been brainwashed into supporting the Vietnam War).
- Nixon had performed well in the primaries.

- Nixon was a compromise candidate, acceptable to most Republicans, in contrast to his rivals for the nomination, who were on the extreme wings of the Republican Party. **Nelson Rockefeller** was an East Coast liberal. Reagan (see Chapter 4) was as conservative as Barry Goldwater.
- Nixon stopped Southern Republicans defecting to Reagan, when he promised them he would promote big defence spending in the South and go slow on racial integration.

Key question
Did Nixon's running mate help him win the election?

Key figure

Nelson Rockefeller (1908–79)
Repeatedly elected Governor of New York state (1950–70), where he greatly improved cultural and educational facilities, Rockefeller was a liberal-moderate Republican. He failed to get the Republican presidential nomination in 1964 and 1968, but was Ford's Vice President (1974–7).

(g) Getting elected in 1968. Step 7 – Selecting a running mate

Nixon's surprising choice as running mate in 1968 was Maryland's Governor Spiro Agnew, the son of poor Greek immigrants. 'Spiro who?' asked the press. Nixon had asked others, including Michigan Representative Gerald Ford (see page 67), but they had declined.

Nixon chose Agnew because he considered him impressive and thought he would help win votes in border states (such as Maryland itself), amongst the 'silent majority' (see page 30) and in the South. Agnew had gained massive publicity after the spring 1968 riots in Baltimore, when he had summoned leaders of the black community and castigated them as 'circuit-riding, Hanoi-visiting, caterwauling, riot-inciting, burn-America-down type of leaders' who had been 'breaking and running' instead of stopping the riots. Some white Americans liked that performance, and Nixon thought Agnew would be helpful against the right-wing, racist, independent presidential candidate, George Wallace.

Agnew looked good. He was tall, handsome and physically imposing in a way that Nixon never was, but it is doubtful that he added much to the ticket. Agnew spent his first news conference after the Convention declaring that he was not a bigot; Nixon spent his defending his choice of Agnew, after which he avoided mentioning Agnew in public again. The Democrats ran 30-second TV commercials with laughter accompanying the words 'Agnew for Vice President'.

Agnew enlivened the campaign with some gaffes. Asked why he was not campaigning in ghetto areas, he replied, 'When you've seen one slum, you've seen them all.' When he saw Maryland reporter Gene Oishi asleep on their flight to Hawaii, he asked, 'What's wrong with the fat Jap?'

Wallace's choice of running mate really damaged his chances. Vice-presidential candidate General Curtis LeMay said he would use nuclear weapons immediately in Vietnam. That gave Nixon the chance to be statesmanlike and moderate, saying LeMay was irresponsible. The Democrat candidate Hubert Humphrey warned voters against both Wallace and Nixon on the grounds of their irresponsible choices of running mate, asking them to imagine President Agnew (if Nixon were elected and died in office).

When Nixon won the election, he triumphantly told his staff that they had picked the right man in Agnew, a man with capacity, brains, energy and quality. 'Well, we sure concealed that from the American people during the campaign', muttered one aide.

(h) Getting elected in 1968. Step 8 – winning over Middle America

In his 1968 acceptance speech at the Republican Convention, Nixon identified himself with what he called 'the silent majority' or 'Middle America', whose voice he alone appreciated and listened to (see page 15).

According to historian Iwan Morgan, Nixon was always most effective when practising the politics of division. In this speech he divided the 'silent majority' from the liberal élites, the hippy protesters, the ghetto rioters. His stance won him a great deal of support, and not from the usual Republican voters: 'My source of strength was more **Main Street** than **Wall Street**' (1984 interview). In 1970 he was described as having appealed to the 'unyoung, unpoor, and unblack … middle-aged, middle-class, and middle-minded', in other words, all who opposed 1960s radicalism and change. He was particularly effective when he promised them a restoration of law and order in the cities, repeatedly saying:

> In the [past] 45 minutes … this is what has happened in America. There has been one murder, two rapes, 45 major crimes of violence, countless robberies and auto thefts.

He promised less (and therefore cheaper) government. His attacks on the massive bureaucracy that implemented welfare and poverty programmes led some voters to hope that he would dismantle the welfare state that Democrats since Roosevelt had introduced: 84 per cent of Americans believed that 'there are too many people receiving welfare money who should be working'. In 1960, three million Americans received ADC (Aid to Dependent Children); by 1970, it was 8.4 million. One in nine children, and one in three black children, were on welfare.

(i) Getting elected in 1968. Step 9 – the Southern Strategy

After Johnson had played a massive part in ending segregation in the South, many Southern white voters no longer felt at home in Johnson's Democratic Party. Nixon wooed them by promising to slow down the pace of school desegregation in the South and by rejecting President Johnson's policy of cutting off federal funds to school districts that refused to desegregate. This so-called **Southern Strategy** was very effective; it transformed Southern voting patterns.

Key question
How did Nixon win over Middle America?

Key terms

Main Street
A synonym for the usually conservative, average, ordinary, small-town US resident.

Wall Street
The financial centre of the USA, whose big-earners traditionally vote Republican.

Southern Strategy
Nixon's plans to win Southern voters from the Democrats.

Key question
What was the Southern Strategy and how did it help Nixon's election?

Key question
How did the Vietnam
War help get Nixon
elected?

(j) Getting elected in 1968. Step 10 – promising peace in Vietnam

In March 1968, President Johnson had surprised Americans when he announced that he would not stand for re-election, but would seek peace in Vietnam.

Nixon has been accused of sabotaging the chance for a Democrat-engineered peace by discouraging South Vietnamese President Thieu from participating in the autumn 1968 peace talks, but Thieu did not need discouraging. Johnson knew Nixon was talking to Thieu, but could not denounce Nixon publicly without revealing that he had been bugging Republican phones. Nixon's intervention was illegal: the Logan Act said no citizen should privately negotiate with foreign governments. His anxiety lest the Democrats expose this wrongdoing contributed to the illegal intelligence operations during his presidency (see page 49).

The Vietnam War contributed greatly to Nixon's victory:

- The war was seen as 'Johnson's war', which damaged the electoral hopes of Nixon's opponent, Johnson's Vice President, Hubert Humphrey.
- Nixon's promise that if elected he would bring 'peace with honour', while vague, appealed to voters.
- Nixon's promise to phase out American troops and leave the fighting to the South Vietnamese was appealing.
- Nixon promised to end the draft.

(k) Getting elected in 1968. Step 11 – let the Democrats implode

(i) The Democratic Convention

Key question
How did the
Democrats help get
Nixon elected?

A divided and weakened Democratic Party helped Nixon win the presidency.

Johnson foisted Humphrey, who had not won a single primary, on the Convention. Outside the hall, Chicago's (Democrat) Mayor Richard Daley ordered his police to crush student demonstrators. News pictures and reports of students targeting the police (calling them 'pigs', blowing marijuana smoke in their faces, and giving them the finger) and having sex in public places all combined to helped Nixon, the candidate of 'law and order'. He shot ahead of Humphrey in the polls.

(ii) Democrats vs Humphrey

With Johnson's Vice President as the Democratic nominee, there was nowhere for the large numbers of anti-war Democrats to go. Resentful about the way their anti-war candidates had been treated and rejected at the Convention, hating the war even more than they hated Richard Nixon, many continued to attack

Humphrey ('Dump the Hump'), disrupting his meetings and making it impossible for his speeches to be heard. These hecklers told reporters they would probably vote for Humphrey in the end, but wanted to 'push him toward the left'. They pushed Humphrey towards defeat in 1968, and introduced reforms that led to another Nixon victory in 1972 (see page 45).

(iii) Nixon vs Humphrey

Nixon, who had more staff than Humphrey, held ticket-only rallies. His aides sent long-haired ticket holders away, saying their tickets were counterfeit. When some hecklers got through, Nixon ordered his Secret Service detail to rough them up. They refused, but off-duty local police happily did it. Nixon handled hecklers far better than Humphrey, using them to confirm his point that the USA had become lawless under the Democrats. Johnson's poor record on law and order, and the unpopular and expensive Vietnam War, which had led to inflation and higher taxes, all handicapped Humphrey and helped Nixon.

(l) Getting elected in 1968. Step 12 – the 1968 presidential election

Key question
What happened in November 1968?

(i) A close race

Nixon had been considerably ahead of Humphrey for much of the autumn, but Humphrey rallied dramatically in the final days of the campaign, when he broke away from Johnson on Vietnam and advocated a bombing pause. Anti-war Democrats came back to him.

(ii) A nasty race

The race was close and nasty. A Republican TV commercial showed Hanoi battle scenes, black ghetto rioters, a starving child, then Hubert Humphrey talking about the 'politics of joy'. A Democratic radio commercial sounded a thump, thump, thump, and then a voice-over said in an incredulous tone, 'Spiro Agnew? A heartbeat from the presidency?'

(iii) Playing politics with peace

'We do not want to play politics with peace', said Nixon, but, as he noted in his memoirs, 'that was inevitably what was happening'. When President Johnson declared a halt on bombing in Vietnam, Humphrey went past Nixon in the polls for the first time. 'Mr Nixon', asked a journalist, 'some of your close aides have been trying to spread the word that President Johnson timed the Vietnam bombing pause to help Vice President Humphrey in Tuesday's election. Do you agree with them?' 'No', lied Nixon. 'I don't make that charge,' although he admitted that lots of his supporters did!

Nixon's biographer Stephen Ambrose found the 1968 election campaign particularly distasteful ('so many lies'). In 1968 Johnson claimed that peace was at hand. The Nixon administration did the same in 1972. 'In each case, in its quest for votes, the administration treated the American people with cynical contempt', sighed Ambrose.

(iv) Counting the votes

The 1968 race was one of the closest in American history. Though he won comfortably in the **electoral college**, Nixon took only 43.4 per cent of the popular vote, the lowest winning margin since 1912. Nixon had hoped to carry the white Southern and Northern blue-collar workers, but he had to share them with the independent candidate George Wallace, who, like Nixon, had campaigned on anti-big government, anti-inflation, anti-welfare, anti-riots and anti-liberals **planks**.

(v) Nixon's cabinet

President-elect Nixon quickly chose his first cabinet. His appointments were generally well received, being moderate and sensible, with the exception perhaps of 29-year-old Ron Ziegler as press secretary. Nixon knew the importance of the press: 'In the modern presidency, concern for image must rank with concern for substance.' Nixon was convinced that the press hated him and said he was 'prepared to do combat with the media', who were 'far more powerful than the President in creating public awareness and shaping public opinion'. If this was so, choosing the inexperienced Ziegler was unwise.

(m) The problems facing the new President in January 1969

The newly elected President faced many difficult problems:

- The American people were deeply divided over the Vietnam War; there were frequent demonstrations and violence.
- Nixon wanted to achieve 'peace with honour' in Vietnam.
- There was a massive federal deficit.
- Inflation was at 4.7 per cent, and a flood of imports endangered America's balance of trade.

Nixon's stated aim was 'to bring the American people together', but how difficult that would be was evident at his presidential inauguration, the first in US history to be marred by protest. Hundreds of young anti-war protesters shouted, 'Ho, Ho, Ho Chi Minh, the NLF (see page 2–3) is going to win', burned American flags, spat at the police, and threw sticks, stones, beer cans and bottles at the presidential limousine.

Key terms

Electoral college
Under the constitution, each state's voters vote for delegates who then vote on behalf of that state in the electoral college. The number of delegates depends upon the state's population. The leading candidate in a state takes all that state's delegates. Whoever wins a majority of delegates becomes President.

Planks
Stated policies of a candidate in an election.

Key question
What problems faced Nixon in 1969?

Key date
Nixon became President: January 1969

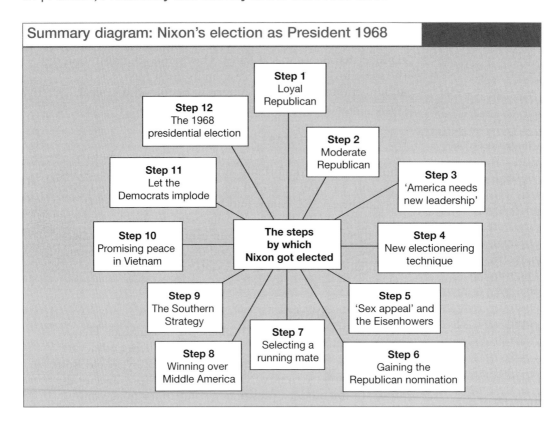

Summary diagram: Nixon's election as President 1968

- **Step 1** Loyal Republican
- **Step 2** Moderate Republican
- **Step 3** 'America needs new leadership'
- **Step 4** New electioneering technique
- **Step 5** 'Sex appeal' and the Eisenhowers
- **Step 6** Gaining the Republican nomination
- **Step 7** Selecting a running mate
- **Step 8** Winning over Middle America
- **Step 9** The Southern Strategy
- **Step 10** Promising peace in Vietnam
- **Step 11** Let the Democrats implode
- **Step 12** The 1968 presidential election

The steps by which Nixon got elected

3 | Getting Re-elected in 1972

From the moment he was elected President in 1968, Nixon had his eye fixed firmly on re-election in 1972. As with all presidents, much of what he did in his first term was designed to win him another term.

(a) Getting re-elected in 1972 – ensuring Middle America's vote

In 1970 *Time* magazine described Nixon as 'the embodiment of Middle America'. Nixon ensured that exasperated conservatives in the Sun Belt states in the South and West, in the suburbs, and blue-collar workers, knew that he shared their dislike for liberal Supreme Court rulings (for example, the 1966 **MIRANDA** vs ARIZONA ruling, which seemed to give the accused more rights than the victim) and for liberal calls for **busing**, equal rights for African Americans, women and homosexuals. Like Middle America, Nixon was tired of anti-war protests, ghetto riots, and the lack of law and order.

Nixon set up the Middle America Committee: 1969

Key date

Key question
How did Nixon ensure that he won Middle America voters?

Key terms

MIRANDA
Supreme Court ruling that improperly obtained confessions be excluded from trials.

Busing
Supreme Court rulings on integrated education meant some white children were sent (by bus) to black schools, and vice versa.

Key question
How did Nixon's policies on race win white votes?

Key date

Supreme Court ruled pro-busing to further desegregation in North: April 1971

Key terms

Affirmative action
Giving economically disadvantaged African Americans extra opportunities (even if whites were better qualified) in education and employment in order to compensate for previous unfair treatment.

Welfare
Since Roosevelt's New Deal, the USA had a welfare safety net, which helped the very poor, sick, unemployed and elderly in varying degrees.

Supreme Court
Rules on whether or not laws and actions are in line with the Constitution.

Constitutional amendment
The USA's Founding Fathers wrote out rules by which the country was to be governed in the Constitution. New rules or amendments can be added.

(b) Getting re-elected in 1972 – race and votes

In order to get re-elected in 1972, Nixon wanted to continue his 'Southern Strategy' (see pages 30–1) and win white voters across America who had concerns about racial integration (especially busing), **affirmative action** and **welfare**.

(i) Busing

The Nixon administration tried (but failed) to slow down desegregation in Southern schools. For example, in 1969, the Nixon Justice Department argued in a federal court for a delay in desegregation, despite the Supreme Court's 1967 ruling that desegregation should be immediate.

In accordance with such rulings, Nixon slowly and reluctantly facilitated the desegregation of Southern public schools. When the Justice Department began to respond to a 1971 **Supreme Court** ruling on busing that aimed to further desegregation in the North, Nixon told them to 'Knock off this crap. Do only what the law requires and not one thing more.'

Busing was opposed by over 80 per cent of Americans, who wanted their children educated in their own neighbourhood. In 1972 Nixon attacked liberals who supported busing, which was 'wrenching … children away from their families and from the schools their families may have moved to be near.' He sought (unsuccessfully) a **constitutional amendment** against busing, which helped win him votes.

(ii) Supreme Court judges

In 1968 Nixon had promised Southern Republicans he would select judges who would slow down the pace of integration. In 1969 he successfully nominated conservative Warren Burger as chief justice. He also nominated racially conservative Clement Haynsworth. Although no Supreme Court nominee had been rejected since 1930, the Senate rejected Haynsworth. Nixon then nominated another racist Southerner, G. Harrold Carswell, whose lack of ability was attested by a White House aide: 'They think he is a boob, a dummy … He is.' One Republican senator tried to support Carswell by saying that even if he were mediocre, 'there are a lot of mediocre judges and people and lawyers. They are entitled to a little representation, aren't they, and a little chance?' However, 13 other Republicans joined in the successful Senate rejection of the candidate. Nixon told the press he felt his nominations had been rejected because they were Southerners, which won him Southern votes.

(iii) Affirmative action

Although the Democratic Party demanded more affirmative action, the traditionally Democrat **unions** and Nixon condemned it as reverse discrimination. Although in practice the Nixon administration gave minorities considerable help (for example, it required firms with federal contracts to set goals and timetables for minority hiring), Nixon's words on race appealed to the average white American voter, who did not want to pay the financial and social cost of integration and racial equality. A *Newsweek* poll in 1969 showed that a majority of Americans believed that blacks had a better chance of getting a good job or house or school than whites.

(iv) Welfare

Nixon told advisers:

> The American people are outraged [by the welfare system], and, in my view, they should be … I do not want this swept under the rug or put aside … This whole thing smells to high heaven and we should get charging on it immediately.

Nixon wanted to:

- stop discrimination against low income fathers who did not desert their children
- make welfare recipients work (a 1969 *Newsweek* poll said 80 per cent believed that over half those on welfare could get a job if they so desired)
- decrease the bureaucracy
- equalise payments across the United States.

In August 1969 Nixon announced his Family Assistance Plan (FAP) and got a 65 per cent approval rating. He knew his plan did not have much chance of getting through Congress. It was too expensive for conservatives and did not go far enough for liberals. However, it won Nixon votes. When the Nixon administration decreased the funding of 'Great Society' anti-poverty schemes such as the Job Corps and the Youth Programme, it appealed to taxpayers who felt they were subsidising the idle.

(v) Suppressing the Black Panthers

White America hated the **Black Panthers**. When in 1969, 28 Black Panthers were killed by the police and hundreds imprisoned, white voters were delighted.

Key terms

Unions
Groups of workers (for example, **teamsters**) organised themselves into unions in order to negotiate better pay and/or working conditions.

Teamsters
Truck drivers.

Black Panthers
A group of militant black activists who used revolutionary rhetoric, ostentatiously carried guns, monitored police brutality and distributed free meals to the ghetto poor.

(c) Getting re-elected in 1972 – law and order

Law and order: statistics

1969	602 bombings or attempted bombings
1970	1577 bombings or attempted bombings
1969–70 bombings	56 per cent resulted from campus disorders, 19 per cent from black extremists, 14 per cent from white extremists, 8 per cent from criminal attacks. There were 41 deaths and 37,000 bombings threats
Spring 1969	300 colleges had demonstrations, 20 per cent of which included bombings or trashing of buildings; gun-toting black students at Cornell University demanded the establishment of a black studies programme

Gun-toting black students at Cornell University demand change. Why do you suppose the students carried guns?

Autumn 1970	Boston University evacuated buildings on 80 occasions because of bomb threats

The nation seemed to be falling apart with unprecedented political and racial violence and a perceived rise in criminality. Nixon seemed to be intent on restoring law and order, which pleased conservative voters. On the second day of his presidency, a *New York Times* headline called the nation's capital a 'city of fear and crime', and the Washington *Daily News* asked him to root out the 'fear that stalks the streets of Washington'. A White House secretary was mugged just outside the East Gate and Nixon's secretary, Rose Mary Woods, had $7000 worth of jewellery stolen from her apartment in Washington's new Watergate building when she accompanied Nixon to Europe. Nixon sent Congress a bill to decrease crime in the city in which they lived. They responded with the District of Columbia Crime Control Act of 1970, which facilitated search procedures and made bail harder to obtain.

Radicals were dealt with harshly, including the Black Panthers (see page 36) and the **Chicago Eight**, who were persecuted in 1970 for travelling across state lines to foment anti-war riots. Youthful protesters seemed to many to present the greatest problem, as these were the children of the middle and upper classes.

(d) Getting re-elected in 1972 – rebellious youth

Student protests began under Johnson and continued under Nixon. A 1969 *Newsweek* poll showed that 84 per cent of Americans believed that student demonstrators were treated too leniently. There were votes to be had for a President who could handle the problem.

October and November 1969 saw America's greatest ever anti-war protests, the **Moratorium**. Tens of thousands of all ages marched on the White House and in every major city.

Although by spring 1970, anti-war protests had decreased, there were still protests: in favour of civil rights, in favour of the Black Panthers, against capitalism, or against nothing in particular. Radical students blew up buildings at the University of Colorado because scholarship funds for black students were frozen. Students at San Diego, California, set fire to banks. Ohio State students demanded the admission of more black students and the abolition of Reserve Officer Training Corps (ROTC); in a six-hour battle with the police, seven students were shot, 13 injured and 600 arrested, after which the state governor called in the National Guard. A pro-Black Panthers demonstration set Yale Law School library books on fire.

When Nixon ordered the invasion of Cambodia in search of Communists in spring 1970, anti-war protests erupted again in more than 80 per cent of American universities. Police and National Guardsmen frequently clashed with students, most famously at Kent State, Ohio, where students had rioted downtown and firebombed the ROTC building. When Kent State students held a peaceful protest rally, the National Guard shot four dead and wounded 11. Two of the girls were simply walking to class. In the next week, two more students were killed and 12 wounded at Jackson State, Mississippi, when police opened fire on the women's dormitory. Some Americans felt the government was deliberately murdering dissenters.

Nixon used several strategies, with varying degrees of success, for dealing with the students.

(i) Discredit them

Nixon antagonised students (and some middle-class parents) when he talked of 'these bums … blowing up the campuses'. Nixon did not handle the Kent State and Jackson State tragedies well, blaming the 'politics of violence and confrontation' and failing to express sorrow at the deaths. The father of a dead girl hit the national headlines when he said, 'My child was not a bum.'

However, when Nixon denounced violent and intimidatory protesters, and declared that what was new about such people was their numbers and 'the extent of the passive acquiescence, or

Key terms

Chicago Eight
In 1969 the Nixon administration charged eight New Left leaders with conspiracy. They included Tom Hayden of SDS and Bobby Seale of the Black Panthers. Five were convicted, by an exceptionally hostile judge. Eventually their convictions were overturned on appeal.

Moratorium
In this context, suspension of normal activities to facilitate national anti-Vietnam War protests in 1969.

Key dates

Moratorium protests: October–November 1969

Kent State students killed: May 1970

Key question
How did Nixon deal with student protests?

even fawning approval, that in some fashionable circles has become the mark of being "with it"', Middle America agreed with him. Over half of Americans blamed the students for what had happened at Kent State.

Nixon used student behaviour to win votes, as in the 1970 congressional mid-term elections, when he campaigned in San Jose on behalf of Republican Governor Reagan of California. Outside the building where Nixon spoke, demonstrators beat on the walls. When Nixon walked out to the car he climbed atop the presidential limousine and gave them his traditional V-for-victory sign (as used by Churchill during the Second World War). Amidst jeers and boos, eggs and rocks the size of baseballs were thrown at the presidential car – an unprecedented occurrence, which Nixon hoped would shock Middle America and win him votes. It probably did. According to Nixon's biographer Stephen Ambrose, 'At no time in the [1972] campaign did Nixon make a point of his accomplishments. Instead, he ran against pot, permissiveness, protest, pornography and dwindling patriotism' (the report on pornography that Johnson had commissioned, published in October 1970, said pornography had no great adverse effect on society, with which Middle America disagreed).

(ii) Hold your own protest

When New York's liberal mayor John Lindsay criticised Nixon ('the country is virtually on the edge of spiritual – and perhaps even a physical – breakdown') the administration encouraged New York construction workers in an anti-Lindsay and anti-anti-war protest (May 1970). Most voters sided with Nixon and Agnew, who asked whether Americans wanted to be ruled by a democratically elected President or 'a disruptive radical and militant minority', and who failed to differentiate between the mainstream anti-war movement and increasingly violent splinter groups.

(iii) Threaten, monitor and litigate

Anti-war demonstrators were convinced that Nixon was another Hitler who planned to send troops into the campuses, but Nixon did not ask for any new legislation. Instead he:

- Urged the university officials to enforce their own rules, to show 'backbone'.
- Said federal scholarships and loans would cease for convicted student criminals or those who had 'seriously' violated campus regulations.
- Adjusted the draft (August 1972) so that students aged over 20 were no longer threatened.
- Secretly monitored disruptive groups.
- Took protesters to court. In spring 1970, 10,000 people were arrested in Washington DC. Although most of the arrests were thrown out of the courts because they violated the demonstrators' civil rights, the litigation kept the protesters too busy and broke (with legal fees) to cause more trouble.

(iv) Talk to them
LSD in the White House
In April 1970, Tricia Nixon hosted a White House tea for her fellow Finch College alumni. Invited guests included Grace Slick, of the acid-rock group Jefferson Airplane. Slick planned to bring along yippie (see page 9) leader Abbie Hoffman as her date and to lace the punch with LSD, which would be hidden under her fingernails. The journalist whom Slick told of the idea, tipped off the White House. The invitation was withdrawn. Most Americans' sympathy (and votes) gravitated towards the Nixons.

The Lincoln Memorial
Nixon, like many American voters, could hardly understand or communicate with any rebellious young. The feeling was mutual. Nixon made an impromptu visit in the middle of the night to the Lincoln Memorial, where he tried to convince a group of amazed students, who had driven all night to come to Washington to protest against the Vietnam War, that he understood them and wanted the same things they did. One girl told a reporter:

> I hope it was because he was tired, but most of what he was saying was absurd. Here we had come from a university [Syracuse] that's completely uptight – on strike – and when we told him where we were from, he talked about the football team and surfing.

The incomprehensible counterculture
Nixon's Lincoln Memorial visit represented an attempt to try to understand the disaffection, but the counterculture was beyond his and Middle America's comprehension. One extreme group of discontented students, the 'Up Against the Wall Motherfuckers', tried to explain how they felt:

> What we are trying to say, is that the whole fucking struggle isn't anti-imperialist, capitalist, or any of that bullshit. The whole thing is a struggle to live. Dig it? For survival. The fucking society won't let you smoke your dope, ball your women, wear your hair the way you want to. All of that shit is living, dig, and we want to live, that's our thing.

This counterculture was well illustrated at the Woodstock rock festival in August 1969, where Jimi Hendrix performed the 'Star Spangled Banner', and, one participant recalled, 'everyone swam nude in the lake, balling [getting laid] was easier than getting breakfast, and the pigs [police] just smiled and passed out the oats [drugs]'. For three days and three nights, the rolling hills of upstate New York rocked to free musical entertainment.

Where these young people saw liberation and freedom, Middle America saw anarchy, and worried about youthful behaviour and role models (several great rock stars, Janis Joplin, Jim Morrison and Jimi Hendrix all died from drug overdoses within a 10-month period from 1970 to 1971).

President Nixon greets Elvis Presley in the Oval Office in 1970. Presley (whose secret addiction to prescription drugs was to hasten his early death) had offered to help in the war on drugs. Why do you suppose Presley and Nixon liked the idea of Presley helping in the war on drugs?

Key date

Nixon ended draft: 1972

The counterculture and the protests played really badly in Middle America and helped contribute to Nixon's 1972 victory, as did the fact that the President seemed to be halting them. This had been accomplished through increased legal and illegal administration actions. The prosecutions and surveillance, the end of the draft, along with the exhaustion of many radicals, had all combined to dramatically decrease the number of campus protests.

(e) Getting re-elected in 1972 – women
(i) The traditional family
Some of Nixon's policies on women pleased conservatives. He vetoed the 1971 Child Development Act, which would have provided free childcare for the poor, because it was too expensive, and because he felt a communal approach to childcare would 'Sovietise' family life. The veto pleased those who valued the nuclear family and believed that mothers should stay at home and look after the children. Nixon's opposition to abortion (perhaps thinking of the Catholic vote) prompted Democratic Representative Bella Abzug of New York to call him 'the nation's

Key term

Sovietise
Resemble the social and political structure of the USSR.

What happened to the New Left?

The New Left student movement quickly imploded, because:

- The authorities were clearly not going to grant any of their demands.
- Some students wanted a revolutionary terrorism, others felt politics was a farce and activism was a waste of time.

SDS had dissolved into splinter groups:

- The 'Motherfuckers' and 'Crazies' advocated anarchy.
- The Progressive Labour faction seemed to favour Stalinism.
- The Revolutionary Youth Movement (RYM) called for violent revolution.
- The 'Weathermen' favoured terrorist violence: in October 1969, they started a 'Days of Rage' campaign in Chicago. They aimed to provoke mass violence. Their manifesto ('You Don't Need a Weatherman To Tell You Which Way the Wind Blows') said the great contemporary issue was 'between US imperialism and the national liberation struggles against it'. They wanted 'a classless world', freedom from the 'iron grip of authoritarian institutions' and their 'pigs' – teachers, social workers and the army. The Weathermen went underground, randomly attacking established institutions. In March 1970, several Weathermen accidentally blew themselves up when building a bomb in Greenwich Village, which deprived the movement of important leaders.

---

chief resident male chauvinist' in 1973. In his frequent male chauvinism, he was in tune with the vast majority of Middle American males.

(ii) Top government jobs for women

Nixon was probably right when he said, 'I seriously doubted jobs in government for women make for many votes from women', but when an anxious adviser pointed out that only 3.5 per cent of his appointees were women, Nixon tried to get more women in top positions. Pat called publicly for a female Supreme Court judge and was furious when her husband did not appoint one. He seriously considered New York Republican lawyer Rita Hauser, but when she said the Constitution did not bar same-sex marriage, he said, 'There goes a Supreme Court Justice. I can't go that far … that's too far.'

> Nixon adviser Daniel Moynahan on women: '[There will be] violence if women are not granted equality [because] … by all accounts, the women radicals are the most fearsome of all.'

(f) Getting re-elected in 1972 – the economy

Nixon always said that people's votes were determined by their wallets. He was concerned by the inflation inherited from Johnson, who, rather than raising taxes (which would be unpopular), had financed the Vietnam War and the 'Great Society' by increasing the federal government's debt. Nixon also inherited declining productivity in American industry, which was

> **Key question**
> Did Nixon's economic policies win votes?

Nixon's New
Economic Policy:
August 1971

**New Economic
Policy**
Nixon's new policy
of August 1971
froze wages and
prices for 90 days.
When he discovered
that Lenin had had
an NEP, he dumped
the phrase but not
the policy.

How did Vice
President Agnew
contribute to Nixon's
re-election?

Did Nixon's
environmental policies
win him votes?

New Federalism
Nixon's plans to
redirect power away
from Congress and
the federal
bureaucracy, and
back to the states
and local
communities, who
could spend it on
education and other
local issues as
needed.

faced with increased competition from Japan and Western
Europe.

By August 1971 the economy was in big trouble, with inflation,
high unemployment, a looming trade imbalance, and the dollar
under attack from speculators in the international money market.
Nixon's **New Economic Policy** (NEP) of August 1971 introduced
the first peacetime wage-price freeze and devalued the dollar
(making US exports cheaper and more competitive). These
measures did not help solve the underlying problems of the
American economy but did help Richard Nixon get re-elected
(NEP got a 75 per cent approval rating). When Nixon abandoned
the controls, prices rocketed in what became known as the great
inflation of 1973, but by then he had been re-elected.

(g) Getting re-elected in 1972 – revenue sharing

As part of his **New Federalism** Nixon wanted to share federal
revenue directly with the states and thereby decrease the red tape
and bureaucracy traditionally involved in the distribution of
federal funds. Voters liked this.

(h) Getting re-elected in 1972 – the Vice President

Spiro Agnew was to Nixon as Nixon had been to Eisenhower –
the 'hatchetman' who did the President's political dirty work in
his speeches. Wags christened Agnew 'Nixon's Nixon'. In 1972,
Nixon kept Agnew on the ticket, impressed by his hard-hitting
attacks on 'Radiclibs' (radicals/liberals) in the 1970 mid-term
elections. Agnew appealed to Middle America and right-wing
Republicans, as when he attacked the East Coast liberal
establishment, the 'snivelling, hand-wringing power structure
[that] deserves the violent rebellion it encourages'. They were an
'effete corps of impudent snobs who characterise themselves as
intellectuals'.

(i) Getting re-elected in 1972 – the environment

In Nixon's first term, several high-profile incidents suggested that
Nixon was incorrect when he claimed, 'people don't give a shit
about the environment'. In January 1969, offshore oil rigs leaked
crude oil onto 200 miles of beautiful Southern Californian
coastline. Thousands of dying oil-covered seabirds aroused great
public sympathy and antagonism towards the oil company
president who reportedly said, 'I'm amazed at the publicity for
the loss of a few birds'. Equally dramatically, the polluted
Cuyahoga River in Ohio caught fire. Between 1965 and 1970, the
percentage of Americans worried about air pollution rose (from
28 to 69 per cent), as did the percentage concerned about water
pollution (from 35 to 74 per cent). In 1969, only 1 per cent felt
the environment was the greatest domestic problem; by 1971, it
was 25 per cent.

Nixon was responsible for perhaps the most significant
advances in environmental protection in American history, for
example, with legislation on clean air (1970), coasts (1972),

endangered species (1969) and an Environmental Protection Agency (1970).

'In a flat choice between smoke and jobs, we are for jobs', he told a speechwriter, so he was careful not to penalise blue-collar workers with his environmental initiatives. However, when he declared, 'We have to bring the parks to the people', that played well with blue-collar workers who could not afford long-distance trips to national parks. Nixon put 80,000 acres of federal lands into state hands: 642 parks, many within an easy drive of cities, were created.

(j) Getting re-elected in 1972 – foreign policy
(i) Vietnam
Foreign policy was Nixon's speciality. He used it to win votes. Just as in 1968 he had promised 'peace with honour' in Vietnam, so when on the eve of the 1972 election, his National Security Adviser Henry Kissinger announced (in defiance of Nixon's orders) that 'Peace [in Vietnam] is at hand', it played well with the great silent majority.

(ii) SALT
Nixon appealed to many voters with the **SALT** agreement, the first meaningful attempt to put a brake on the nuclear arms race between the USA and the USSR.

(iii) Communist China
Nixon's opening up of relations with Communist China, after 20 years of tense hostility, was both statesmanlike and partly motivated by the desire for re-election. Before his 1972 visit to China, Nixon got the Chinese government's promise that 'no

Key question
How did Nixon's foreign policy contribute to victory in 1972?

Key dates
Kissinger announced 'peace is at hand': November 1972

SALT treaty with the USSR: 1972

Key term
SALT
The Strategic Arms Limitation Treaty signed by Nixon and the Soviet leader Brezhnev in 1972.

President Nixon's famous meeting in 1972 with Chinese Communist leader Mao Zedong. Why do you suppose Nixon wanted to publicise his visit to Communist China?

Key date
Nixon visited
Communist China:
1972

Democrat is to go to China before the President'. His visit had saturation media coverage: Americans were fascinated by pictures of the recently forbidden, exotic country they had hated since China turned Communist in 1949. On his return from China, Nixon waited for nine hours in Alaska so his plane could land in Washington DC at the 9 pm prime TV news hour.

(iv) Lieutenant William Calley

Army Lieutenant William Calley commanded the platoon responsible for the massacre of around 500 Vietnamese civilians at My Lai. His defence was that, in guerrilla warfare, 'they were all enemy. They were all to be destroyed', and that he was following orders. Calley was sentenced to life imprisonment by an army jury of Vietnam veterans. Nixon ordered his release from a stockade and a return to comfortable officer quarters, which appealed to voters (a majority, when polled, felt Calley was a scapegoat).

Key question
How and why did
Nixon beat
McGovern?

(k) Getting re-elected in 1972 – defeating McGovern
(i) The end of Muskie, Wallace and Kennedy

In 1972, Nixon was faced with far less formidable opposition than in 1968. The early moderate Democratic front-runner Edmund Muskie dropped out in May 1972. An assassination attempt permanently disabled George Wallace and put him out of the race for the Democratic nomination. Wallace had campaigned on an anti-busing and anti-East Coast establishment platform. With him gone, the white Southern vote was up for grabs.

Another potential Democratic nominee, Senator **Edward Kennedy**, had been involved in a scandal. His car had gone off the bridge at Chappaquiddick Island, Massachusetts, in July 1969. His 29-year-old passenger, Mary Jo Kopechne, had drowned. Kennedy had been extremely slow in informing the authorities. For years, Kennedy supporters had asked, 'Would you buy a used-car from this man [Nixon]?' Nixon supporters now responded gleefully, 'Would you go for a ride with this man [Kennedy]?'

Key figure

Edward 'Ted' Kennedy (1932–)
Younger brother of John and Bobby Kennedy, Ted was elected senator for Massachusetts in 1962. Repeatedly re-elected, he was a candidate for the Democratic nomination for the presidency in 1980, but his personal life (especially the Chappaquiddick event) severely damaged his prospects. A liberal, he promoted a great deal of legislation to help the less privileged.

(ii) The Democratic National Convention

The 1972 Democratic National Convention delighted Nixon. It was, according to Ambrose, 'the high watermark of the New Left's participation in national politics'. Middle America watched in horror as some delegates booed Humphrey and Johnson and cheered Ho Chi Minh.

Due to new party rules governing the selection of the presidential candidate, the Democrats chose their most left-wing candidate, George McGovern, who seemed to be the candidate of the counterculture. He selected Senator Thomas Eagleton as his running mate, while other delegates nominated China's leader Mao Zedong and Nixon's Attorney General's extrovert wife, Martha 'the mouth' Mitchell.

(iii) McGovern's liberalism

Republicans played on conservative fears of McGovern, christening him the '3As' candidate: **'acid, abortion and amnesty'**. McGovern said he wanted to give $1000 to every American to redistribute income and decrease poverty. He wanted to legalise marijuana and abortion, and cut defence spending. When his vice presidential running mate revealed he had been treated for manic depression and given electric shock therapy, McGovern initially said he was 1000 per cent behind him, then dumped him. The whole episode cost McGovern many votes.

Both parties played it dirty. The Nixon administration broke into the Democratic campaign headquarters (see page 49), and McGovern likened Nixon to Hitler.

(iv) Counting the votes

Not surprisingly, Nixon won by a landslide, with 60.7 per cent of the popular vote. He carried every state except Massachusetts. He was the first Republican presidential candidate ever to gain the majority of Catholic votes. The unions, traditionally Democrat, rejected McGovern because he opposed the Vietnam War and defence spending, so Nixon carried 52 per cent of the blue-collar vote, as opposed to 38 per cent in 1968. Several Southern governors, including Jimmy Carter of Georgia, refused to support McGovern because Southerners so disliked him. Nixon's Southern white support rose from 38 per cent in 1968 to 72 per cent in 1972.

(v) The Democratic Congress

While electioneering, Nixon rarely mentioned the word Republican, preferring to wage a personal campaign, based on his achievements in the first term. He was the only President ever to win two terms without his party having a majority in either the House of Representatives or the Senate in either term. That caused him problems in his second term, as did the dirty tricks that developed into the Watergate scandal.

'Acid, abortion and amnesty'
In 1972, Republicans accused Democratic presidential candidate George McGovern of favouring drugs ('acid'), irresponsible sex ('abortion') and unpatriotic draft dodgers (to whom he would give 'amnesty', i.e. freedom from prosecution).

Key term

President Nixon's suggestion for a bumper sticker: 'NIXon McGovern'

Summary diagram: Getting re-elected in 1972

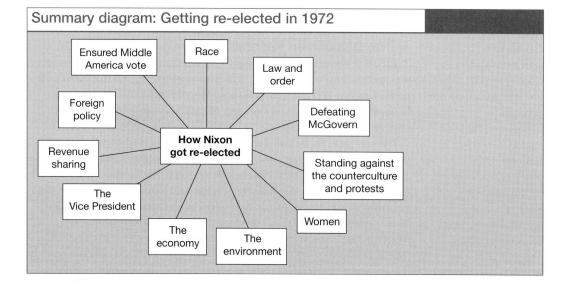

- Ensured Middle America vote
- Race
- Law and order
- Foreign policy
- Defeating McGovern
- Revenue sharing
- **How Nixon got re-elected**
- Standing against the counterculture and protests
- The Vice President
- Women
- The economy
- The environment

4 | The Watergate Scandal

(a) Nixon's White House team

(i) Bob Haldeman and John Ehrlichman

Haldeman managed Nixon's 1968 presidential campaign, then ran the White House as Nixon's chief of staff. Sometimes Haldeman felt Nixon went too far, for example, ignoring Nixon's order that thousands of State Department employees be given lie detector tests to ascertain who had leaked Kissinger's negotiations with North Vietnam. He and Ehrlichman physically controlled access to Nixon. Ehrlichman joined Nixon's campaign staff in 1960. In 1969 he was appointed as Nixon's domestic affairs adviser.

After his fall, Nixon put a great deal of blame on Haldeman and Ehrlichman. He said they were responsible for the Watergate cover-up, and that he had not sacked them early enough because of his personal loyalty to them.

(ii) John Mitchell

Lawyer John Mitchell helped manage Nixon's 1968 presidential campaign and was Nixon's **Attorney General** from January 1969 until he resigned (March 1972) in order to head Nixon's Committee to Re-elect the President (**CREEP**). Mitchell approved wiretaps without court authorisation, prosecuted anti-war protesters, and tried to block publication of the Pentagon Papers (see page 48). Like Nixon, he was antagonistic towards the press. When the *Washington Post*, owned by Katharine Graham, was about to publish something on Watergate, Mitchell threatened 'Katie Graham's gonna get her tit caught in a big fat ringer if that is published'. Mitchell's wife, nicknamed 'Martha the mouth' by the press, was always in the news: 'a heavy drinker and gossip … in delicate mental health' (historian Melvin Small).

(iii) The significance of Mitchell, Haldeman and Ehrlichman

Nixon's biographer Stephen Ambrose believed Nixon's choice of vindictive cynics such as Mitchell, Haldeman and Ehrlichman was disastrous. They helped bring out the worst in him. Nixon had suffered vindictive cynicism under Kennedy, who had harassed him with an **IRS** audit and an investigation into a loan to his brother, and probably bugged his phone. Given Nixon's experiences and advisers, it is not surprising that the Watergate scandal occurred.

(iv) The other Watergate conspirators

John Dean was Associate Deputy Attorney General to Nixon, and from 1970, White House counsel.

Another lawyer, Charles Colson, was appointed as counsel to Nixon in 1969, and then worked on CREEP. Haldeman recalled rumours of wild schemes hatched by Colson, for example, feeding LSD to an anti-Nixon commentator just before he went on TV. 'If

Key question
Who was involved in Watergate?

Key terms

Attorney General
Head of the Justice Department in the federal government.

CREEP
Committee to Re-elect the President, established by the Nixon administration prior to the 1972 presidential election.

IRS
(Internal Revenue Service) US tax collection agency, which monitors taxpayers, checking whether they pay the correct sum.

Nixon said, "Go blow up the Capitol", Colson would salute and buy loads of dynamite', said Ehrlichman.

Jeb Magruder was appointed Special Assistant to Nixon in 1969. He encouraged supportive phone calls and telegrams to the White House whenever the President was in need of support. He worked under Haldeman, and Mitchell in CREEP.

Ex-**FBI** and **CIA** employee James McCord was appointed security director of CREEP in 1972.

Ex-CIA employee E. Howard Hunt wrote spy novels in his spare time. After he retired in 1971, Colson and Ehrlichman appointed him to the White House staff. Working under Gordon Liddy, he was a member of the **'plumbers'** whose job was to stop White House leaks (see page 47). With a red wig, thick glasses and a speech-alteration device provided by the CIA, he took charge of surveillance of Senator Edward Kennedy in 1971–2 (see page 45).

Gordon Liddy campaigned for Nixon in 1968 and joined the White House staff in 1971. He was one of the 'plumbers'. He and Hunt organised the break-in of Daniel Ellsberg's psychiatrist's office (see page 49). They borrowed cameras and burglary equipment from the CIA. Hunt photographed Liddy standing proudly outside the psychiatrist's office (complete with name sign on the door), and then handed the camera back to the CIA with the film left in. 'Idiots', said Dean to the President. In 1972, Liddy joined CREEP. In 1973, he held a lighted candle to his arm to show a lawyer that nothing could induce him to 'spill the beans'!

(b) What exactly was 'Watergate'?

Watergate was the name of an office block in Washington DC. Confusingly, the word has become a kind of shorthand that sums up Nixon's illegal actions while President. The story of how the name of an office building came to be shorthand for corruption, illegality and abuse of power is a long and complex one.

(c) Leaks and the Pentagon Papers

Nixon was excessively concerned about leaks, especially after the press broke the story of his secret bombing of Cambodia in May 1970. The administration ordered the FBI to wiretap 11 officials (including the Secretaries of State and Defence), four journalists and Don Nixon, whom the President called his 'poor damn, dumb brother', who got favours by using his brother's name. Nixon said that nothing that the President ordered done to secure internal order and national security could be considered illegal.

The White House Special Investigation Unit (better known as the 'plumbers') was set up in summer 1971 because the

Key terms

FBI
The Federal Bureau of Investigation was set up in 1924 to help deal with crime.

CIA
The Central Intelligence Agency was set up in 1947 to monitor Communist threats early in the Cold War.

'Plumbers'
Those on the White House staff whose job it was to halt leaks of information.

Key question
What was 'Watergate'?

Key terms

Pentagon Papers
A collection of government documents that reflected badly on the Democratic presidents who had got the USA into Vietnam. The papers were leaked to the press by civil servant Daniel Ellsberg.

Brookings Institution
A liberal Washington think-tank.

Canucks
French-Canadians, of whom New Hampshire had a sizeable population.

DNC
Democratic National Committee, which had its headquarters in the Watergate building in Washington DC.

Pentagon Papers were leaked. Nixon felt the contents damaged his policy of continued involvement in Vietnam until 'peace with honour' was achieved and that national security required that classified documents be kept secret. Fearing more leaks, Nixon wanted to discredit the leaker, Daniel Ellsburg. The FBI refused to tap Ellsburg's phone and to undertake surveillance, so the 'plumbers' were set up to do this. Liddy, Hunt and Colson worked with the 'plumbers' to try to discredit Ellsburg.

'That fucking Colson is going to kill us all', opined Attorney General Mitchell, when Colson wanted to burgle, firebomb or set fire to the **Brookings Institution**, in order to access foreign policy documents. Ehrlichman said no. However, the 'plumbers' did break into the Los Angeles office of Ellsburg's psychiatrist on 3 September 1971, where they found nothing to discredit Ellsburg. As subsequent testimony from Ehrlichman, Dean and Colson varied, it is hard to tell how much Nixon knew about all this.

(d) CREEP

The administration's main preoccupation in 1972 was the presidential election. Nixon was not confident of victory: his prolongation of the Vietnam War was unpopular in many quarters. He therefore established CREEP. CREEP was involved in criminal surveillance, political subversion and illegal fundraising. It collected over $60 million in campaign contributions, 'funny [illegitimate] money' that came in via suitcases. McDonald's chairman donated $255,000, and the company was allowed to continue an unauthorised price increase on a quarter-pounder cheeseburger, while Walter Annenberg paid $250,000 million to get London, the prime ambassadorial posting.

According to historian Iwan Morgan, the 'dirty tricks' of the Nixon campaign 'went far beyond the customary rough-and-tumble of American elections'. The White House ordered surveillance of Democratic Senator Edward Kennedy, hoping to catch him womanising. CREEP worked to discredit the moderate Democratic candidates, for example, informing the press a week before the New Hampshire primary that early Democratic front-runner Senator Edmund Muskie had insulted **Canucks** (Muskie had not). Furious, frustrated and upset, Muskie wept before the TV cameras, which greatly damaged his reputation.

(e) The Watergate break-ins

Key date

Watergate break-in burglars apprehended; Nixon and Haldeman discussed using CIA to halt FBI investigations of break-in: June 1972

Liddy (see page 48) ran CREEP's surveillance. He suggested electronic eavesdropping, kidnapping of political opponents, disruption of Democratic political meetings, and employing prostitutes to compromise Democratic delegates to the National Convention.

CREEP organised two illegal break-ins into the Democratic National Committee (**DNC**) headquarters in the Watergate building in Washington DC. The second break-in (17 June 1972) was discovered. The five burglars (James McCord and four Cuban Americans) were arrested, as were Liddy and Hunt, who were caught in the building opposite with walkie-talkies, co-ordinating the burglary. The President was not worried: 'I think the country does not give much of a shit when somebody bugs somebody else.'

(f) Why break into the Watergate building?

Why had they broken into the DNC? After all, as Nixon said in 1990, it was 'a pathetic target', not a place where strategy was planned. There have been several suggestions:

1. The break-in was a CIA plot to bring down Nixon because of his plan to decrease CIA power under his proposed administrative reforms.
2. Colson and Hunt wanted to expose Democrat links to radical groups.
3. Dean ordered the break-in to get hold of a DNC list of expensive prostitutes that mistakenly included his fiancée.
4. It was hoped to find out about a prostitution ring supposedly operating out of DNC and about the prominent Democrats who used it.
5. Magruder said, 'We were really after everything', especially, some believe, information on Nixon's involvement in Castro assassination plots in 1959–60 and his financial dealings with reclusive billionaire Howard Hughes.
6. When the break-in was authorised, in early 1972, Nixon was behind the Democratic front-runner, Edmund Muskie, in the polls, so information on the Democratic campaign would be useful.

We will probably never know for sure if and how much the President knew about the break-in, but there is no doubt he was involved from the start in the cover-up. He complained to aides that the Democrats had been doing this sort of thing for years – 'they never got caught … everytime the Democrats accuse us of bugging, we should charge that we were being bugged and maybe even plant a bug and find it ourselves'! On the White House taping system, which Nixon knew was in operation, we can hear the President saying to Haldeman:

> 'Did Mitchell know [about the break-in]?'
> 'No.'
> 'Well who was the asshole that did? Is it Liddy? He must be a little nuts.'
> 'He is.'

(g) Getting caught

Within days of the break-in, the FBI traced the plumbers' **laundered money** to CREEP. On 23 June 1972, Nixon and Haldeman discussed using the CIA to stop the FBI: a clear obstruction of justice. The CIA would not co-operate, so Nixon tried to pay the burglars ($430,000) to keep quiet: again,

Laundered money
When money is to be used illegally, it is frequently laundered or 'made clean' by being put into a bank not connected with the payer. In this case, the campaign money was laundered through a Mexican bank with the aim of disguising that it came from CREEP.

Key term

Key date

Watergate burglars convicted: January 1973

Key terms

Deep Throat
The unidentified (at the time) FBI source who gave Woodward and Bernstein vital information during Watergate. In 2005, former FBI employee Mark Felt confessed to being Deep Throat.

Bipartisan
When Republicans and Democrats forgo political partisanship and co-operate on an issue.

obstruction of justice. In January 1973 the burglars were convicted, with sentences ranging from 20 years (Liddy) to 40 (the Cubans).

(h) The press and Watergate

The press in general worked hard to uncover the plot. *Washington Post* reporters Bob Woodward and Carl Bernstein wrote a best-seller, *All the President's Men*, which rather suggested that they had done all the work themselves. What made their myth particularly appealing was the mysterious character '**Deep Throat**', the unidentified (until 2005) administration leaker, who gave them stories.

(i) Senate hearings

In February 1973, the Senate established the **bipartisan** Select Committee on Presidential Campaign Activities, chaired by Sam Ervin (a Democrat Senator from North Carolina, and, according to Nixon, an 'old fart'). On 23 March 1973, McCord agreed to talk about Magruder, Mitchell, Dean, Haldeman and Colson. Then Magruder and Dean agreed to talk. From 17 May to 7 August, Ervin's committee held 37 days of hearings. Television networks covered over 300 hours of testimony. Former Attorney General John Mitchell admitted meeting the conspirators three

The myth that Woodward and Bernstein had done all the work in exposing Watergate was confirmed in a very successful 1976 film, *All the President's Men*, in which the rather ordinary-looking Woodward was played by Robert Redford (left), whom many considered to be quite exceptionally handsome. Dustin Hoffman played Bernstein (right). Why do you suppose this was such a successful film?

times before the break-in. The nation watched transfixed: Ervin ('I'm just a country lawyer') and another committee member, Republican Howard Baker ('What did the President know and when did he know it?'), became national heroes.

John Dean had run the Watergate cover-up before he, Haldeman and Ehrlichman resigned on 30 April. On 22 May Nixon announced that they had been involved in the cover-up without his knowledge. Dean's testimony now suggested Nixon's involvement in the cover-up, but Haldeman and Ehrlichman and Mitchell denied this.

The judge in the Ellsberg case now revealed the break-in in Ellsburg's psychiatrist's office. Then, on 16 July, White House aide Alexander Butterfield revealed the existence of the White House taping system, which had been kept highly secret (even Nixon's own family were not aware that their private conversations were being taped).

(j) Special prosecutors
(i) Cox and Jaworski
In May 1973 Congress forced Nixon to appoint the first ever special prosecutor, Harvard law professor Archibald Cox, a Democrat and Kennedy family friend. Cox and his team (nicknamed the 'Coxsuckers' by the White House) concentrated upon getting hold of the Nixon tapes. Nixon sacked Cox and abolished his office on 20 October 1973, which was constitutionally 'right', but unwise. When Attorney General Elliot Richardson resigned rather than carry out the sacking, there was public outrage at this **'Saturday Night Massacre'**. Nixon's approval ratings sank to 17 per cent. He received a record near-half million telegrams, most of which were hostile.

Under this pressure, Nixon named Leon Jaworski as special prosecutor (31 October). The House Judiciary Committee gave $1 million to hire 106 staff, including Yale lawyer and future First Lady Hillary Rodham Clinton, for an impeachment investigation. Faced with the public outcry, Nixon decided to surrender seven White House tapes.

(ii) Disgrace and disarray
When in October 1973 Agnew, the champion of law and order, became the first Vice President to resign (for tax evasion and accepting bribes), the Nixon administration was in increasing disgrace and disarray. Nixon's own finances came under investigation. Investigators said he had received $1.1 million in income in his first term, but paid less than $80,000 in taxes. Furthermore, his houses at Key Biscayne and San Clemente had greatly increased in value due to improvements made out of the public purse.

Nixon was under tremendous strain. Outside the White House, pickets carried signs saying 'Honk for Impeachment', so car horns were sounded throughout every day. There was talk that Nixon was drinking heavily and emotionally unstable. Invited to an informal dinner at the White House, Barry Goldwater,

Key dates

Senate established Select Committee on Presidential Campaign Activities: February 1973

Haldeman and Ehrlichman resigned: April 1973

Senate investigated Watergate: May–August 1973

Existence of White House taping system revealed: 16 July 1973

Key term

'Saturday Night Massacre'
When Nixon sacked the Watergate special prosecutor and the attorney general resigned.

sickened by Nixon talking 'gibberish', embarrassed the President's family when he called out, 'Act like a President'.

(k) The surrender of tapes
(i) The first seven tapes

The seven White House tapes Nixon surrendered on 26 November 1973 contained an 18½-minute gap in a Nixon–Haldeman conversation. Nixon's loyal secretary Rose Mary Woods said she had accidentally deleted this. Subsequent expert testimony said the tapes had been tampered with. Nixon claimed two other subpoenaed tapes did not even exist. When Nixon assured reporters, 'I am not a crook', most Americans were either embarrassed and/or disbelieving. The line was 'used by stand-up comedians across the country, in and out of Congress', according to Ambrose.

(ii) Indictments and more tapes

On 1 March 1974, seven of Nixon's aides were indicted for the cover-up. The President, it was discovered later, was named as a co-conspirator, but not indicted. Rather than face **impeachment**, Nixon surrendered edited transcripts of other requested tapes in April 1974. The transcripts included many 'expletives deleted', but nothing incriminating. Jaworski wanted the actual tapes and asked the Supreme Court to rule on this. On 24 July, the Supreme Court ruled unanimously, in USA vs RICHARD M. NIXON, PRESIDENT, that the subpoenaed tapes must be released and that the President could not claim **executive privilege**. The 23 June tape (one aide called it the 'smoking gun') proved Nixon had ordered the cover-up and engaged in a conspiracy to obstruct justice.

After the proof that the President had ordered the cover-up, the House Judiciary Committee approved three articles of impeachment on the grounds of:

- obstruction of justice (by participating in the cover-up)
- abuse of power (by invading the civil rights of individuals such as Ellsburg, by misuse of government agencies such as the FBI, CIA and IRS, and by authorising wiretapping)

The charges against Nixon examined by the House Judiciary Committee

Possible involvement in: obstruction of justice; conspiracy to obstruct justice; conspiracy; conspiracy to misuse government agencies; cover-ups; illegal wiretaps; destruction of evidence; election fraud; forgery; perjuries; money-laundering; bribery; financial misdealings; break-ins; offers of clemency; providing political favours for contributions; failure to fulfil the oath of office; failure to answer subpoenas; interference with federal prosecutors; obstruction of Congressional investigations; bombing **Cambodia**; illegal impounding of funds; the Agnew case.

Key dates

Seven White House tapes surrendered: November 1973

Seven Nixon aides indicted: 1 March 1974

Supreme Court said tapes must be released; tapes proved Nixon ordered the cover-up: July 1974

Key terms

Impeachment
Under the US Constitution, Congress has the power to bring an errant President to trial, to impeach him.

Executive privilege
Cold War presidents contended that in such a time of national emergency, they, as the executive branch of government, needed certain privileges, such as keeping some things secret because of the demands of national security.

Cambodia
As part of the war against Communism in Vietnam, Nixon bombed and invaded neighbouring Cambodia, through which Vietnamese Communists travelled to get to Southern Vietnam.

- abuse of Congress (by ignoring subpoenas issued by the Judiciary Committee).

Polls suggested that 75 per cent of Americans believed Nixon guilty of the first charge, and 66 per cent favoured impeachment.

(l) Explanations for Nixon's behaviour
(i) Family problems

Key question
Why did Nixon do it?

Some psychobiographers see Nixon's family background (see page 21) as explaining his actions.

President Nixon faced exceptional strain, with unprecedented protests, riots and disorder. His presidential inauguration was the first to be spoiled by protests and violence. His daughter Julie received dozens of kidnap and murder threats. Unable to attend her graduation because of threatened protests, Nixon resorted to holding a make-believe graduation at **Camp David** in spring 1970. Even without him there, students had chanted, 'Fuck Julie'. In 1977, David Frost told Nixon that he was 'perhaps … the last American casualty of the Vietnam War' (the war bore responsibility for much of the unrest).

(ii) 'Everybody's trying to bug everybody else'

Nixon's predecessors had behaved similarly in many ways, but had not been caught. Kennedy and Johnson had ordered a great deal of wiretapping. Kennedy had his brother Bobby's office bugged. As Nixon said, 'most people around the country think it's [bugging] probably routine, everybody's trying to bug everybody else, it's politics.' Nixon saw nothing wrong in any of this. His Nixon's biographer Joan Hoff described him as **aprincipled**.

(iii) The Radford case

In December 1971, Ehrlichman discovered that the **JCS** had been spying on the **NSC**, using naval officer Charles Radford to steal classified documents from the NSC files. Radford, when caught, claimed that this military intelligence operation aimed at 'bringing Nixon down' – or at least, getting rid of his national security adviser Henry Kissinger. Thus, President Nixon's enemies used the same methods he used. The Radford incident proved to Nixon that:

> this country … this bureaucracy … [is] crawling with … at best unloyal people and at worst treasonable people … We have no discipline in this bureaucracy! We never fire anybody. We never reprimand anybody. We always promote the sons-of-bitches, that kick us in the ass!

(iv) Presidential freedom

In the permanent state of Cold War crisis, the presidency had been gaining power at the expense of Congress. Accustomed to lack of restraint in foreign policy, Nixon desired the same in domestic politics. Nixon felt the President represented the American people. He continually received high approval ratings.

Key terms

Camp David
Presidential retreat in the rural hills of Maryland.

Aprincipled
Unable to see what was acceptable and what was unacceptable behaviour.

JCS
The Joint Chiefs of Staff were the heads of the army, navy and air force.

NSC
The National Security Council advised the President on foreign policy.

Congress did not. Therefore, he felt he had the popular mandate to do what he saw fit.

(v) Siege mentality

Nixon had a point when he described the Democrats as holding 'all four aces in Washington – the Congress, the bureaucracy, the majority of the media, and the formidable group of lawyers and power-brokers who operated behind the scenes in the city'. This led to what Colson subsequently called a 'siege mentality' in the Nixon White House. 'It was "us" versus "them".' CREEP was out to get 'them'.

The media was sometimes unfair to Richard Nixon. In spring 1970, the magazine *Parade* reported that he had made the nation pay for a $60,000 'wind wall' around his swimming pool at his San Clemente home, to protect him from the strong prevailing offshore wind. The wall was in fact a bullet-proof glass shield upon which the Secret Service insisted, and which Nixon had not wanted. *Parade* refused to print a retraction. When Nixon visited China the press reported that he had looked at the famous Great Wall and said, 'This is a great wall'. They omitted the rest of the sentence ('and it had to be built by a great people'), without which the statement was inane. Similarly, in the 1977 Frost interview, Nixon said, 'When the President does it, that means it's not illegal.' What he went on to say is rarely mentioned: he was talking about actions in a national security context.

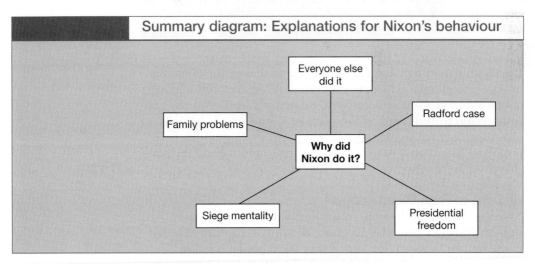

Summary diagram: Explanations for Nixon's behaviour

Why did Nixon do it?
- Everyone else did it
- Radford case
- Family problems
- Siege mentality
- Presidential freedom

Key question
Why did President Nixon resign?

(m) The effect of Watergate

(i) Why did Nixon resign?

On 8 August 1974, Nixon resigned. Why did he resign?

Key date
Nixon resigned: 9 August 1974

(ii) Financial and legal concerns

If Nixon resigned he would get his $60,000 presidential pension and $100,000 for staff expenses. On the other hand, if he was impeached, 'I'll be wiped out financially', by legal fees and his $500,000 bill for unpaid taxes. He had paid virtually no tax while

Mrs Nixon kisses Mrs Ford, as the Nixon family leave the White House for the last time. Nixon's daughters and their husbands walk behind. What contribution could you say Pat Nixon and her daughters made to Richard Nixon's presidency?

President, obtaining a big tax write-off in exchange for donating his vice presidential papers to the National Archives and making dubious capital gains in selling real estate without paying any tax. Also, Nixon feared criminal prosecution if impeached. Anxious about the national trauma, the House Judiciary Committee promised Nixon on 6 August 1973 that he would face no further charges if he resigned.

(iii) Loss of Republican support

Nixon was not sure Republican senators would continue to support him and deny the necessary two-thirds majority required in the Senate to secure his impeachment. Although initially Republican Senator Barry Goldwater said, 'Well, for Christ's sake, everybody bugs everybody else', he changed his mind with the 5 August 1974 release of the 23 June 1972 tape of the conversation between Nixon and Haldeman that showed presidential complicity in the cover-up:

> Dick Nixon has lied to me for the very last time. And to a helluva lot of others in the Senate and House. We're sick to death of it all … Nixon should get his ass out of the White House.

Polls showed 66 per cent of Americans favoured impeachment, while only 27 per cent opposed.

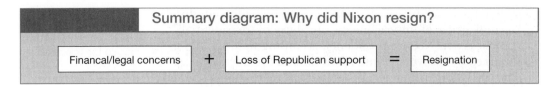

Summary diagram: Why did Nixon resign?

| Financial/legal concerns | + | Loss of Republican support | = | Resignation |

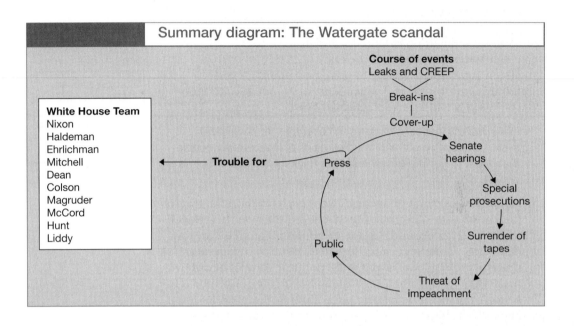

Summary diagram: The Watergate scandal

Course of events
Leaks and CREEP

White House Team
Nixon
Haldeman
Ehrlichman
Mitchell
Dean
Colson
Magruder
McCord
Hunt
Liddy

Break-ins

Cover-up

Trouble for ← Press

Senate hearings

Special prosecutions

Surrender of tapes

Public

Threat of impeachment

Key question
How and why was Watergate important?

5 | The Results and Significance of Watergate

1. Nixon was the first President to resign while in office. Vice President Gerald Ford became President, declaring, 'Our long national nightmare is over'.
2. Nixon 'departed the presidency with a villainous reputation unmatched by any other leader of a modern democracy' (according to historian Iwan Morgan). When scholars rank presidents, Nixon always comes out at or near the bottom.
3. Nixon's own assessments of the significance varied. In 1977 he said he had let the country down. In 1978, he said, 'Some people say I didn't handle it properly, and they are right. I screwed it up and I paid the price.' In 1988, he told the press the cover-up was 'a great mistake', but that the break-in was 'a small thing … break-ins have occurred in other campaigns as well'. In a 1990 memoir he said that Watergate was 'one part wrongdoing, one part blundering, and one part political vendetta by my opponents'.
4. Historian Melvin Small considered the Nixon administration:

   the most scandal-ridden administration in American history … Whereas some presidents participated in some of those illegal activities much of the time, and others did almost all of them on occasion, none of them committed all the illegitimate acts that constituted Watergate all the time.

5. While the break-in and the cover-up are remembered, the second article of impeachment, the abuse of (presidential) power, is not. Nixon's presidency, according to Morgan, was 'marked by the worst abuse of presidential power in US history'. Morgan claimed Watergate was more than a scandal. It was a constitutional crisis, 'the greatest constitutional crisis the country had faced since the civil war' (historian William Chafe).

6. Most subsequent presidential scandals have the word 'gate' (from Watergate) stuck on the end.

7. Nixon contributed greatly to increased popular cynicism toward and distrust of government. In March 1977, Nixon confessed to TV interviewer David Frost:

> I let down my friends, I let down the country. I let down our system of government and the dreams of all those young people that ought to get into government but think it's all too corrupt and the rest.

> Bumper sticker: 'DON'T BLAME ME, I'M FROM MASSACHUSETTS' (the only state won by McGovern).

8. Although government agencies were perhaps more important in exposing the affair, the press believed the role they played in the Watergate scandal made them the great guardians of democracy. Woodward and Bernstein inspired a generation of reporters to dig away at potential political scandal in order to make their name. The press role in Watergate confirmed Nixon's oft-stated belief (see page 25) that the press had always been his enemy ('75 per cent of these guys hate my guts'). Their relationship was indeed particularly bad and perhaps played a part in the tenacity with which the press investigated the Watergate affair.

9. Congress enacted several laws to try to limit presidential power and avoid another Watergate, for example, the Budget and Impoundment Control Act (1974) (see page 60) and the Ethics in Government Act (1978). Historians disagree over their effectiveness.

10. Some observers felt that there had been a drunk and/or a madman in the White House. Kissinger frequently discussed the President's 'stability' with colleagues. A frightened Pentagon official feared Nixon was losing control during the Cambodian invasion. When briefing congressional leaders on the Arab–Israeli war in 1973, Nixon started to roll his head and make jokes about Kissinger's sex life. 'The President's acting very strange' wrote House Speaker Tip O'Neill (see page 82).

11. The Republican Party suffered greatly in the 1974 congressional elections: the four Republicans on the House Judiciary Committee who had voted against impeachment lost their seats. The presidential pardon for Nixon probably cost Gerald Ford the 1976 election (see page 69). The party moved to the right: when Nixon resigned, conservatives criticised his policies. When Ford was defeated by Jimmy Carter, a defeat that owed a great deal to Nixon, the conservatives took control of the Republican Party, which

dramatically affected American politics, government, economic affairs and foreign policy for many years afterwards (see Chapter 4).

12. Nixon's biographer Joan Hoff contended that Watergate was the inevitable product of the 'aprincipled American political system', 'a disaster waiting to happen'. She lamented that the popular belief that it was all Nixon's fault stopped much-needed reform of the American political and constitutional system, claiming that Ronald Reagan's military and diplomatic actions and his 'violations of the democratic process … far exceeded those for which Nixon was almost impeached' (see pages 117–18).

13. Loyal aide Bob Haldeman believed that Nixon's **New American Revolution**, a vote-winning plan to devolve federal funds and greater power to the 50 states over issues such as health and education, was the 'hidden story of Watergate'. Seventy-seven per cent of Americans favoured the plan, which Nixon said would decrease bureaucracy and thereby lower taxes. Haldeman and Nixon believed that because the revolution represented a threat to the power of Congress and the federal bureaucracy, both took the opportunity presented by Watergate to attack and stop Nixon.

Key terms

New American Revolution
Nixon's plan to devolve power from the federal government to state governments, to decrease bureaucracy and save money.

Administration
When Americans talk of 'the Nixon administration', they mean the government as led by that particular President.

Key question
In what ways did Nixon abuse power?

(a) 'Abuse of power' and 'abuse of Congress'?
(i) 'Abuse of power'
In August 1971, John Dean sent a memo to staff that clearly demonstrated willingness to abuse presidential power:

> How can we maximise the fact of our incumbency in dealing with persons known to be active in their opposition to our **Administration**? Stated a bit more bluntly – how can we use the available federal machinery to screw our political enemies?

The authorisation of the break-ins of Ellsburg's psychiatrist's office and the Watergate building are probably the best-known examples of the abuse of power. An example of the President's (attempted) involvement occurred in summer 1971 when a Long Island newspaper published a series on the finances of Nixon's best (some say only) friend, Bebe Rebozo. Nixon ordered Haldeman to 'figure out a plan … to harass … Use the power we have', particularly the IRS. Ironically, although the Kennedys used the IRS to embarrass political enemies such as Nixon, the IRS usually refused to be used by Nixon, so in this case he was guilty only of attempting to misuse power. On the other hand, owners of newspapers hostile to Nixon were hounded by the IRS (as Nixon himself had been).

Key question
Was Nixon guilty of 'abuse of Congress'?

(ii) Nixon's poor relations with Congress
An aide recalled how Nixon felt it was 'somewhat demeaning' to have to ask Congress for support. Nixon was unusual in that he was a Republican President who never had a Republican Senate or House of Representatives with which to work, but he did not even get on with the Republicans in Congress. An aide of

Gerald Ford said, 'Nixon couldn't hide his disdain for the Congress and he treated some individuals in Congress very badly'. In 1970 Nixon repeatedly accused Congress of bringing the US government into disrepute by opposing his programmes. He described Congress as:

> cumbersome, undisciplined, isolationist, fiscally irresponsible, overly vulnerable to pressures from organised minorities, and too dominated by the media.

Ehrlichman said congressmen were 'furtive mediocrities', and Congress was a place where:

> members consume time in enormous quantities in their quaint Congressional processes. They recess; they **junket**; they arrive late and they leave early; they attend conferences out of town, fly off to give speeches, sip and chat and endlessly party. And only sometimes do they focus on legislation.

(iii) Attempted curtailment of congressional power

Nixon certainly tried to circumvent congressional power, for example over the appointment of directors of government agencies, for which Congress took him to court. He delayed, evaded and on 27 occasions flat-out ignored congressional requests for information on executive actions. His predecessors had occasionally claimed executive privilege in keeping certain actions quiet, but Nixon went much further.

Nixon also challenged Congress by **impounding** money Congress had allocated to spend on programmes such as the Clean Water Act of 1972. He only wanted to spend 25 per cent of what Congress had appropriated, because he was concerned about balancing the budget and/or because he wanted to increase presidential power, depending on one's viewpoint. In 1974 the House Judiciary Committee wanted to include impoundment in the impeachment charges, but lawyers said that Nixon's position was supported by the constitution and statutory powers. Those sympathetic to Nixon say that the water pollution legislation was used by the Democratic Congress to embarrass the President, on a popular issue in an election year, that the amount they wanted to spend was unrealistically high and probably could not have been spent.

Key terms

Junket
The taking advantage of political office by accepting perks such as lavish entertainments.

Impounding
When the President refuses to spend money allocated by Congress.

Summary diagram: 'Abuse of power' and 'abuse of Congress

Abuse of power	Abuse of Congress
Screw enemies	Treat them badly
Break-ins	Insult them
Use IRS	Try to curtail their power
Phone-tapping	Ignore their requests for information

Key question
Why did President
Ford pardon Nixon?

Key term

**House Minority
Leader**
Leader of the
political party in
the minority in the
House of
Representatives.

Key date

President Ford
pardoned Nixon:
September 1974

(b) The pardon of President Nixon

(i) Vice President Agnew and Vice President Ford

When Spiro Agnew became the first Vice President to resign
(10 October 1973) (see page 52), Nixon chose Republican **House
Minority Leader**, Gerald Ford, as Vice President.

Haldeman claimed Nixon chose Ford because he reasoned that
as the House knew Ford's ability so well, they would never
impeach the President lest Ford replace him. Nevertheless, when
Nixon resigned, Ford became President.

(ii) President Ford and the pardon

The pardon

With his resignation, Nixon avoided an impeachment trial.
When President Ford pardoned him, Nixon avoided any criminal
prosecution.

On 8 September 1974, President Ford said a pardon of former
President Nixon was the best way to end the 'American tragedy',
because the national trauma would be prolonged if Nixon went
on trial. It was better, Ford thought, to let the slow process of
healing begin. Amidst national outrage, Ford's approval rating
sank from 71 to 49 per cent.

Why did Ford pardon Nixon?

Privately, Ford gave several reasons for the pardon:

- A former President in the dock in a criminal court would
  degrade the presidency as well as the individual.
- It would be difficult, even impossible, to meet Supreme Court
  standards for an unbiased jury.
- The indictment and trial would take a long time, and the
  nation would continue its unhealthy and divisive obsession with
  Watergate.
- If Nixon were found guilty, whoever was President would have
  to pardon him, so why not sooner rather than later?
- Nixon's family and a Ford envoy to Nixon suggested that Nixon
  was, according to the envoy, 'an absolute candidate for suicide;
  the most depressed human being I have ever met'. The pardon
  made Nixon more depressed and for a dangerously long time
  he refused hospitalisation because of his phlebitis, despite the
  possibility of a life-threatening embolism. In his speech
  announcing the pardon, Ford said 'the American tragedy'
  needed to be ended, and 'I feel that Richard Nixon and his
  loved ones have suffered enough.'
- It was Christian to show mercy.
- Ford believed resignation from office was an admission of guilt.
- Possibly Ford was concerned for Republican electoral prospects
  in 1976 if Nixon's misdemeanours were still being pored over
  by the press.

A deal?

Many contemporaries were convinced that Nixon and Ford had
made a deal, a pardon in exchange for the presidency. There is
no evidence of any deal (although Nixon tried to get one).

A wise decision?
When Gerald Ford died in 2007, Senator Edward Kennedy, who had opposed the pardon at the time, said he now felt it to be the right decision. Some Americans felt that Ford should have made Nixon sign a statement of guilt in exchange for the pardon. The pardon never specified for what Nixon was being pardoned. Ford always carried a Supreme Court decision in his wallet that a pardon 'carries imputation of guilt, acceptance, a confession of it'. Pardoning Nixon certainly helped finish Ford's political career (see page 75).

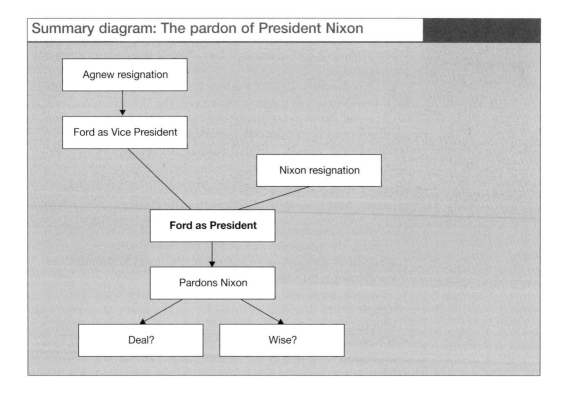

Summary diagram: The pardon of President Nixon

(c) What happened to the Watergate conspirators?
(i) Richard Nixon

For many Americans, the sentencing of Nixon's aides to imprisonment constituted a tacit conviction of the ex-President too.

While friends and supporters helped him financially, enemies gloated over Woodward and Bernstein's book on *The Final Days* of his presidency. Readers were agog at the depiction of a dangerously unstable drinker, who talked to portraits on the White House wall, and had not had sexual relations with his (drunken) wife for 14 years. Despite her husband's protests, Pat Nixon read it, then suffered a stroke.

In retirement, Nixon worked incessantly and quite successfully to rehabilitate his reputation and to ensure his financial security. A series of foreign visits, books, articles and interviews reminded people of his exceptional knowledge of foreign affairs. Joan Hoff

Key question
Did the Watergate Conspirators receive just treatment?

"They are leaders who have made a difference.
Not because they wished it, but because they willed it."

-RN

Four Republican Presidents (left to right: Ronald Reagan, Richard Nixon, George H.W. Bush and Gerald Ford) amongst the life-size bronzes of world leaders whom Nixon had known, in the Richard Nixon Library, established to house records of, and tributes to, Nixon's life and career. For what reasons might a President build a presidential library?

notes the unusual process of 'rehabilitation through internment services', whereby Nixon's attendance at funerals such as those of his old political enemy Hubert Humphrey (1978) and his wife Pat (1993) made people feel both nostalgic and sorry for him.

(ii) The other Watergate conspirators

Haldeman, Ehrlichman, Dean, Mitchell, Colson, Hunt, Liddy, McCord and Magruder were all convicted, on charges such as conspiracy, obstruction of justice, perjury, burglary and wiretapping. Their jail sentences varied between four months and 20 years, but all were released early. With the exception of Mitchell, all wrote about Watergate. Haldeman went back into business. Colson worked on prison reform. Hunt wrote more spy novels. Liddy became a writer and 'shock jock' (right-wing) radio talk show host. McCord worked for the University of Michigan athletics department, and got that university into trouble by giving money from his illegal gambling ring to athletes. Magruder became a Presbyterian minister, admitting in 2003 for the first time that President Nixon gave orders for the break-in, which Dean confirmed. After criticism for not providing this evidence during his 1974 trial, Magruder was arrested for disorderly conduct and subsequently for drunk driving.

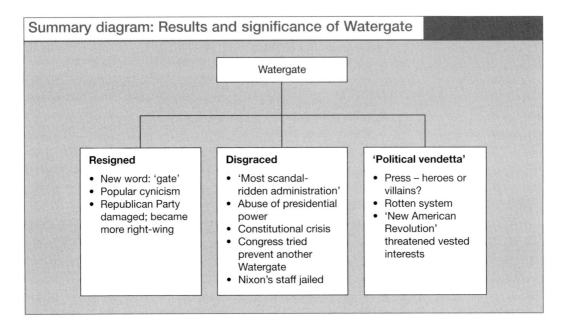

Summary diagram: Results and significance of Watergate

Watergate

Resigned
- New word: 'gate'
- Popular cynicism
- Republican Party damaged; became more right-wing

Disgraced
- 'Most scandal-ridden administration'
- Abuse of presidential power
- Constitutional crisis
- Congress tried prevent another Watergate
- Nixon's staff jailed

'Political vendetta'
- Press – heroes or villains?
- Rotten system
- 'New American Revolution' threatened vested interests

Study Guide: AS Question

In the style of Edexcel

How far do you agree that the key factor influencing Richard Nixon's election as President in 1968 and 1972 was the popularity of his policies on the Vietnam War? (30 marks)

Exam tips

The cross-references are intended to take you straight to the material that will help you answer the question.

This is a question asking you to explain why Richard Nixon was elected and re-elected as President. Every history essay will require you to make decisions about how you are going to organise your response. Here you must chose whether or not to deal with the campaigns separately. You will not need lengthy descriptions of his campaigns, but you need to identify the factors that gave him voter appeal in the elections. The key to success in the examination is to make sure your answers focus on the question – and the best way to ensure that focus in this essay is to identify the factors accounting for Nixon's success, let those factors drive your paragraph points, and then draw on evidence from both campaigns to support the points you make. You will still be able to show when a factor was more influential in one campaign than the other.

The other important decision you have to make relates to what information you select. Much that is interesting about Nixon may not be strictly relevant and useful for this question. When you only have about 35 minutes to write an answer, you need to concentrate on what is central to include. In this case, you can omit information about how Nixon came to be chosen as the Republican Party's candidate (page 25) and just concentrate on why he won the struggle against his Democratic rivals in 1968 (pages 26–33) and 1972 (pages 34–6).

You must consider in detail the popularity of Nixon's Vietnam policies (pages 26–7, 29, 31–2, 38 and 40), as it is the key factor in the question. In addition to the appeal of Nixon's statements on, and policy towards, Vietnam, consider the following factors:

- Nixon's appeal to Middle America: the significance of his approach to welfare, race, law and order (pages 26, 30–1 and 34–41).
- His foreign policy: how did this increase support at home between 1968 and 1972 (pages 44–5)?
- Electioneering: were his campaigns better than those mounted by the Democrats (pages 26–7)?
- Weaknesses of his opponents: were the Democrats more divided, and less appealing (pages 31–2 and 45–6)?
- His economic policy (pages 42–3).

Finally, you should come to an overall conclusion. How much did Nixon's Vietnam policies influence his success in both elections? Was his attention to the domestic (i.e. within the USA) concerns and the prejudices of Middle America actually more important in both campaigns?

NB. Foreign policy is not part of the syllabus: only its impact on US domestic affairs is relevant.

3 Presidents Ford (1974–7) and Carter (1977–81)

POINTS TO CONSIDER

As single-term presidents who had difficulties with Congress, neither Ford nor Carter was perceived as successful on domestic issues. This chapter investigates their lack of success (explaining why neither won re-election) and illuminates important political and social themes.

Key dates

1974	Ford became President
	Ford pardoned Nixon
	Acute racial tensions over desegregation of Boston schools
1976	Ford defeated by Carter in the presidential election
1977	Miners' strike
1978	Carter's energy legislation
	Supreme Court supported affirmative action but not quotas
1979	Three Mile Island partial nuclear meltdown
1980	Billygate
1980	Race riots
	Reagan defeated Carter in presidential election

1 | Gerald Ford – Background

(a) Youth and education

Ford was born in Omaha, Nebraska, in 1913. In 1914, his mother left her husband ('I heard that he hit her frequently', Ford recalled) and took their son to Grand Rapids, Michigan. At church, she met then married Gerald R. Ford Sr, a businessman.

Ford worked hard in the family business, and won an athletics scholarship to attend the University of Michigan. He worked at a hospital and sold his blood every eight or ten weeks to finance his liberal arts degree. Although one of the best college football players in the country, Ford rejected offers from professional teams, believing 'professional football probably wouldn't lead me anywhere'.

Ford coached Yale University's team (1935–8), then studied for a law degree, graduating in the top third of his class (1941). He

Key question
Why did Ford's background appeal to American voters?

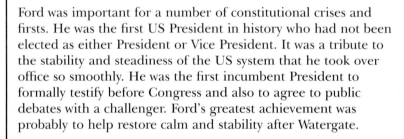

Profile: Gerald Rudolph Ford (1913–2007)

1913		– Born in Omaha, Nebraska
1941		– Yale law degree
1948		– Elected to the House of Representatives (Republican)
1965		– Elected House Minority Leader
1973		– After Agnew's resignation, became Vice President
1974	August 9	– After Nixon's resignation, became President
	September 8	– Pardoned Nixon
	October 17	– Voluntarily appeared before House of Representatives to explain pardon
1976	August	– Won Republican nomination, but had been greatly damaged by the conservative challenge from Ronald Reagan
	November	– Defeated by Jimmy Carter in presidential election
1976–7		– Retired from politics
2007		– Died

Ford was important for a number of constitutional crises and firsts. He was the first US President in history who had not been elected as either President or Vice President. It was a tribute to the stability and steadiness of the US system that he took over office so smoothly. He was the first incumbent President to formally testify before Congress and also to agree to public debates with a challenger. Ford's greatest achievement was probably to help restore calm and stability after Watergate.

saw active navy service in the Second World War, then returned to Grand Rapids. He was elected to Congress in 1948.

(b) Congressman Ford 1948–74

Constituents and fellow congressmen liked hard-working Republican Congressman Ford, who was elected House Minority Leader in 1965. In 1968, Nixon, who considered Ford the consummate legislator, asked Ford to be his running mate. Ford declined, hoping to be Speaker of the House.

Although Ehrlichman (see page 47) 'wasn't impressed' with Ford ('not excessively bright') and Ford felt the Nixon White House believed that congressional Republicans existed 'only to follow their instructions', Ford was very loyal to the Nixon administration. A White House aide described Ford as 'the tool of the Nixon administration – like a puppy dog … They would wind him up and he would go "Arf, Arf".' When the Watergate scandal broke, Ford worked to block congressional investigations into the financing of the break-in (see page 49).

When Vice President Agnew resigned (see page 52), loyal, likeable Jerry Ford was the only candidate acceptable to both the White House and Congress (the most relieved man in America was House Speaker Carl Albert, who had been next in line for the presidency since the Vice President had resigned – Albert had recently driven his car through a saloon window).

Despite wife Betty's protests, Ford accepted the vice-presidency. Leading Republicans preferred Rockefeller (see page 29) or Ronald Reagan (see page 98), but as Congress had to confirm him, it had to be Ford who, when sworn in, joked, that he was **'a Ford, not a Lincoln'**.

(c) Vice President Ford

Ford defended Nixon himself, but in March 1974 shocked 1000 Chicago Republicans:

> What lessons can the Republican Party learn from Watergate? … Never again must America allow an arrogant, élite guard of political adolescents like [CREEP] … to bypass the regular party system and dictate the terms of the national election … [I am] not blaming the President for CREEP. He picked people he thought would do a good job.

When the 'smoking gun' tape (see page 53) was released, Ford broke with the administration. After Nixon resigned, Ford, usually an undistinguished speaker, impressed **staffers** in his **inauguration** speech (August 1974):

> My fellow Americans, our long national nightmare is over. Our constitution works. Our great republic is a government of laws and not of men. Here, the people rule.

Time magazine wrote that a 'time for healing' was needed: Watergate and Vietnam had adversely affected American political institutions, divided American society, and damaged the American economy. These themes ran through and dominated Ford's presidency.

Key terms

'A Ford, not a Lincoln'
Ford was saying that he was not going to be a great President like Abraham Lincoln, playing on the public's familiarity with cars. Fords were the cars of ordinary Americans; Lincolns were expensive, prestige cars.

Staffers
In this context, the White House staff.

Inauguration
The President usually undergoes an elaborate inauguration ceremony on Capitol Hill, at which he is sworn into office. In the unprecedented 1974 situation, Ford was inaugurated inside the White House.

Key date

Ford became President: August 1974

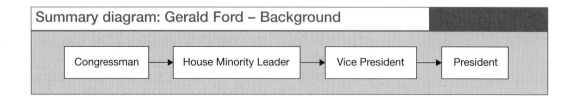

Summary diagram: Gerald Ford – Background

Congressman → House Minority Leader → Vice President → President

Key question
Why was Ford not re-elected?

Key question
When and why did voters decide Ford was corrupt?

Key terms

Equal Rights Amendment (ERA)
Congress passed the ERA in 1972. Designed to help women and minorities in employment and education, it was never ratified by sufficient states.

ROE vs WADE
The Supreme Court decision legalising abortion.

Key date

Ford pardoned Nixon: 1974

2 | Gerald Ford – The Half-a-Term President

As President, Ford seemed unable to get anything right.

(a) Just another corrupt politician

The press and people were desperate for a 'regular guy' in the White House. When the pyjama-clad President-elect picked up the morning newspaper off his front porch and waved to the press, they felt they had one. *Newsweek* said he was, 'nothing any different from your next-door neighbour'.

It helped that Ford had what Betty called 'one big scrappy family'. Susan, their 17-year-old daughter, insisted on wearing jeans in the White House. Her brother Jack showed Beatle George Harrison around the residence. Many Middle America parents sympathised when it was rumoured that Jack smoked pot.

Betty Ford was fun. She liked Citizen's Band (CB) radios and talked to truck drivers in Washington DC, who called her 'First Mama'. She was photographed pushing the fully clothed Ford into a Camp David pool. She was also feisty. She shocked many when she praised the **Equal Rights Amendment (ERA)** and **ROE vs WADE** ('great, great decision'), said she 'wouldn't be a bit surprised' if her daughter had an affair, and assumed her children had experimented with pot; she said she would if she were young. The President speculated as to how many million votes that lost him, but many Americans admired her refreshing honesty, especially after she spoke freely about her 1974 breast cancer scare, in order to encourage self-examination.

The American people wanted to believe in their President, but the honeymoon period ended when Ford pardoned Nixon. His popularity never recovered. The 'regular guy' was just another politician after all. His popularity never recovered from the pardon.

A nice, regular guy
Some thought Gerald Ford was too nice. After Nixon nearly died (see page 61), Ford was in Los Angeles campaigning for Republican candidates. Aides urged him not to visit Nixon, but Ford responded, 'If there's no place in politics for human compassion, there is something wrong with politics. I'm going to leave it to Pat.' He asked Pat if a visit would help. She said, 'I can't think of anything that would help Dick more.' Ford visited Nixon, and probably lost himself some votes.

Although some believed Ford when he testified, 'There was no deal, period', others believed he had struck a deal with the outgoing President (see page 61). One congressman said, 'Jerry Ford will deal on anything and don't forget it.'

(b) Vietnam

Initially Ford, like 60 per cent of Americans, opposed amnesty for **draft dodgers**. Then he decided clemency would help heal the nation. It was not unconditional amnesty: some liberals called it 'shamnesty'. Offenders had to turn themselves in. Some got alternative service, some a full pardon, some were jailed. Neither liberals nor conservatives were satisfied.

Key question
How did Vietnam cost Ford votes?

(c) President vs Congress
(i) Ford's pardon of Richard Nixon

Nixon bequeathed an aggressive legislature to Ford (see page 58). The pardon increased the tension. Republican congressmen blamed it for the loss of 43 House seats in 1974.

When Congress demanded more information on the pardon, Ford volunteered to be the first President to testify since Lincoln. The congressional interrogation was 'amazing' according to Ford's biographer, J.R. Greene:

Key question
How well did Ford handle Congress?

> Congress had a President on the ropes, defending and explaining his most private decision-making ... clearly, the locus of power in the federal government had shifted from the White House to **Capitol Hill**.

One Washington reporter talked of a 'Power Earthquake'.

(ii) Ford's failure with Congress

Ford's relations with Congress were so poor that he vetoed 66 (mostly spending) bills in his 29 months' presidency. Congress overrode his veto 12 times. Some say that Ford's failure to work with Congress was not all his fault. He became President at a low point in the prestige of the presidency, had no genuine electoral mandate and the Republicans were very much in the minority in both houses of Congress. On the other hand, Richard Reeves, in *A Ford Not A Lincoln* (New York, 1975), depicted Ford as a vain, ignorant, vacuous man, without principles or goals, distinguished only by a talent for ingratiation, which alone accounted for his accession to the presidency. Reeves said that Ford lacked the ability to inspire. Barbara Kellerman, in *The Political Presidency: Practice of Leadership* (Oxford, 1984), studied Ford's attempts to obtain a tax cut from Congress, and came to similar conclusions. In his first days as President, Ford advocated a tax increase. Congress did not want that. A few weeks later, Ford asked Congress to approve a $16 billion tax cut. When Congress agreed to $7 billion, Ford accepted it. This seemed to reveal a President without a clear sense of direction, a President who compromised too soon and too easily, and one without the essential persuasion skills.

(iii) The CIA and moral leadership

Although the CIA was not supposed to have any domestic authority, the plumbers' use of CIA equipment in the Ellsburg break-in (see page 49) demonstrated CIA intervention in

Draft dodger
One who avoided being called up to fight in the Vietnam War.

Capitol Hill
The location of the US Congress, the words Capitol Hill are often used as a synonym for Congress.

Key terms

Key terms

Angola
When the Portuguese empire in Africa came to an end, Angola emerged as an independent nation. Ford wanted to support an anti-Soviet Angolese faction.

Cyprus crisis
Cyprus' population was 80 per cent Greek, 20 per cent Turkish. A Greek-backed coup resulted in a Cypriot government that declared union with Greece. Turkey invaded to protect the Turkish minority.

Dissident
One who disagrees with the official party line, in this case, Moscow's.

domestic affairs. When CIA Director William Colby tried to clean up the agency, the *New York Times* got wind of dubious foreign activities, such as the attempt to overthrow the Chilean government (1970–3).

Ford thought he had better let Vice President Rockefeller (see page 29) investigate the CIA before Congress did. When it became clear that Rockefeller's commission (1974–5) had uncovered material about CIA assassination plots under Kennedy and that Ford did not want it published, the Senate began to investigate and monitor the CIA. In 1975, Congress stopped Ford using the CIA in **Angola**.

Ford, says J.R. Greene, had missed an opportunity to 'corner the post-Watergate market on morality'. In the CIA affair, Congress, not the President, seemed to provide the moral leadership.

(iv) Foreign policy

Congress also reasserted foreign policy leadership during the **Cyprus crisis**. Ford backed Turkey, but Congress favoured Greece and cut off military aid to Turkey. Congress had taken control of US foreign policy for the first time in many years.

In summer 1975, Congress pushed Ford around again, suggesting he meet Soviet **dissident** Alexander Solzhenitsyn. About to meet Soviet leader Brezhnev, Ford was reluctant, especially as he considered the volatile Solzhenitsyn to be a 'goddamned horse's ass'. Senators suggested some ridiculous dates for a meeting, including 4 July, when Ford was fully booked. When Ford finally issued an invitation, Congress dropped the whole idea.

(d) President vs press

The press also turned against Ford after the pardon, picking up on Lyndon Johnson's joke about Ford having played football once too often without a helmet. The TV showed Ford falling on the ski slopes in Colorado, and falling down the plane ramp in Austria – one network showed that 11 times in one newscast. A *New York* magazine cover showed Ford as Bozo the Clown.

Key question
How did Ford alienate right-wing Republicans?

Key term

Congressional mid-term elections
Some voters elect senators and representatives in presidential election years, some elect them in the middle of a President's term.

(e) The right-wing Republican theme

Republican Party right-wingers disliked Nelson Rockefeller. They hated him because of his challenge to Goldwater in 1964, and considered him a spendthrift (he had spent New York state into recession) and a womaniser (he was divorced). After he promised to pay his $1 million back taxes, Rockefeller was sworn in as Vice President (December 1974). The confirmation battle left Ford four months without a Vice President and caused tension within the Republican Party.

After the Nixon pardon and disastrous **congressional mid-term elections**, right-wing Republicans openly criticised Ford. A conservative New Hampshire newspaper called him 'Jerry the Jerk'. Right-wing Californian Governor Ronald Reagan challenged him for the Republican nomination in 1976. 'Ford thought Reagan was a phoney', said one that Ford aide, 'and

Reagan thought Ford was a lightweight, and neither one felt the other was fit to be President'.

(f) Women's rights

Key question
Did Ford's policies please women voters?

Women's lives had changed dramatically since the early 1960s. The skyrocketing divorce rate (40 per cent) and new attitudes to work, sex, family and personal freedom seemed to indicate a cultural revolution.

Over two-thirds of female college students agreed 'the idea that the woman's place is in the home is nonsense'. Most women now expected to work for most of their lives, even with young families. More women entered traditionally masculine occupations such as medicine and law, although they only received 73 per cent of the salaries paid to professional men. Women remained overwhelmingly dominant in low-paid jobs and constituted 66 per cent of adults classified as poor. The phrase 'feminisation of poverty' entered the language.

Although Betty Ford championed the Equal Rights Amendment, her husband did nothing to help women.

(g) Racial equality

Key question
Did Ford deal with racial inequality?

Although African Americans were making great gains (see box), there was still a long way to go, particularly in education.

Black progress – statistics
- Number of blacks in Congress in 1959 – 4; in 1969 – 10; in 1980 – 18.
- Number of blacks in college in 1997 – 1.1 million (a 500 per cent increase over 1960).
- Number of black mayors in 1960 – none; in the 1970s – Los Angeles, Detroit, Cleveland, Birmingham, Oakland, Atlanta.
- Proportion of black families earning over $10,000 (in **constant dollars**): in 1947 – 3 per cent; in 1960 – 13 per cent; in 1971 – 31 per cent.

However, in the 1970s …
- Although 35–45 per cent of black families were classified as middle class, black male teenage unemployment was 50 per cent. When middle-class residents moved out, ghetto communities became even more rundown.
- Half of all black teenagers in New York City dropped out of high school before graduation.
- Compared to a white child, a black child was twice as likely to die before reaching the age of one, twice as likely to drop out of school, and four times as likely to be murdered.

Constant dollars
To make comparisons between dates more meaningful, economists factor in changes in the cost of living or the value of the currency, etc.

Key term

(i) School desegregation

In 1969 the Supreme Court ruled that separate, but equal schools were 'no longer constitutionally permissible'. By 1974, the percentage of black school children attending segregated schools in the South was down from 68 to 8 per cent. However, *de facto* segregation remained in the North.

(ii) The desegregation of schools in Boston

Boston's public schools were clearly separate and unequal. In 1965, 25 per cent of Boston students were black but only 0.5 per cent of teachers were black and none was a principal. **NAACP** initiated a federal district court case, complaining about inferior educational materials and a textbook in which the song 'Ten Little Niggers Sitting on a Fence' was used to teach arithmetic. In June 1974 the court found Boston guilty of unconstitutional segregation of schools and ordered busing of black students from Boston's Roxbury area to the predominantly white South High School in neighbouring Irish American South Boston. The city authorities refused to comply. White anti-busing groups such as Restore Our Alienated Rights (ROAR) sprang up. When Massachusetts Senator Edward Kennedy, whose children attended private schools, advocated busing, ROAR marchers chased him into the Federal Building and pounded on the barricaded glass doors until they shattered.

On Boston's first desegregated day, black parents greeted white students, but South Boston High white parents surrounded the school, jeered and threw objects at black students. Nine children were injured, 18 buses damaged. Whites then boycotted city schools. White adults 'welcomed' black students to school throughout the year by holding bananas, calling them apes and chanting obscenities. Schools installed metal detectors because knife fights became common.

Ford opposed busing, but had troops ready when Boston erupted (December 1974). A white South Boston High student was stabbed. White parents surrounded the school. Black students had to escape out the back. However, when Boston's education authorities were held in contempt of court, the busing increased and the violence decreased.

(iii) The permanent underclass

Senator Edward Kennedy talked of 'the great unmentioned problem of America today', the development of 'a permanent underclass in our society'. Those less sympathetic criticised

Key terms

NAACP
The National Association for the Advancement of Colored People was the oldest and most respected black civil rights movement.

Flip-flop
When a politician reverses a political stance.

Key date

Acute racial tensions over desegregation of Boston schools: 1974

New York City bankrupt!
New York City's population was as big as Sweden's, its budget as big as India's. The city spent more than it received in taxes and federal and state aid. When Ford refused to help, an October 1975 *New York Daily News* headline was: 'FORD TO CITY – DROP DEAD'.

Ford **flip-flopped** (there was a presidential election coming up) and Congress rapidly passed his bill to bail out New York City.

'welfare mentality', when welfare became an accepted way of life for successive generations that, without a decent education, found it hard to escape. Ford had no real ideas or impact on these problems.

(h) Labour
Faced with inflation, unemployment, pressure to be more productive and increased automation, **labour** felt increasingly displaced and devalued.

A 1951 Supreme Court ruling had declared **common situs picketing** illegal. The issue generated more White House post than any other in the Ford years – even the pardon. Ford introduced a bill to allow common situs, but then vetoed it to appease Republican right-wingers. 'If I sign the bill, I won't get nominated', he told his Secretary of Labour, who had written a bill at his request and now resigned.

(i) The economy
After the Second World War, Americans experienced a prolonged economic boom. This was clearly over by the 1970s. Ford inherited inflation, exacerbated by rising oil prices. In August 1974, unemployment rose to 5.4 per cent and the **GNP** and the **Dow Jones Industrial Average** dropped. Bewildered voters expected the President to do something about this.

Initially, Ford wanted to raise taxes to combat inflation, but his 'Whip Inflation Now' (WIN) programme did not help. Faced with **stagflation** (slow economic growth, with high unemployment and rising pries), Ford proposed cutting taxes (January 1975). The *New York Times* said, 'President Ford has not turned the economy around … but at least he has turned himself around.' Voters were unimpressed.

(j) Foreign policy
The Republican Right attacked Ford for attending the **Helsinki Conference**, where, they alleged, the USA had agreed to Soviet domination of Eastern Europe. Ford argued in vain that the East European provisions were balanced by the signatories' commitment to human rights.

There was little foreign policy success with which Ford could woo voters.

(k) The struggle with Ronald Reagan
By late 1974, Ronald Reagan was privately asserting that Ford was a 'caretaker' who had been 'in Congress too long'. Backed by Republican right-wingers, Reagan challenged Ford for the Republican nomination, running as an outsider untainted by the corruption of Washington DC. Expecting a Reagan attack on Vice President Rockefeller, Ford threw Rockefeller off the ticket and sacked several others (the so-called 'Sunday Morning Massacre'). This antagonised Republican moderates.

Reagan attacked Ford's foreign policy as aimless. He emphasised the Helsinki 'betrayal'. When Ford considered a US

Labour
Blue-collar, unionised workers

Common situs picketing
When an entire construction site was picketed (that is, access was halted by union members) even though a union only had a dispute with one (or two) contractors on the site.

Key question
Were Ford's economic policies a vote winner?

GNP
A country's gross national product is the aggregate value of goods and services produced in that country.

Dow Jones Industrial Average
Stock price average compiled by Dow Jones & Co. indicating market trends in the USA.

Stagflation
Slow economic growth, with high unemployment and rising prices.

Helsinki Conference
1975 accord where the West recognised Soviet control of Eastern Europe in exchange for Soviet concessions on human rights.

Key terms

Panama Canal
The US built
(1903–13) and ran
the canal, which
bisected North and
South America,
thereby joining the
Pacific and the
Atlantic. By the
1970s, some
Americans thought
the Canal Zone
should be returned
to the Panamanians.

Saturday Night Live
A popular TV
programme starring
comedians such as
Chevy Chase.

Key question
How did Carter defeat
Ford?

Key date

Ford defeated by
Carter in the
presidential election:
1976

retreat on the **Panama Canal**, Reagan won North Carolina with
'When it comes to the canal, we built it, we paid for it, it is ours
and we should tell [Panama] we are going to keep it', only the
third time a challenger had defeated an incumbent President in a
primary.

Press secretary Ron Nesson made a huge error, appearing on
Saturday Night Live skits that mocked Ford's intelligence and
physical co-ordination. Nesson even persuaded Ford to take part.
A letter to the *Washington Post* said, 'If Ford agreed to Nesson's
appearance, I don't see how I can vote for a man who could be so
dumb.'

When Ford used the incumbency (for example, promising
federal contracts in states in order to win primaries) and Reagan
made errors (such as naming the liberal governor of Pennsylvania
as his running mate, which alienated conservatives), Ford finally
got the nomination. However, Reagan had humiliated him.
Furthermore, Ford had to appease Reagan by choosing
unimpressive Kansas Senator Bob Dole as his running mate.
Reagan had given Ford a bad start against the Democratic
candidate, Jimmy Carter.

(l) The struggle with Jimmy Carter

In the lowest presidential election turnout since 1948 (only 54 per
cent of all eligible Americans voted), Carter won 49.9 per cent of
the vote, to Ford's 47.9 per cent.

The disillusioned electorate
'Why don't people vote? Because it's doesn't make a difference' –
a welfare worker.

In the Carter years, around half of the electorate never
bothered to vote, clearly feeling alienated from the political
process. Polls illustrated Americans' loss of confidence in
politicians and government:

- Percentage who felt government will 'do what is right most
  of the time'; in 1969 – 56 per cent; in 1979 – 29 per cent.
- Percentage believing government officials were 'smart
  people who know what they are doing' in 1969 – 69 per
  cent; in 1979 – 29 per cent.
- Percentage who felt that US affairs were run for the benefit
  of a few big interests rather than all the people; in 1969 –
  28 per cent; in 1979 – 65 per cent.
- Percentage who agreed that the 'people running the country
  do not really care about what happens to you'; in 1966 – 26
  per cent; in 1977 – 60 per cent.

Carter won because:

- Although hardly discussed in the campaign, the pardon of
  Nixon cost Ford votes.
- The Reagan challenge divided and exhausted the Republicans
  and gave Carter a head start.

- Ford made poor strategic decisions. He underestimated Reagan. He failed to emphasise his commitment to tax cuts throughout the campaign. He underestimated Carter, whom he considered a 'flash in the pan'. He could not believe the Democrats 'were about to rest their hopes on an outsider with little more going for him than a winning smile'.
- Carter ran a similar campaign to Reagan, emphasising that he had not been part of the corrupt Washington scene, and claiming that Ford had ratified the Soviet takeover of Eastern Europe.
- Ford campaign strategist Stuart Spencer told Ford straight: 'Mister President … you are not now perceived as being a strong, decisive leader.'
- New financial laws (1976) deprived the Republicans of their big advantage in fundraising for the first time in years.
- Dole (see page 75) was dogged by press stories of an illegal corporate contribution to his 1973 election. The Democrats planted a story that said Reagan had asked Ford to dump Dole. Furious, Dole refused to prepare for his October debate against Democratic vice presidential candidate Walter Mondale, and performed badly.
- Ford's image was that of a bumbler.
- Ford's administration seemed corrupt. When the head of the FBI was accused of using an agency man to install a window sash for free in his home, Carter said Ford should have sacked him. Ford also suffered from talk that corporate friends with whom he played golf received special favours, and had too much access to him. Revelations from John Dean (see page 47) damaged Ford. Dean claimed Ford had moved to stop investigations into Watergate (he gave no proof) and said Ford's Secretary of Agriculture Earl Butz disparaged blacks. Butz had to resign.
- The second Carter–Ford debate was a tie until Ford said:

> There is no Soviet domination of Eastern Europe, and there never will be under a Ford administration. The United States does not concede that those countries are under the domination of the Soviet Union.

Ford meant 'a part of', not 'under the domination of', but when the moderator gave him a chance to clarify, but he made it worse: 'I don't believe that the Poles consider themselves dominated by the Soviet Union'. Ford stubbornly refused to explain until three days after the debate, which seemed to confirm he was not up to the job. Carter surged in the polls.

- Most people agree it was the announcement of the economic slowdown just days before the election that was the turning point for Carter. Already, inflation was in double figures and Americans were worried about oil shortages and gasoline prices.

Key term

Bicentennial
The USA's 200th birthday was on 4 July 1976. Americans had made their declaration of independence from Britain on 4 July 1776.

- Carter said he would tackle big problems such as energy, welfare, health care and urban decay. Ford never really articulated his vision for the American people. When advisers prodded him on this, he was not interested.

However, although Ford lost the election, he was probably right when he claimed during the 4 July 1976 **Bicentennial** celebrations, 'I guess we've healed America'.

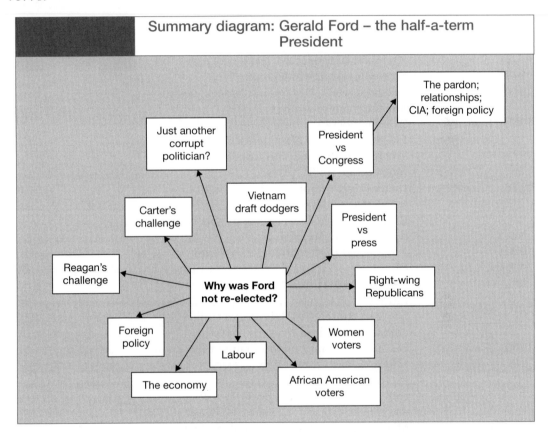

Summary diagram: Gerald Ford – the half-a-term President

Key question
Was Carter well prepared to be President?

3 | Jimmy Carter – Background

(a) Youth, education and employment

Born in 1924, Jimmy Carter grew up on the family's 350-acre farm in a predominantly black community in Plains, Georgia. His father was a moderately successful businessman. His mother, a registered nurse, was exceptionally liberal, providing free health care for the black community and allowing a black visitor in her living room. Jimmy inherited concern for the poor from his mother, and devout religious beliefs from both parents.

After graduation from high school (1941), Carter attended local scientific and technical colleges, joined the navy (1946), then married Rosalynn, whom he had known since childhood. When his father died (1953), Carter, his wife and three sons returned to Plains to concentrate upon the family peanut business.

Profie: James Earl 'Jimmy' Carter (1924–)

1924	–	Born in Plains, Georgia, to a peanut farmer, and Georgia state legislator
1946	–	Graduated from US Naval Academy at Annapolis
	–	Served in the navy for five years
1953	–	On his father's death, returned to Georgia to manage the peanut business
1962	–	Elected to Georgia State Senate (Democrat); re-elected 1964
1970	–	Elected governor of Georgia
1974	–	Declared would run for presidency; began non-stop campaigning
1976 July	–	Won Democratic nomination
November	–	Elected President after defeating Ford
1977	–	Treaty with Panama said canal would be returned in 1999
1978	–	Increasingly unpopular due to lack of legislative achievements
	–	Brokered peace between Egypt and Israel (Camp David Accords)
1979	–	Established diplomatic relations with China
	–	Signed SALT II treaty (Congress never ratified)
	–	Iranians students took hostages from US embassy in Tehran
1980 April	–	Secret US military mission failed to rescue hostages
	–	Interest rates hit 20 per cent
November	–	Defeated by Reagan in presidential election
1981–present	–	Mediated several international conflicts (for example, North Korea in 1994) and wrote books

As President, Carter seemed unable to deal with the most pressing contemporary issues (the economy, the energy crisis and Iran). However, he was important in that his election represented disillusionment with the tainted nature of Washington politics, and because he reflected the increasing political and social conservatism of many Americans. Often far removed from the liberal wing of his Democratic Party, he anticipated President Reagan in his criticism of big government.

(b) State senator 1963–6 and governor of Georgia 1970–4

Carter served as a Georgia state senator. Although he ran on a segregationist platform, once elected governor of Georgia, he helped impoverished blacks. He also streamlined the state government and pleased environmentalists.

(c) Election and early performance

(i) A narrow victory

Key question
What Carter characteristics emerged in 1976–7?

When in 1972 Carter told his mother he intended to run for President, she replied, 'President of what?' His presidential election victory has been described as a political miracle.

In his campaign, Carter concentrated upon values rather than specific issues, and exploited the nation's anti-Washington mood. Many considered the federal government meddlesome, inflexible, bureaucratic, out of touch, untrustworthy and immoral. Carter appealed to the American public to help him improve it.

Carter gave an early sign of the political inexperience that would plague his presidency (see page 80) when he told *Playboy* he had 'committed adultery in my heart many times' and spoke of 'screwing' and 'shacking-up'. However, voters considered Ford's gaffe on Eastern Europe (see page 76) worse.

Neither candidate excited the electorate: 76 per cent of voters said Ford lacked 'presidential quality'; 80 per cent said Carter did. Ford staffers said 'vast numbers of voters have looked at the two men and see no practical difference'.

Although Ford said Carter 'wavers, he wanders, he wiggles, and he waffles and he should not be the President of the United States', Carter won (see page 75). He carried Southern, union, black and rural Protestant votes, but lacked a strong popular mandate. His had been a lacklustre victory.

(ii) Problems inherited by Carter

Key question
What problems did Carter inherit?

Carter inherited problems that would have taxed any President:

Key term

Liberalism
Toleration and/or approval of federal government interventionism, and 1960s' campaigners such as as feminists and civil rights activists.

- The country was still divided and disillusioned by memories of Vietnam and Watergate, both of which had weakened the presidency.
- **Liberalism** was increasingly discredited. There seemed to be a movement towards more conservative political, social and cultural values, which was dividing the Democratic Party (see page 87).
- The United States suffered from crises in energy, welfare, health care and inner cities.
- The Washington establishment that Carter had attacked during his campaign looked down upon him as a Southern hick, which did not augur well for future collaboration.

Carter added to these problems. He was quickly adjudged to be aloof, self-righteous and a micromanager (in his first six months, he personally reviewed all requests to use the White House tennis courts). His liberal Vice President, Walter Mondale, noted that

Carter thought politics was sinful. The worst thing you could say to Carter if you wanted to do something was that it was politically the best thing to do.

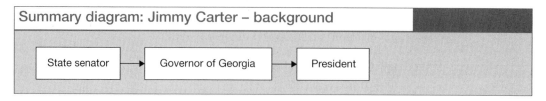

Summary diagram: Jimmy Carter – background

State senator → Governor of Georgia → President

4 | Why did President Carter Fail to Get Re-elected?

The first elected President in half a century who failed to win a second term, Carter was, according to former presidential speechwriter Jim Fallows, 'ignorant' of how power could and should be exercised. He and his staff (nicknamed the 'Georgia Mafia' or 'Peanut Brigade') were inexperienced, insular, uncoordinated and error prone.

(a) 'Can Carter cope?'
(i) The lack of vision
According to his biographer Burton Kaufman:

> he was a President who never adequately defined a mission for his government, a purpose for his country, and a way to get there.

Key question
Was Jimmy Carter successful presidential material?

(ii) Strategic errors within the White House
From the start, Carter made strategic errors:

- He did not delegate authority along clearly established lines.
- He micromanaged and lost the big picture (for example, he limited the number of pens at signing ceremonies to four).
- He and his staff got bogged down in paperwork.
- An NSC member said if Carter 'saw a problem he wanted to solve it, and that was all there was to it – no prioritisation'.
- He tried to do too much too quickly, failing always to grasp the complexity of the initiatives he proposed.

(iii) Strategic errors on legislation
Carter presented Congress with a **legislative docket** that would have taxed the skills of an experienced President. House Speaker Tip O'Neill felt Carter 'didn't seem to understand' the need to master the legislative process. After Congress rejected his proposals for a Consumer Protection Agency, and gutted his energy programme, Carter admitted he should have held more meetings with senators.

Legislative docket Set of bills and proposals given by the President to Congress.

Key term

(iv) Strategic errors in relation to close associates
Carter's personal loyalties made voters doubt his political wisdom. He supported his Office of Management and Budget (OMB)

director and friend Bert Lance over his dubious banking and business practices longer than was politically prudent, especially given Carter's stance on public morality.

Many felt Rosalynn Carter had become too powerful, especially when she had participated in discussions on a cabinet purge. The media referred to her as 'Mrs President'. *McCall's* magazine asked, 'Is Rosalynn really running the country?' However, one journalist said, 'I'll be damned if I ever want my country run by a President who is too dumb to consult with his wife!'

(v) Public perceptions

During 1977, Carter's public approval rating had dropped from 75 per cent (March) to 50 per cent (October). By December, only 18 per cent had 'a lot' of confidence in his ability – even Democrats were asking, 'Can Carter cope?' People wondered whether he was really up to the job. In 1978 his approval rating hovered around a low 31 per cent. In 1979, 41 per cent of Americans believed their country was 'in deep and serious trouble'. By 1980, it was 64 per cent, and Carter had the lowest approval rating of any President ever – even lower than Nixon at the time of Watergate.

(b) Corruption scandal – 'Billygate'

Carter was elected as an outsider, untainted by Washington corruption, but became involved in several scandals, the worst of which was 'Billygate'.

The President's older brother Billy was commonly lampooned as a beer-bellied (he advertised his own brew, 'Billy Beer') **redneck**. His self-deprecatory humour made him a popular talk-show guest and lecturer.

In 1978, Billy and other Georgia businessmen and legislators visited Libya. In January 1979, Billy hosted a reception for a Libyan 'friendship delegation'. His pro-Libya and pro-Arab sentiments were interpreted as anti-Semitism, to which Billy responded, 'The only thing I can say is there is a helluva lot more Arabians than there is Jews.' President Carter said he hoped that the American public would 'realise that I don't have any control over what my brother says', and that 'he has no control over me'. However, as Carter's chief aide Hamilton Jordan said, 'That damn Billy Carter stuff is killing us'. 'If Billy is not working for the Republican Party, he should be', joked one Atlanta newspaper.

After several weeks in an alcohol treatment centre, Billy was sober (which made the celebrity circuit lose interest in him) and short of money. In July 1980, he belatedly registered as a foreign agent and admitted receiving a $220,000 'loan' from the Libyan government. This was investigated by the Senate and Justice Department. 'Billygate' raised a political storm. The media speculated on the President's involvement.

The Senate acquitted President Carter of all but unwisely trying to use (at Rosalynn's suggestion) Billy's Libyan contacts to try to help free the Iranian hostages (see page 90). The American

Key question
Was Carter corrupt?

Key term

Redneck
Poorly educated, working-class white Southerner, frequently characterised by racism and beer drinking.

Key date

Billygate: 1980

public decided that President Carter was not corrupt, just incompetent.

(c) Carter vs Congress

The antagonism between Congress and the President (see page 70) continued in Carter's presidency, even though he was a Democrat President with a Democrat Congress. Much of the problem lay with Carter himself. He had run on an anti-Washington platform, and Congress resented and resisted his pledge to end the **pork-barrel politics** that characterised Capitol Hill. Not surprisingly, congressional Democrats felt no obligation to help him.

Always convinced that he was right, Carter never developed a solid base of dedicated supporters on Capitol Hill. When House Speaker Tip O'Neill offered to help the new President establish good working relations with Congress, Carter said he had been a governor and knew how to deal with legislators. O'Neill warned him that most members of Congress had firm political bases in their states and minds of their own.

Communication with Congress was often poor (Hamilton Jordan boasted that he never bothered to answer calls from Congress). Congress disliked Carter's resistance to compromise and bargaining, and his frequent threats to go over their heads directly to the people who had elected him. 'I can talk to your constituents easier than you can', Carter boasted to congressmen. When he tactlessly cancelled the production of some expensive planes after Congress declared production should go ahead, Congress felt he was deliberately embarrassing them.

Carter failed to get congressional co-operation, for example, with his energy programme.

(d) The energy crisis

A major new political theme of Carter's presidency was the rapidly worsening energy crisis. The United States was economically self-sufficient after the Second World War, but became increasingly dependent on Middle Eastern oil in the 1970s. More than half of US oil had to be imported. In the harsh winter of 1976–7, there was a shortage of natural gas, and schools and factories had to close. The severity of the crisis was evident when fuel stations closed on Sundays or cut their hours to conserve supplies and long queues developed at the petrol pumps. The United States' first energy riot occurred in Levittown, Pennsylvania, when truckers barricaded expressways: in two nights of violence, 100 were injured and 170 were arrested.

Carter's proposed energy legislation was farsighted, but Congress diluted it beyond recognition. Where had Carter gone wrong? First, his energy legislation had been drawn up without consultation with Congress. Second, he had failed to lobby Congress consistently. Third, voters remained unwilling to pay higher prices for fuel. They were unimpressed by the President's handling of the energy crisis, which persisted and worsened.

Key question
Why was Carter unable to get on with Congress?

Corrupt Congress?
In February 1980, it was revealed that FBI agents posing as wealthy Arabs in a sting operation had successfully persuaded 12 government officials and seven members of Congress to take bribes for a fictitious oil sheik in return for political favours.

Pork-barrel politics
When a legislator will not pass legislation unless he can see benefit for his own constituents.

Key term

Key question
How well did Carter handle the energy crisis?

Carter's energy legislation: 1978

Key date

Key question
Did Carter win over
women voters?

(e) Women voters

Carter was sensitive to women's rights, insisting that at least one female candidate be considered for each cabinet post. He appointed two female cabinet members and more women to high-level posts than any previous President.

Carter supported the Equal Rights Amendment (ERA), which Congress had passed in 1972, but which still needed **ratification** by four more states. Although the President said Rosalynn could speak for him 'with authority', many women voters felt he should not have left the campaign for ERA to her, but should have done more himself. Some were also annoyed by his opposition to federal funding of abortion except in cases of rape, incest or the endangerment of the mother's life.

Key question
Did Carter please
black voters?

(f) African American voters

(i) Carter's appointments

Sensitive to minority rights, Carter insisted that at least one minority candidate be considered for each cabinet post. Several prominent blacks turned him down, but Patricia Harris became Secretary of Housing and Urban Development. Carter appointed 38 black federal judges and Andrew Young as US ambassador to the United Nations.

(ii) Affirmative action

Under Carter, the federal Equal Economic Opportunities Commission (EEOC) worked against discrimination in the labour force, while the 1977 Public Works Act said minority contractors should get 10 per cent of federal grants for public works.

Since the mid-1960s, affirmative action laws had been passed to help minorities and women in education and employment. In BAKKE vs REGENTS OF THE UNIVERSITY OF CALIFORNIA (1978), the Supreme Court upheld Allan Bakke's complaint that Davis medical school had discriminated against him by accepting minority students with lower grades. The Supreme Court thus supported affirmative action, but declared the quota system (16 Davis places were reserved for disadvantaged students) unconstitutional.

African Americans were not happy with BAKKE, or with Carter, in whose administration there was some support for the ruling. Blacks felt Carter was not committed to busing (see page 73) or to the 1978 fair housing bill. The congressional Black **Caucus** resented his fiscal conservatism, favouring a great expansion of social welfare programmes.

(iii) Black rioting

Blacks suffered disproportionately during the great recession of the Carter years. When hundreds of black teenagers reported for snow-shovelling work in Washington DC in 1979 and found the jobs already filled, they broke into and looted stores. The same thing happened in Baltimore. Black officials told Carter they blamed him for not helping the poor and unemployed.

Key date

In BAKKE vs REGENTS OF THE UNIVERSITY OF CALIFORNIA, the Supreme Court supported affirmative action but not quotas: 1978

Key terms

Ratification
Any amendments to the US constitution have to be ratified by three-quarters of the states.

Caucus
A political group usually sharing similar ideas.

In the 1980s, economic problems prompted the worst summer of racial violence since the 1960s. In Liberty City in Miami, Florida, an all-white jury acquitted four white policemen charged with beating to death a black insurance salesman. There followed three days of looting, shooting, overturning of cars and burning of property. Sixteen people died, over 400 were injured and an estimated $100 million property was damaged. 'Black folks ain't worth a damn in this country', said the president of NAACP. There was sporadic violence in Miami throughout the year and similar scenes in Chattanooga, Boston and Wichita.

Race riots: 1980

Miners' strike: 1977

Key dates

Losing the black vote
Blacks felt Carter gave them little help. Although he made a highly publicised visit to South Bronx to show his anxiety over blighted urban areas and supported several mayoral recommendations for national legislation, he never planned to spend on the cities, just to improve existing programmes.

Although Carter had appointed more minority federal judges than any previous President (28 blacks, 14 Hispanics), channelled government contracts to minority firms, strengthened Justice Department enforcement of voting rights laws and increased the effectiveness of EEOC, these measures did not help poor blacks. Although Carter finally helped get the **Humphrey-Hawkins** full employment bill through, black leaders felt resentment that it had taken him so long.

In the second half of 1979, blacks were upset that Carter forced Andrew Young to resign because of his unauthorised meeting with a representative of the Palestinian Liberation Organisation (see page 90). Carter appointed another black to replace Young, but the black community was not appeased.

**Humphrey-
Hawkins**
This bill said the federal government should be the employer of last resort during a recession. The final Act (October 1978) was a much watered-down version of the original bill.

Key term

(g) The labour vote

Although blue-collar workers traditionally voted Democrat, labour had several grievances with Carter. Unions felt Carter should concentrate less upon inflation and more upon the unemployment problems. They disliked his ideas about voluntary wage guidelines. They considered Carter unsupportive over a national health insurance bill, a federal minimum wage, the Humphrey-Hawkins proposal, a common situs bill (see page 74) and the miners' strike.

In December 1977, 165,000 United Mine Workers went on strike because mine owners refused to recognise the miners' right to engage in wildcat strikes to protest against contract infractions or safety standard violations. After three months, coal stocks fell to emergency levels. Schools closed and there were shortened work weeks in the Eastern USA. Then, 109 days later, the miners returned to work. Carter criticised and alienated the miners. Two-thirds of those polled felt Carter handled the strike badly, although his biographer Burton Kaufman believed there was little he could have done.

Key question
How did Carter alienate the labour vote?

Many of the loyal Democrat voters who stayed at home on voting day were labour.

A taxpayers' revolt
High taxation was a big issue to voters, and especially to labour. A taxpayers' revolt occurred in California, when 75-year-old businessman Howard Jarvis collected over one million signatures to force a referendum on Proposition 13, which proposed to slash property and local government taxes. Californian voters approved Proposition 13 by 2 to 1, prompting other states to emulate them.

(h) The poor

Key question
Why did the poor not turn out to vote for Carter?

As a Democrat, Carter was expected to care and do more about poverty than his Republican predecessors. He faced several problematic demographic trends. First, the fastest growing section of American population was the elderly. This made for increasingly expensive social security and health care, which Carter wanted to rationalise and reform without increasing federal expenditure (he wanted to balance the federal budget). Second, many people were migrating to the Sun Belt, the population of which had increased by 9 per cent between 1972 and 1977, compared to 2 per cent for the rest of the nation. As middle-class taxpayers fled the Northern (Snow Belt) cities, this exacerbated urban blight in poverty-stricken Northern city centres.

The number living below the poverty line was growing (from 11.2 per cent in 1974 to 12.5 per cent in 1976) and included 50 per cent of all black female heads of household. Carter made little progress on these problems, despite $4 billion being allocated for public works in 1977 and increased federal aid to the poor (for example, food stamps helped 21 million in 1980, compared to 18.5 million in 1976). The problem was the taxpayer voters did not want to subsidise the poor, of whatever age, colour or sex, and Carter, a fiscal conservative, wanted to balance the budget.

(i) Environmentalists
(i) Environmentalism

Key question
Did Carter's environmental policies win votes?

The environmental movement had become politically important by the time of Carter's presidency. His predecessors had set up the Environmental Protection Agency (EPA) and the Occupational Safety and Health Administration (OSHA). Congress had passed the Clean Air Act (1970), Endangered Species Act (1973) and Toxic Substances Control Act (1976). Catalytic converters and unleaded gasoline, introduced in the mid-1970s, cut car pollution by 75 per cent in the following decades. A Consumer Product Safety Commission had been set up, owing much to the campaigning of Ralph Nader. Middle-class liberals flocked to join environmentalist organisations, whose membership rose from 125,000 in 1960 to one million in 1970, two million in 1980 and 6.3 million in 1990.

Two highly publicised events during the Carter presidency increased environmental awareness. State authorities admitted that Love Canal, near Niagara Falls, in Upper New York State, was a 'great and imminent peril' to health: full of industrial waste that had oozed into the ground, it had led to high rates of miscarriages and birth defects in the local population, who were relocated in 1978. Then, in 1979, at Three Mile Island in Pennsylvania, the radioactive core of the nuclear reactor overheated and partially melted down. The radioactive steam was confined to the interior of the reactor. No one was hurt, but the accident turned American public opinion against nuclear power – thereby increasing US dependence on oil.

Key date
Three Mile Island partial nuclear meltdown: 1979

(ii) Carter and the environment

Carter was the first successful presidential candidate who campaigned on environmental issues. He obtained legislation to prevent chemicals from polluting the environment, control surface mining, protect the outer continental shelf, expand National Park and wilderness land (the 1980 Alaska Lands Act set aside one-third of the state as wilderness), re-authorise the clean air and clean water acts, and seek alternative sources of energy. However, Carter's ambitious energy programme failed to get through Congress intact. Americans did not want to pay more for petrol (many had to travel long distances to work or to shops). Although impressive, Carter's achievements were insufficient for environmentalists. Equally dissatisfied were the traditionally Democrat labour unions, who believed that environmentalists threatened their jobs.

Union members sported bumper stickers saying 'IF YOU'RE HUNGRY AND OUT OF WORK, EAT AN ENVIRONMENTALIST'.

(j) The economy

Carter was unlucky to be President at a time of staggering inflation, increasing unemployment and rising energy prices.

Key question
How did economic problems contribute to Carter's defeat?

(i) Inflation

An April 1978 poll showed that 63 per cent of Americans believed that inflation was their greatest concern, and that Carter was not managing it; only 32 per cent approved his economic record.

In or near double figures for much of Carter's presidency, inflation meant more expensive mortgages, loans, food and energy. Carter tried to halt it by decreasing government expenditure (for example, holding down federal workers' wages) and voluntary wage and price controls. Labour, Congress and business disliked those proposals, which added to the growing sense of crisis and of failure of presidential leadership.

When Carter appointed conservative Paul Volcker as chairman of the Federal Reserve Board, he helped the economy revive – eventually. Backed by Carter, Volcker was tough on inflation. He curbed the money supply. This led to recession initially, but revival under Reagan (see page 111).

(ii) Unemployment

Unemployment was a problem throughout Carter's presidency, rising to 8.2 million in summer 1980. There was 24 per cent unemployment in the car manufacturing city of Detroit.

(iii) Business

The business community never had any faith in Carter's ability to manage the economy. Business feared that his energy proposals would damage industry and was also anxious about mounting trade deficits and their negative impact on the dollar, which had slumped on the world currency markets.

(iv) Political disaster

Economic problems led to political disaster for Carter in mid-1979 when, attempting to signal regeneration, Carter asked for the resignation of all cabinet secretaries and top aides. This only made voters feel that their President was losing control.

(v) Economic disaster in the presidential election year

By the presidential election year of 1980, the economy seemed to be spinning out of control. Republican nominee, Ronald Reagan, made great political capital out of Carter's apparent inability to solve economic problems.

(k) Left-wing Democrats and big government
(i) Carter vs traditional Democrats

In many ways, Carter was a precursor of Reagan (see page 106) in wanting to curb excessive governmental regulation of the economy. Carter signed several deregulatory acts, such as the Airline Deregulation Act of 1978, which stimulated airline competition and lower fares. In his second State of the Union address, Carter said:

> Government cannot solve our problems. It cannot eliminate poverty, or provide a bountiful economy, or reduce inflation, or save our cities, or cure illiteracy or provide energy.

Key term

Traditional Democrats
Liberals such as Senators Kennedy and McGovern still wanted massive federal intervention and expenditure to make the USA a more equal society, following in the tradition of the New Deal and Great Society.

However, many liberal Democrats disagreed. Liberal historian Arthur Schlesinger Jr said if Franklin Roosevelt had believed that, 'we would still be in the Great Depression'.

A Carter aide warned him against liberal **traditional Democrats** on Capitol Hill, such as Edward Kennedy and George McGovern, who were 'as antiquated and anachronistic group as are conservative Republicans'. Carter's fiscal frugality (he wanted to balance the federal budget to combat inflation) alienated traditional Democrat voters, who wanted a more comprehensive health care system. Urban leaders, the black community and labour felt they received no help from the President. As a result, Kennedy challenged Carter for the Democratic nomination in 1980.

Carter's problems at the start of his presidency

- Inflation.
- Unemployment.
- High taxes.
- Urban blight.
- Lack of confidence amongst the business community.
- Energy crisis.
- Dollar in trouble on international money markets.
- USA did not seem to be winning Cold War.

Carter's problems in the summer of the presidential election year (1980)

As above, but also:

- Racial unrest in the ghettos.
- Democratic Congress had rejected the vast majority of his legislative proposals.
- Democratic Party unenthusiastic about his candidacy.
- Lowest approval rating of any President ever.
- Senate hearings on Billy Carter.
- Kennedy defeated him in several Democratic primaries; persisted in divisive challenge even when he knew he could not beat Carter.
- Hostages in Iran.
- US allies openly criticised Carter's foreign policy.
- Republican nominee Reagan had a 28-point lead over Carter.

Given all these problems, it is surprising that Carter came so close to Reagan in the presidential election.

(ii) Losing Senator Edward Kennedy

A May 1978 poll showed that registered Democratic voters preferred Ted Kennedy as their 1980 presidential candidate by 53 per cent to 40 per cent. In May 1980, it was 54 per cent to 31 per cent. Luckily for Carter (who told some congressmen that if Kennedy challenged him, he would 'whip his ass'), Kennedy was:

- generally considered too liberal
- handicapped by the stigma of challenging the incumbent President from within his own political party
- still tainted by the Chappaquiddick scandal (see page 45)
- halting and rambling in an abysmal TV interview, in which he seemed sympathetic to the Iranian revolutionaries (see page 90) who had taken 50 Americans hostage.

Although Kennedy defeated Carter in five out of the eight states on **Super Tuesday**, it eventually became clear that Kennedy could not win. However, he kept in the race, keeping the Democratic Party divided and greatly helping Reagan's campaign.

Although Carter was chosen as the Democrats' candidate, the greatest excitement at the Democratic Convention was over a

Super Tuesday
A day on which there are several primaries is known as 'Super'.

Key term

Kennedy speech that appealed to the Democrats to maintain their liberal traditions.

Key question
How did foreign
policy contribute to
Carter's defeat?

(l) Foreign policy

(i) Polls

Although Carter had several foreign policy successes (when he engineered the Camp David agreements between Israel and Egypt in 1978, his popularity revived), voters never rated his foreign policy for long. In late 1977, only 38 per cent of Americans approved of Carter's foreign policy. *Newsweek* said, 'the President's uncertain diplomatic strategy has left allies perplexed, enemies unimpressed, and the nation is vulnerable as ever in an increasingly dangerous world'. By 1980, 54 per cent of Americans believed the US world position was only 'fair' or 'poor'; 62 per cent felt their country was 'becoming weaker'; 81 per cent believed the USA was in serious trouble. Only 18 per cent rated Carter 'a very strong leader'.

(ii) The Cold War

Overall, voters did not perceive their country to be winning the Cold War under Carter.

First, he frequently equivocated. For example, when Senator Church declared in 1979 there was a Soviet combat brigade in Cuba, Carter said it was no threat, then demanded the Soviets remove it. Second, many felt Carter underestimated Soviet power. While he called for another SALT treaty (see page 44), the Soviets invaded Afghanistan (1979). When Carter got tougher (for example, boycotting the 1980 Olympics in the USSR) voters liked it.

(iii) Latin America

Carter was inconsistent in relation to Latin America. In his presidential election campaign, he said, 'I would never give up complete control or practical control of the Panama Canal Zone' (see page 75). When as President he decided it was morally right to turn the Canal over to Panama, Congress and some voters were displeased.

When Cuban Leader Fidel Castro said anyone dissatisfied with his Communist regime could leave his country (April 1980), Carter accepted 125,000 refugees into the United States, although the March 1980 Refugee Act said the United States should take no more than 19,000 Cubans annually. Carter had made no provision for the influx of refugees, and tent cities sprang up in Florida. The American public was furious, even more so when the refugees clashed with the National Guard and destroyed federal property. Sixty per cent of the American public opposed the influx, and only 19 per cent supported it. 'The perception, aided by a negative Miami press, that we have "dumped" this problem on the taxpayers of Florida is widespread', said one Carter aide.

(iv) Losing the Jewish vote

American Jews traditionally voted Democrat. Although Carter's advisers told him to avoid getting involved in the Middle East, and he said he would 'rather commit suicide than hurt Israel', he also said that Israel treated the Palestinian community within Israel unfairly and was the biggest obstacle to Middle East peace. This upset American Jewish leaders and Congress, whose sympathies lay with Israel, and lost him many Jewish American votes.

(v) Iran

The greatest crisis of Carter's presidency was the Iranian crisis. As with the economy, developments in Iran made Carter a victim of events over which he had little or no control.

The Iranian revolution

In 1978, Islamic fundamentalists led a revolution against the repressive, pro-American Shah Mohammad Reza Pahlavi. In January 1979, the Shah left Iran, never to return. Iranians who had resented US military and political support for the Shah stormed the US embassy in Tehran and held it for a few hours. Many Americans felt powerless, and 50 per cent of them felt Carter was 'too soft' on Iran.

The seizure of the American hostages

On 4 November 1980, Iranian militants seized the US embassy in Tehran. They took 60 Americans hostage in protest against Carter allowing the Shah into the United States to receive cancer treatment.

Carter's response

Carter tried to negotiate the hostages' release, stopped Americans buying Iranian oil, and froze Iranian assets. His approval rating rocketed to 61 per cent. Then, in April 1980, he attempted a military rescue, with what historian James Patterson called a 'harebrained scheme'.

The failed rescue mission

One of the US rescue mission helicopters broke down as it entered Iranian airspace. A second got lost in a sandstorm. When a third developed hydraulic problems, the mission was aborted. Then one of the helicopters crashed, setting the others on fire. Eight Americans died, four were badly burned. Critics say the plan was too complex, and dependent upon too many variables. Some contend the mission needed more than six helicopters and two spares.

The impact on Carter's re-election campaign

This failed rescue mission was a major reason for Carter's defeat by Reagan. Congress was upset that it had not been consulted. Secretary of State Cyrus Vance was 'volcanic' when Carter gave the rescue mission the go-ahead without consulting him, so he resigned. Many felt that Carter simply messed up everything.

The hostage crisis dragged on throughout the presidential election year. The Republicans repeatedly warned that the

Democrats would try to use the hostage crisis for votes. When, on the eve of the election, Carter announced that the hostages might be freed soon, voters were suspicious (speculation that Reagan's team interfered with the negotiations so the hostages would not be released during Carter's presidency remains unproven).

Key question
Why did Reagan defeat Carter in 1980?

(m) Ronald Reagan
(i) Carter and Reagan errors
'If Reagan keeps putting his foot in his mouth … we can close down campaign headquarters', said a Carter aide. Reagan's gaffes included his claim that air pollution in Los Angeles had been 'substantially controlled', after which his plane was unable to land there because of smog.

However, Carter made errors too. By concentrating upon Reagan's fitness for office, Carter brought down attacks upon his own competency. Carter publicly admitted he had been 'carried away' in excessive criticism of Reagan as racist, divisive and a warmonger. Reagan maintained his 'nice guy' image by expressing 'sorrow' and 'regret' that Carter was being 'nasty'.

A leading Californian Democrat warned Carter not to 'make a mistake that every person in this room has made at one time or another, and underestimate Ronald Reagan', but Carter did.

(ii) The Carter–Reagan debate
Despite Reagan's reputation as the 'great communicator', Carter felt that he had to debate with him (October 1980). Reagan made no gaffes, and came across as warmer than Carter with his frequent 'aw shucks' and 'there you go again' interjections. Reagan asked Americans:

> Are you any better off than you were four years ago? Is there more or less unemployment in the country? Is America as respected throughout the world as it was? Do you feel that our security is safe, that we are as strong as we were four years ago?

That was highly effective. Polls mostly showed that Reagan had won the debate.

(iii) Summarising why Reagan beat Carter in 1980
Reagan won because of several reasons. Carter seemed unable to do anything to improve the economic crisis (stagflation, unemployment and a weakened dollar). He failed to get congressional assent to most of his legislative initiatives. This made him seen inept. People asked, 'Can Carter cope?'

Key date
Reagan defeated Carter in presidential election: 1980

Carter's own party was not fully behind him. He had alienated liberal Democrats. Furthermore, he and the Democratic Party were losing many of their traditional blue-collar supporters, who resented 'reverse discrimination' in favour of blacks, who, they believed, perpetrated most of the crime in America.

Forty per cent of those who voted for Reagan gave their main reason as, 'it's time for a change'. Reagan was a brilliant campaigner. He performed well in and 'won' the eve of election debate. Demographics favoured Reagan. The population of the Sun Belt was rising at the expense of the Northeast and Midwest. The migrants were usually white conservatives. Carter lacked a coherent vision for America, while Middle America envisioned a return to traditional values under Reagan. Social issues mobilised conservative voters. The well-organised 'New Right' or 'Religious Right' was already one of the United States' most visible and powerful political forces, and it backed Reagan. Harris pollsters talked of the Moral Majority during this election: an estimated five million evangelical Christians who had never voted before, now voted for Reagan.

Carter had no great foreign policy victories, but several disasters, especially the Iranian hostages. Reagan promised strong leadership and a revival of US power.

(iv) The results and significance of the 1980 elections

Although the Democrats had won their greatest majority in Congress since the Second World War in 1974, the Republicans won a similar victory in 1980. Conservative voters had been effectively mobilised. Reagan's was not a decisive victory. Only 28 per cent of the potential electorate voted for him (25 per cent voted for Carter); 47 per cent stayed at home, making the non-voters the biggest group in US politics. Most of them were poor and/or unemployed, and they were the traditional Democratic constituency. These statistics suggest disillusionment with politics in general, and Democrat disillusionment with Carter in particular.

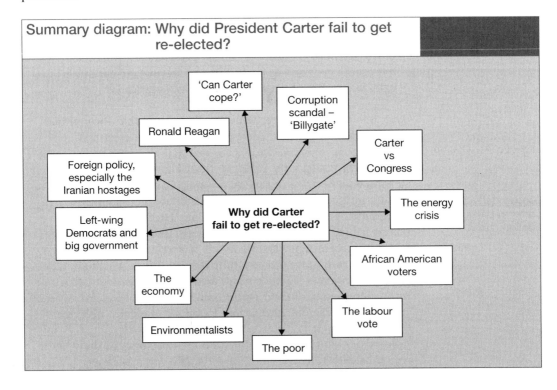

Summary diagram: Why did President Carter fail to get re-elected?

5 | The New Right

(a) The beliefs of the New Right

Key question
What characterised a
New Right or
Religious Right voter?

Key terms

New Right
This group of right-
wing voters became
influential in the
late 1970s; their
beliefs were a
reaction to the
counterculture of
the 1960s, and
included opposition
to abortion, busing
and Darwinism.

Religious right
Although not all
members of the
New Right were
religious, members
of the Religious
Right were usually
part of the New
Right.

Some members of the **New Right** were also known as the
Religious Right. A New Right voter was usually:

- Disgusted by 1960s' excesses and permissiveness (too much sex, drugs and rock-and-roll).
- Deeply patriotic.
- Anti-Communist.
- A great believer in free enterprise and a balanced budget.
- A church-goer ('born-again' Christians constituted 24 per cent of church-goers in 1963, but 40 per cent in 1978).
- A great believer in family values.
- Opposed to the teaching in schools of Darwinian ideas on evolution.
- Anti-sex education in schools.
- Anti-busing ('busing maximises the amount of time the child is away from his home, promotes race mixing, and destroys the authority of parents', said one member of the Religious Right).
- Anti-affirmative-action.
- Anti-feminism ('women's lib') and the Equal Rights Amendment.
- Anti-abortion (and ROE vs WADE), pro-'right to life'.
- Anti-pornography.
- Against the abolition of prayer in schools.
- Against IRS moves to deny tax-exempt status to private schools, including Christian academies with all white pupils.
- Anti-crime (violent crimes had risen from 783,000 in 1970 to 1.3 million in 1980).
- Anti-federal government bureaucracy.
- Anti-homosexuals (particularly those teaching in schools or in the Armed Forces).

(b) Important individuals in the New Right

(i) Jerry Falwell

Key question
What sort of people
led the Religious
Right and how
effective were they?

Falwell was a Baptist minister, whose *Old Time Gospel Hour* was
broadcast on 225 TV stations and 300 radio stations each week.
His mostly Baptist 'Moral Majority' aimed to 'fight the
pornography, obscenity, vulgarity, profanity that under the guise
of sex education and values clarification literally pervades the
literature' of American schools. 'We are going to single out those
people in government against what we consider to be the Bible,
moralist position.' Falwell helped raise millions of dollars for
Ronald Reagan's presidential campaign. Some estimated that the
Moral Majority registered around two million voters in 1980.

(ii) Phyllis Schlafly

Lawyer and Catholic mother of six children, Phyllis Schlafly,
'Sweetheart of the Silent Majority', mobilised opinion against the
Equal Rights Amendment and abortion. 50,000 people joined her
Eagle Forum, mailing legislators against the Equal Rights

Amendment, because, they said, it would sanction gay marriage, unisex toilets and women in combat, and destroy the traditional family. Schlafly campaigned for women's skirts to be two inches below the knee.

New Right activists used mail effectively to fundraise and recruit. 'Our purpose is to organise discontent … The shriller you are, the easier it is to recruit supporters.' One anti-abortion mailing said:

> Stop the baby killers … These anti-life baby killers are already organising, working and raising money to re-elect pro-abortionists like George McGovern. Abortion means killing a living baby, a tiny human being with a beating heart and little fingers … killing a baby boy or girl with burning deadly chemicals or a powerful machine that sucks and tears the little infant from its mother's womb.

Graphic pictures were included in that effective mailing. Seventy per cent of those contacted by the National Right to Life Committee turned out to vote in 1978 (that was twice the national average) and 50 per cent of them donated a minimum of $25. Such efforts helped account for the defeat of several liberals, such as McGovern, in the 1980 congressional elections.

Summary diagram: The New Right/Religious Right

Anti-			
Liberals	Democrats	Communist	Permissiveness
Big government	Darwin	Busing	Sex education in schools
Crime	Homosexuals	Affirmative action	
Pornography	Feminism		Women's rights

Study Guide: AS Question

In the style of Edexcel

Why did Jimmy Carter win the presidential contest in 1976 and yet lose to Ronald Reagan only four years later? (30 marks)

Exam tips

The cross-references are intended to take you straight the material that will help you to answer the question.

This question is asking you to explain the outcomes of presidential elections, but it needs a different focus from the question at the end of Chapter 2 (page 64). This time you are not being asked to judge the importance of one factor in relation to another. Here essentially you are thinking about the differences in Carter's position in 1976 and 1980.

How will you organise your material? You could analyse the reasons for success in 1976 and then focus on what was different in 1980. Or you could take the key factors which explain electoral success or failure, establishing in each case how 1980 was different. If you decide on the 'separate elections' approach, take care not to drift into describing the two campaigns.

The key factors you could consider are:

- Effectiveness of the election campaign: was the Democratic Party more divided in 1980 (pages 87–8)?
- Candidate personal appeal: in what ways did the appeal of Carter's opponents differ in 1976 and 1980 (pages 69–76 and 91–4)? How had public perception of Carter himself changed in the interval (pages 80–92)?
- Appeal of policies: why were Carter's promises more appealing than Ford's in 1976, and less appealing than Reagan's in 1980 (pages 75–7 and 91–2)?
- The influence of events and the historical context: for example, how did the economic context help Carter in 1976 and damage him in 1980 (pages 76 and 91)? Was Carter unlucky? What other circumstances were influential (pages 82–3 and 90–1)?

The key to the explanation of the differences will be the way in which Carter had lost the support of the electorate both as a result of poor handling of events and unpopular policies during his four years as President, and as a result of the circumstances beyond his control during that period. Make sure these emerge clearly as you plan and organise your response.

4 President Reagan 1981–9

POINTS TO CONSIDER
Ronald Reagan is one of the most controversial American presidents. While some conservatives felt he was insufficiently conservative, many liberals loathed his conservatism. This chapter looks at the following questions:

- Was he well prepared to be President?
- Was the presidency 'imperilled'?
- Why was he elected and re-elected?
- Was his second term far less successful than his first, and if so, why?
- Was he 'an amiable dunce'?
- What were his achievements?

Key dates

1980	November	Reagan became President
1981	December	Budget director Stockman admitted administration's economic plan did not add up
		Congress passed Reagan's budget, cutting taxes and domestic expenditure
1982		Equal Rights Amendment defeated
1983		Social Security Reform Act
1984	November	Reagan re-elected by near-record margin
1985	December	Congress enforced spending cuts
1986		Major tax reform
	November	Iran-Contra scandal exposed
1987	February	Tower Commission criticised Reagan's delegatory management style
		Reagan's nomination of Robert Bork as Supreme Court justice failed

1 | Preparation for the Presidency

It has been claimed that Reagan was ill-prepared to be President: he came into politics relatively late in life and lacked experience in national politics and working with other political leaders.

Key question
Was Reagan well prepared for the presidency?

President Reagan bids goodbye to British Prime Minister Margaret Thatcher at the White House, February 1981. Thatcher was the first Western leader to visit after Reagan's inauguration. Both had conservative political philosophies, and seemed genuinely to like and admire each other. A Reagan aide said that when Reagan struggled in international meetings, Thatcher would protect him 'like a mother hen'. Why do you suppose she did that?

However, it could be argued that Reagan had a great deal of relevant experience and truly earned his 'great communicator' nickname. Before he entered politics he had gained experience in a variety of communication fields – a successful radio announcer, film actor and TV performer, an impressive speechmaker and a syndicated newspaper columnist.

(a) Youth

Reagan was born in smalltown Illinois, in 1911. 'Our family didn't exactly come from the wrong side of the tracks, but we were certainly always within sound of the train whistles.' As a politician, Reagan was open about his alcoholic father. He told stories of how he had to put his drunken father to bed (he presumably wanted to demonstrate how he had taken responsibility at an early age). Journalist Lou Cannon felt Reagan had some of the characteristics typical of offspring of alcoholics: he was a loner, adept at reading emotional signals, struggled with intimate relationships, believed in the importance of self-help and was manipulative in pursuit of his goals.

At his small, local college, Reagan preferred sport (he always said it was a healthy alternative to war, satisfying the human need for combat) and drama to academic study.

Profile: Ronald Reagan 1911–2004

1911	–	Born in Tampico, Illinois
1932	–	Graduated from Eureka College; sportscaster in Iowa
1937	–	Start of Hollywood acting career
1947–52	–	Elected president of the Screen Actors Guild; developed into a conservative Republican
1954–62	–	Hosted *General Electric Theatre*, a TV programme
1967–74	–	Served two terms as governor of California
1968 and 1976	–	Unsuccessful bids for the Republican nomination for the presidency
1980	–	Won the Republican nomination; defeated the Democratic incumbent Jimmy Carter (51 to 41 per cent of the popular vote)
1981–9	–	40th President of the United States
1981 March	–	Amazing recovery from a near fatal assassination attempt
May	–	Congress passed his budgetary proposals
1982	–	Recession, followed by economic growth
1983	–	Proposed strategic defence initiative (SDI)
1984	–	Re-elected (59 per cent to Mondale's 41 per cent)
1985	–	Signed legislation for mandatory government spending cuts to balance federal budget by 1991
1985–6	–	Co-operated with Congress on tax reform
1986	–	Embarrassed by Iran-Contra controversy
1988	–	Signed Intermediate Range Nuclear Forces Treaty (INF treaty), which helped slow down the nuclear arms race and bring the Cold War towards an end
1994	–	Disclosed that he had **Alzheimer's disease**
2004	–	Died

Key term

Alzheimer's disease
A degenerative brain disease that causes dementia.

Reagan helped to restore the prestige of the presidency after the disasters of the Vietnam War and the Watergate scandal, and the unimpressive presidencies of Ford and Carter. Since Roosevelt's New Deal in the 1930s, the USA had been moving in the direction of the welfare state. Some historians think that Reagan successfully halted and reversed that process. He contributed greatly to the ending of the Cold War. Most Americans rate him highly: right-wingers generally approve of his policies, and often consider them successful; left-wingers generally consider him likeable, and appreciate his restoration of the prestige of the presidency.

Key question
How did Reagan's earlier careers help prepare him for the presidency?

(b) Earlier careers
(i) Sportscaster
Reagan's four years as a highly successful sportscaster in Iowa gave him experience in captivating an audience.

(ii) Hollywood actor
In 1937, Reagan broke into Hollywood movies ('I decided a little lying in a good cause wouldn't hurt', so he invented acting experience for his CV). In his 50 movies, Reagan learned to give audiences a range of convincing performances, including a particularly evil villain in *The Killers* in 1964.

Reagan was already obsessed with politics. One actor was deeply impressed by Reagan's monologues on politics, society and economics, but recalled that everyone else avoided him in the studio canteen!

(iii) Trade union leader 1947
An active trade unionist, he was elected President of the Screen Actors Guild. As a union president, he acquired valuable negotiating skills. Previously a political liberal, he now moved to the right.

(iv) Television star
From 1954 to 1962 Reagan hosted a highly popular prime-time TV programme, *General Electric* [GE] *Theatre*, which trained him how to connect with a TV audience.

Reagan spent 16 weeks yearly touring GE plants, aiming to boost company morale and encourage a sense of identity amongst the company's 700,000 employees. Overall, Reagan met over a quarter of a million people in over 40 states and made over 4000 hours of speeches, sometimes as many as 14 daily:

> The trips were murderously difficult ... But I enjoyed every whizzing minute of it. It was one of the most rewarding experiences of my life ... No barnstorming politician ever met the people on such a common footing.

Here again, Reagan obtained valuable training and public recognition that would help him win and retain the presidency. He learned how to give an audience the vital feelgood factor. Tens of thousands of voters saw and were impressed by him. General Electric extended his tours to include speeches to business and civic groups. One observer saw him get a 10-minute standing ovation for a knowledgeable speech to 3000 teachers on education, although when his speeches became too anti-government and controversial, GE fired him.

Thus, by the time Reagan ran for office in 1966, he was an exceptionally experienced and articulate political animal. Generally considered handsome and charming, he did not come across as greedy for power. His self-effacing sense of humour and demeanour made people trust him and feel comfortable in his presence. He projected a positive TV image, which would be vital in winning votes and support for his policies.

(c) Governor Reagan of California 1967–74

After his apprenticeship in the communications industry, Reagan completed two terms as governor of California, the most populous state in the union, with a GNP comparable to Canada's.

Key question
What was the significance of Reagan's two terms as governor of California?

(i) California and the swing to the right

Some people considered that California was leading the nation in swinging politically towards the right and away from 'big government'. Reagan's gubernatorial campaign of 1966 was in tune with that rightward shift.

(ii) California and the politics of personality

The political parties in California were increasingly weak. Without party backing, successful candidates such as Reagan depended upon their own ability to fund raise and impress voters. California led the nation in replacing the **politics of party** with the **politics of personality** (see page 104).

(iii) Reagan's 1966 gubernatorial campaign

In his gubernatorial campaign, Reagan emphasised themes he had long been developing and upon which he would concentrate every time he ran for office:

- Taxes were too high (Reagan never forgot how, when in Hollywood, 91 per cent of his income went in taxes).
- The state bureaucracy was too large.
- Too much power was centralised in Washington DC, at the expense of the states.
- Rising crime should be combated.
- People should be taken off welfare and put to work.
- Federal and state governments should get off people's backs.

The Democrats portrayed Reagan as a Goldwater-style extremist (see page 25), but Reagan was a highly effective campaigner, who projected a reassuring and attractive TV image. He won a landslide victory over the Democratic incumbent (whom another Democrat dismissed as a 'tower of Jell-O [jelly]') in 1966.

Politics of party and politics of personality
When political parties are relatively weak, they lack funding, so candidates have to raise funds for themselves. It was easier for a charismatic personality such as Reagan to raise funds when he ran for political office. Reagan represented the replacement of the politics of party with the politics of personality.

Key term

(iv) Learning from early errors

After 10 weeks, journalists asked Governor Reagan what his legislative programme was. Reagan looked at his staff and made the sort of gaffe that made some contemptuous: 'I could take some coaching from the sidelines, if anyone can recall my legislative programme.'

Reagan demonstrated the ability to learn from mistakes. He learned to court the legislative branch of the state government and to understand the realities of decision-making, while still retaining his sense of purpose and direction. He learned how to negotiate with legislators, but also how to control them by going over their heads to the people.

Reagan on universities
Reagan criticised universities for 'subsidising intellectual curiosity'.

Assessments of Reagan as governor of California differ. Unimpressive at first, he improved. He failed to decrease taxes and the state budget doubled under him. However, many historians contend that in a large state, full of problems, with a difficult Democrat-dominated legislature, he governed reasonably competently. Conservatives approved of his harsh words on black and student rioters, dissatisfaction with whom had helped his election victory (as a student, Reagan himself had participated in a strike, but he said that was 'different').

By the time Reagan ran for the presidency in 1980 he was hardly the political amateur that critics suggested. His media careers had helped him become the 'great communicator', which made him a formidable campaigner, well equipped for the business of government in the TV age. He had a lengthy apprenticeship in executive leadership in California. Any reasonably successful governor of a major state could be considered a potential presidential candidate.

Key question
How did Reagan win the Republican presidential nomination in 1980?

(d) Dreaming of the presidency
(i) 1968, 1972 and 1976
Reagan made a bid for the Republican nomination in 1968, but was soundly defeated by Nixon (see page 28). In 1976, Reagan nearly defeated Ford for the Republican nomination (see pages 74–5), mostly because Ford had pardoned Nixon, but also because the increased number of primaries made party leaders less influential in the choice of delegates. This gave an effective campaigner like Reagan the chance to appeal directly to rank-and-file Republicans. Reagan dominated the Republican National Convention and effectively selected Ford's running mate (see page 75), which put him in a strong position for the nomination in 1980.

(ii) 1980 – winning the Republican nomination
Many commentators felt Reagan lacked experience of national office, and was too old and too right wing to be a successful presidential candidate. However, Reagan won the nomination because:

- His conservatism was masked and tempered by an amiable demeanour.
- Increased popular participation in the Republican nomination progress helped Reagan, who appealed to the rank and file.
- After he had completed his second gubernatorial term (1975), he was free to travel across the United States and meet local and state party leaders, gaining financial support and establishing an effective campaign team.
- In California, Reagan's team had become experts in their use of political consultants, computers, direct mailing systems and polling techniques.
- Reagan was an exceptionally gifted political campaigner, photogenic, radiating warmth and charm, and constantly and persuasively reiterating his long-held beliefs, which let voters know exactly where he was going.

- Reagan won 29 of the 34 Republican primaries. The primaries were good TV: programmes could focus on interesting personalities rather than boring policies. Reagan knew his best camera angles, which was useful in disguising his advancing years. He read effortlessly and effectively from teleprompters, coming across as relaxed and natural.

Democrat House Speaker Tip O'Neill on Reagan's rhetoric

O'Neill said that 'With a prepared text, he is the best public speaker I've ever seen', and that Reagan's address to the nation after the space shuttle *Challenger* exploded in 1986 made him weep.

- The primaries marathon helped put Reagan's finger on the pulse of the nation.
- Moderate Republicans approved Reagan's choice of moderate George Bush as his running mate.

Reagan's ethnic jokes

Reagan told many ethnic jokes. One was overheard by the press in the 1980 campaign, but Reagan lied on TV and said that he had told the joke as an example of jokes politicians should not tell! His favourite ethnic joke was:

> A Californian who disliked Italians was walking down the street with his friend. They met an Italian organ-grinder with a monkey. He threw $5 in the monkey's hat. His amazed friend said, 'You've been telling me for years you hate Italians, now you do that.' 'Well, they are so cute when they are little.'

(e) Winning the presidency
(i) Disadvantages

Key question
How did Reagan win the presidency?

Reagan had disadvantages. If elected, he would be the oldest man to be elected President (nearly 70). He made some bad gaffes during the campaign. Many considered him a right-wing extremist who might lead the country into war. Nevertheless Reagan won the presidency with 51 per cent of the popular vote, to Carter's 41 per cent.

(ii) Why he won (see also pages 91–2)

- Voters felt Reagan would do better on economic problems. He brilliantly exploited that economic issue in the televised debate with Carter (see page 91), asking voters, 'Are you better off than you were four years ago?' Most were not.

Reagan's humour

'A recession is when your neighbour loses his job, and a depression is when you lose your job, and … recovery is when Jimmy Carter loses his' (the unemployment rate was high – in Detroit, it was 24 per cent).

Key term

Coattails
Americans talking of a President whose popularity helps other members of his party get elected, talk of those other members as getting in on the President's coattails.

- Voters thought Reagan would gain the nation greater respect abroad.
- Carter spent most of the campaign absorbed in the fate of the hostages in Tehran.
- Reagan had no record to defend.
- Many voters were attracted by Reagan's strong beliefs, which suggested the leadership and decisiveness Carter lacked. In uncertain times, Reagan came across as an optimistic candidate with a clear programme and sense of direction.
- Reagan used brilliant strategists (one of whom arrived at Reagan headquarters and said, 'I'm here to see old foot-in-the-mouth' – a reference to Reagan's many gaffes).

> **Reagan and women voters**
> Women voters only supported Reagan by a narrow 46 per cent to Carter's 45 per cent. However, 54 per cent of men backed him, and only 37 per cent voted for Carter.

Key date

Reagan became President: November 1980

(iii) The significance of the 1980 presidential election
Interpretations of the 1980 election varied. Some believed voters were moving right, with a Republican President and Republicans in control of the Senate for the first time in 26 years. Others felt Republican congressional gains owed much to Reagan's **coattails** and considered 1980 a personal victory for Reagan. Both were right. Many traditionally Democrat voters voted for Reagan (including Catholics, Jews, Southerners, blue-collar workers, union members, the poor and even one-third of the unemployed), but the Democrats retained control of the House of Representatives, and dominated gubernatorial and state legislature elections. As party cohesion loosened, voters were turning towards impressive individual candidates.

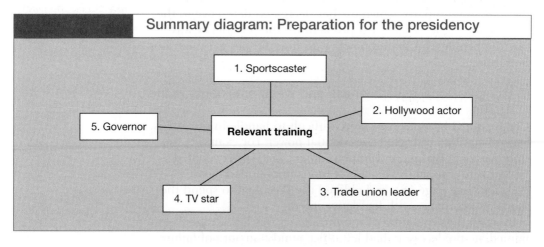

Summary diagram: Preparation for the presidency

1. Sportscaster
2. Hollywood actor
5. Governor
Relevant training
4. TV star
3. Trade union leader

2 | The 'Imperilled Presidency'?

Although Ronald Reagan had been elected to what many considered the most powerful office on earth, some contemporaries (including Gerald Ford) believed the presidency had become an unworkable institution. Like Nixon, Ford said there was no '**imperial presidency**', but an 'imperilled presidency'. Effective leadership was difficult, for several reasons.

(a) Suspicion of government, checks and balances

Suspicion of government was rooted deep in American history, beginning with the colonists who fled from the British government to North America. The American Constitution designed a governmental system to protect citizens from powerful monarchical government. The system was full of checks and balances on the power of the President, especially through Congress.

(b) Congress
(i) Traditional problems with Congress

Reagan needed to obtain congressional assent to his legislative proposals. Any Reagan bill would go through countless congressional committees, during which process it could be changed, often beyond recognition.

Carter showed that even a President whose political party controlled both the House of Representatives and the Senate was not assured of legislative success (see pages 80–2). Why? Congressional committee chairmen got their position from seniority, via repeated re-election by the voters, not from the President. As congressional campaigning was increasingly expensive, money was raised personally rather than through parties. People voted more for an individual who could help them, than for a party, which further decreased deference to the party leader. One of the great problems of the presidency was that the people who shared power with him did not get their jobs from him.

(ii) Congressional assertiveness and weak presidents in the 1970s

Congress had become even more difficult to handle in the 1970s. Several acts had restricted presidential power. For example, the Congressional Budget and Impoundment Act (1974) enabled Congress to compel the release of funds impounded by the President (see page 58), and obliged the President to spend the funds in accordance with legislative intent.

By 1980 the reputation of the presidency was low. Reagan's four immediate predecessors had left office amidst an aura of failure. Johnson's Vietnam War and Nixon's Watergate scandal had undermined Americans' faith in their President and led to an increase in the power of Congress.

Key question
What were the problems faced by Reagan when he took office?

Imperial presidency
During the Cold War, presidential power increased so much that some commentators thought the President was becoming like an emperor – hence 'imperial'.

Key term

(iii) 'Congress has really lost its capability to respond'

By the 1970s, power within Congress had become increasingly diffuse. Committee members' power had increased, making it harder for parties or presidents to control them. Congressional reform 'really messed up the way Congress effectively works ... Congress has really lost its capability to respond', said Ford. A former Johnson aide agreed, saying 'there was no party discipline ... If the President wanted to negotiate with Congress, there were no clear leaders with whom he could talk.'

(c) Problems with the Cabinet (see page 18) and bureaucracy

The loyalty of Cabinet members and bureaucrats could not be guaranteed, particularly if they disagreed with the President's policies. Cabinet members would sometimes 'go native' and accede to the wishes of their departmental bureaucrats rather than those of the President who had appointed them.

The federal government employed around three million civilian and two million military personnel. Bureaucrats hostile or indifferent to a President's wishes could undermine or defeat them. This was a particular problem for Republican presidents such as Reagan, as most senior civil servants were Democrats. Even the Democrat President Franklin Roosevelt, with large Democrat majorities in the House of Representatives and the Senate, said he found it 'almost impossible' to get the Treasury to do what he wanted and found the State Department even worse! Roosevelt's successor Truman pitied his successor: 'He'll sit here, and he'll say, "Do this! Do that!" *And nothing will happen.*'

(d) 'Something is wrong'

In 1981, Americans were still reeling from Vietnam, Watergate and economic problems. Skyrocketing oil prices in 1973–4 had led to a recession, with high inflation, high unemployment, falling industrial output and collapsing world trade. America's problems seemed to be exacerbated by the weakness of Ford and Carter. All combined to lower Americans' morale. It seemed unlikely that the elderly, newly elected President Reagan would be able to effect change: he lacked Washington experience, and faced a Democrat majority in the House of Representatives.

(e) Making the system work

Despite the constraints, there were several factors that could enable Reagan to exercise presidential power effectively:

- He had taken office during a period of crisis. In such periods, Americans were usually willing to follow their President.
- He had won a decisive popular victory in the election; Congress might feel duty-bound to go along with his wishes, particularly if he maintained a high popularity rating.
- In 1976, Harvard professor Richard Neustadt described presidential power as 'the power to persuade and the power to bargain'. Governor Reagan had been willing to bargain. The

'great communicator' was highly persuasive. His charm might win over congressmen, who valued invitations from a congenial President to White House events (they provided good photos for the voters back home). House Speaker Tip O'Neill said:

> Men and women in Congress love nothing better than to hear from the head guy. So they can go back to their districts and say, 'I was talking to the President the other day'.

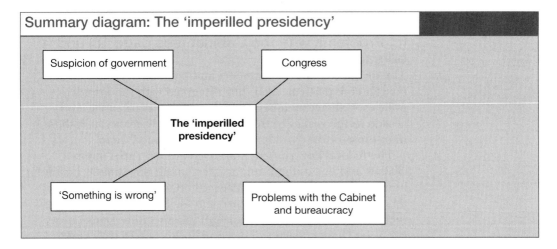

Summary diagram: The 'imperilled presidency'

3 | Reagan's First Term: Aims, Methods and Achievements

(a) Economic aims: Reaganomics

Key question
What was Reaganomics?

> **Reagan on government and capitalism**
> 'Government doesn't solve problems, it subsidises them.'
>   'It's time we realised that profit, property and freedom are inseparable. You cannot have one of them without the others.'

In the 1980 campaign and in his January 1981 State of the Union address, Reagan made clear that he aimed:

- To revive the economy by decreasing taxes, which would encourage people to work harder and buy more.
- To reduce the size and role of the government, cutting public spending and minimising (even eliminating) welfare state arrangements where possible.
- To deregulate state and federal government requirements (this would supposedly liberate business and allow capitalism to flourish, making people more prosperous, enabling them to pay more taxes, thus decreasing the federal deficit).
- To strengthen the nation's defences.

Reagan's economic philosophy became known as **Reaganomics**.

Reaganomics
Reagan's economic philosophy, which emphasised low taxes and deregulation, which it was thought would stimulate the economy.

Key term

Key term

Supply-side economics
Focusing on the supply rather than the demand in an economy. In practice, this meant government should concentrate on achieving inflation-free economic growth, rather than on unemployment and providing welfare state safety nets.

Key date

Budget director Stockman admitted administration's economic plan did not add up: December 1981

Key question
In what ways did Reagan get Reaganomics implemented?

Key terms

Departments of state
Federal government departments such as the State Department (which deals with foreign affairs) and the Treasury.

Federal agencies
These include the FBI (Federal Bureau of Investigation) and the CIA (Central Intelligence Agency).

(i) The old economic consensus

After the Great Depression the consensus was that a government's main target should be to maintain a low level of unemployment. Unemployment rose when demand was too low. Demand could be stimulated by cutting taxes or increasing federal government expenditure. If with full employment demand exceeded supply and inflation resulted, demand could be reduced to counter inflation.

(ii) What were the Reaganites' economic beliefs?

- Reaganites said the low unemployment obsession had pushed up public expenditure and led to budget deficits and stagflation (see pages 75 and 86–7).
- Reaganites believed in **supply-side economics**, which emphasised economic growth.

(iii) Did Reaganomics make sense?

Reagan's budget director David Stockman admitted in a December 1981 interview that the administration's economic plan did not add up and would probably increase the federal deficit. He was right. The administration had justified tax cuts by saying they would help stimulate prosperity, which would ensure that the government still got the same amount of tax revenues as before. As it turned out, the tax cuts, coupled with Reagan's defence spending, resulted in a huge federal budget deficit.

(b) Method No. 1: supporting Reaganomics

Several of Reagan's leading advisers had served in and learned from the Nixon administration. The implementation of any President's programmes depended upon thousands of bureaucrats in the **departments of state** and **federal agencies**. When Nixon had instructed his Cabinet to appoint bureaucrats on the basis of ability first and loyalty second, he made it difficult to obtain the implementation of his policy directives.

Edwin Meese, Reagan's chief of staff in California, worked hard to ensure that the 2000 lower-level political positions went to candidates who sympathised with Reaganomics. There was to be no debate about or opposition to supply-side theory.

Reagan described how he worked hard to ensure that senior members of the administration did not 'go native'. He frequently attended Cabinet meetings to remind everyone who was boss.

(c) Method No. 2: deregulation

Whereas Carter tried to effect change through legislation, Reagan sometimes attempted it through administrative action – or inaction. His administration lightened the burden of regulation on industry and business by cutbacks (averaging 29 per cent) on the staff of regulatory agencies. The number of personnel in the Consumer Product Safety Commission was cut by 38 per cent. There was a 50 per cent fall in prosecutions for illegal disposal of hazardous waste. Reagan used his powers of appointment to ensure that bodies such as the Occupational Safety and Health

Administration made decisions in favour of business and against labour.

Two other essential elements of Reaganomics, tax cutting and a decrease in the rate of growth of public spending, required the agreement of Congress.

(d) Method No. 3: Congressional agreement to the budget – 1981

Historian J.M. Burns defined the classic test of presidential greatness as the President's capacity to lead Congress. Nixon, Ford and Carter failed that test, but Reagan had an early success – the 1981 budget.

> Congress passed Reagan's budget, cutting taxes and domestic expenditure: 1981
>
> **Key date**

(i) Reagan's first budget plan

In his first State of the Union message, Reagan said he wanted to lower taxes, increase defence spending by $7.2 billion, and cut $40 billion from the proposed 1982 federal budget of $740 billion by decreasing government expenditure.

(ii) Congressional co-operation with Reagan over the budget in 1981

In summer 1981, Congress passed Reagan's programme of cuts. The *Washington Post* was impressed. Congress had been:

> dominated by President Reagan and his crusade to cut taxes, strengthen the military, and reverse half a century of growth in social programmes. The Republican Senate and Democratic House … came under Reagan's spell to make more history in a few months than most congresses have made in two full years.

Speaker O'Neill recalled that Reagan:

> pushed through the greatest increase in defence spending in American history together with the greatest cutbacks in domestic programmes and the largest tax cuts [$280 billion] the country has ever seen.

By contemporary standards, the Reagan administration was highly successful in maintaining control over the budgetary process. Congress passed a budget reasonably close to what Reagan wanted. It reduced the budget of 212 federal programmes, most of which aided the working poor, including

---

Reagan jokes

In March 1981, an assassin's bullet nearly killed President Reagan. En route to the operation room, he told his wife Nancy, 'Honey, I forgot to duck' (he had heard that line in a fight film).

About to be operated upon, he said to the doctors, 'Please tell me you are all Republicans.' Voters were impressed.

food stamps, student loans and child nutrition programmes. The Economic Recovery Tax Act cut individual and corporate taxes. How had Reagan done it?

(iii) How did Reagan get congressional co-operation over the budget in 1981?

- Unlike Carter, Reagan came into power with a clear sense of direction and a well-defined order of priorities. **Tip O'Neill** said Reagan and his aides:

> put only one legislative ball in play at a time, and they kept their eye on it all the way through … There was to be only one issue on the agenda – the economy.

- The administration manoeuvred effectively to decrease the traditional length of the congressional debates on the budget.
- Reagan's poll ratings were particularly high after the unsuccessful attempt to assassinate him. This helped make the Democratic House of Representatives co-operative. Democrat House Speaker Tip O'Neill said:

> I can read Congress. They go with the will of the people. The will of the people is to go along with the President. I've been in politics a long time. I know when you fight and when you don't.

Furthermore, he subsequently added:

> I was convinced that if the Democrats were perceived as stalling in the midst of national economic crisis, there would be hell to pay in the mid-term elections.

- Reagan's staff successfully cultivated many **swing voters** in the House.
- Unlike Carter, Reagan was willing to compromise with Congress. He did not get the tax cuts he wanted, but he got enough.
- A Reagan aide said that the tax cut was 'one of the few things Ronald Reagan deeply wanted from his presidency', the only thing he ever put his full political weight behind.
- Reagan gave an impressive televised address to Congress and a masterly televised appeal for the voters' support on 27 July, two days before Congress was to vote. It produced an avalanche of supportive mail and telephone calls, which frightened some congressmen into believing that there would be dire electoral consequences if they failed to support him.
- Reagan's staff increased pressure on congressmen by targeting their districts with radio and TV advertisements, mail and telephone blitzes and administration speakers, and by mobilising local organisations supportive of Reagan's programme. Such grassroots lobbying was not new, but the Reaganites undertook it in a far more sophisticated and skilful manner than ever before.

Key figure

Tip O'Neill (1912–94)
A liberal Democrat, O'Neill represented Boston in the US House of Representatives (1952–87). He was elected House Majority Leader in 1973, then Speaker of the House of Representatives (1977–87).

Key term

Swing voters
Those whose pattern of voting depends on their individual response to each issue; they are not tied to a particular party line.

- Chief of Staff James Baker was responsible for dealing with the **legislature**. He performed brilliantly. One Carter aide recorded:

> It doesn't take much in the White House to pick up the phone and say, 'Is there anything I can do for you in the next two or three months?' In the Carter White House that was regarded as treason. Congress was the enemy. The Democratic Party was the enemy. The Washington establishment was the enemy. Tip O'Neill wanted to help the Democratic President enact a Democratic agenda, but the Carter people didn't understand Tip O'Neill. They regarded him as a horse's ass, and if you call someone a horse's ass in the White House, do you know how fast that gets back to that someone?

Reagan was better. O'Neill recalled how under Carter:

> congressional Democrats often had the feeling that the White House was actually working against us. Once when the city of Boston applied for a government grant for some new roads, I called the Carter people to try to speed it along. Instead of assisting me, however, they did everything possible to block my way. When it came to helping out my district, I actually received more co-operation from Reagan's staff than from Carter's.

(e) Reagan's role in the successful passage of the budget

One of the great debates about President Reagan is exactly how much he contributed to his own successes. In 1981, Reagan was at the height of his powers. He had learned valuable lessons from his governorship, and illness and old age had not yet taken their toll. He charmed congressmen with his amiability and humour and made them feel that they were genuine partners in the policy-making process. When he met them, he was relaxed, full of jokes, and self-effacing. One commentator said Reagan had an 'impressive capacity to be ingratiating'. Tip O'Neill found Reagan:

> exceptionally congenial and charming ... a terrific storyteller, he is witty, and he's got an excellent sense of humour. Some House members said they saw more of him during his first four months in office than they saw Jimmy Carter during his entire four years ... Reagan took Congress very seriously and was always coming over to the Capital for meetings.

Reagan appeared regularly on TV to promote his economic policy. Impressive TV performances just before the congressional votes helped account for his success.

Many Americans disliked Reagan's policies, but liked him. Liberal commentators frequently complained that Reagan was given an 'easy ride' by the media, but he worked for that exceptionally good relationship with the media, always being obliging and polite to them.

Reagan's role in the successful passage of the budget clearly hinged squarely upon his 'great communicator' talents.

Key question
Why did the economy
improve under
Reagan?

Key term

Social Security
A highly valued
entitlement that
insured 140 million
people and sent
benefit cheques to
around 36 million
retirees, disabled
workers and their
families, and
survivors of
deceased workers. It
totalled $161 billion
in 1980.

Key date

Social Security
Reform Act: 1983

Key question
Was Reagan's first
term a success?

(f) The US economy

In Reagan's first two years the economy remained worrying.
Unemployment was 10 per cent and inflation in double figures.
As businesses crashed and the number of homeless increased,
Reagan stayed true to supply-side economics and said prosperity
would return. It did. Not because of supply-side economics (see
page 107), but because of the tight money policies of Carter
appointee Paul Volker (whom Reagan supported) at the Federal
Reserve Board, and because of external factors such as the
discovery of new oil sources, which made the price of oil fall. Also,
massive defence expenditure brought prosperity to US regions
with defence and aerospace industries, such as the West Coast.

(g) Social Security reform

Informed that the fund from which **Social Security** payments
came would be bankrupt by 2000, Reagan suggested almost
immediate cuts in benefits for early retirees, but, faced with near-
unanimous congressional outcry, he appointed a bipartisan
commission headed by economist Allan Greenspan to investigate.
In 1982 the commission recommended raising the retirement age
from 65 to 67 years by 2027, taxing Social Security benefits paid
to the well-off and delaying cost of living increases. In 1983,
Congress made these proposals law.

(h) Conclusions on the first term

(i) 'A new political atmosphere was created'

The effect of the 1981 budget and tax cuts was, according to
historian David Mervin:

> to move the United States in new directions in economic policy;
> fundamental change of a sort that had not been seen for half a
> century. A new political atmosphere was created where minimal
> government, Budget-cutting and low taxation had become the
> norm.

This says Mervin, was the biggest change of direction in the
United States since Roosevelt's New Deal. Reagan had imposed
his policy preferences on the American political system. By this
standard, Mervin says, Reagan was 'brilliantly successful' at the
beginning of his first term when he persuaded Congress to accept
his budget cuts, a substantial tax reduction and a steep increase in

Tip O'Neill tried to explain Reagan's success in late 1981
'People like him as an individual, and he handles the media
better than anybody since Franklin Roosevelt, even Jack
Kennedy. There's just something about the guy that people like.
They want him to be a success. They are rooting for him, and
of course they are rooting for him because we haven't had any
presidential successes for years – Kennedy killed, Johnson with
Vietnam, Nixon with Watergate, Ford, Carter and all the rest.'

defence expenditure. Furthermore, he accomplished this with a Democrat House of Representatives. Reporters spoke of the 'Reagan Revolution'. However, not everyone was convinced that Reagan achieved much in his first term.

(ii) Dissatisfied conservatives and liberals

Some anti-big government conservatives wanted Reagan to demolish the welfare state. However, despite his campaign rhetoric, Reagan knew it would be political suicide to cut programmes such as Social Security and Medicare, especially as elderly voters were a powerful bloc. Reagan was a pragmatist rather than an ideological revolutionary. He knew what was politically possible.

Liberals considered his economic policy unwise, but whether it was or not, he was exceptionally successful in getting it accepted.

(iii) Problems with Congress

Some say he fell far short of his declared policy purposes or point to the thinness of his legislative record in the last three years of his first term.

Reagan never managed to duplicate the domestic policy triumphs of 1981 again. His later budgets were substantially rewritten. He had to accept a succession of tax increases. The legislature disagreed with him over social issues such as busing, abortion and prayer in public schools. Congress was also uncooperative over many of his ambitious attempts to reduce the size of the federal government.

Summary diagram: Reagan's first term – aims, methods and achievements

Aims
- Lower taxes
- Less government
- Deregulation
- National security

Methods and achievements
- Loyal bureaucrats/Cabinet members
- Deregulation
- Congressional agreement to the budget
- Support Volker
- Social Security reform

4 | Reagan's Re-election in 1984

Key question
Why was Reagan re-elected?

In November 1984, Reagan was re-elected for a second term for the following reasons:

- There was an economic upturn.
- Many liked his policies and even those who did not, usually liked him, for example, for the emotional yet dignified way in which he had represented the nation at the 1984 D-Day celebrations in Normandy.
- His 'Morning Again in America' advertisements played on traditional family and American values.
- The 1984 Los Angeles Olympics gave people the feelgood factor.
- Reagan raised $7.2 million, the Democratic candidate Walter Mondale only $657,000.
- Rambling and incoherent (the *Wall Street Journal* headlined, 'Is Oldest US President Now Showing His Age?'), Reagan lost the first debate with Mondale but his aides gave him a brilliant line in the second. The Democrats were saying he was too old (73). Feigning seriousness, he said to Mondale, 'I will not make age an issue in this campaign. I am not going to exploit, for political purposes, my opponent's youth and inexperience.'
- Mondale attacked Reagan's big budget deficits: 'Let's tell the truth. Mr Reagan will raise taxes, and so will I. He won't tell you. I just did.' 'I was in ecstasy', said a Reagan aide. 'The political graveyard is full of tax increasers.' Reagan told voters: 'I wanted to say [in that debate], "You are taxing my patience." But then … why should I give him another idea? That's the only tax he's not thought of.'
- Republicans implied the husband of Mondale's running mate, Geraldine Ferraro, was involved in shady financial dealings in New York. Some worried about a woman being a heartbeat from the presidency. The *Denver Post* asked: 'What if she is supposed to push the button to fire the missiles and she can't because she's just done her nails?'
- Reagan won 72 per cent of the Southern white vote (the South was the centre of the new Religious Right).
- Reagan said he had strengthened US defence and stood up to Communism (for example, in overturning the leftist government of tiny Grenada in 1983), but wanted better relations with the USSR.
- Reagan's aides kept him away from the press to prevent gaffes such as his August 1984 microphone test when he joked, 'My fellow Americans, I'm pleased to tell you today that I signed legislation that will outlaw Russia for ever. We begin bombing in five minutes.' That made the Soviets furious and adversely affected Reagan in the polls. One strategy Reagan's aides used to stop his spontaneous responses to reporters shouting questions was to rev up the engines of his helicopter so he could not hear the questions that he always politely answered.

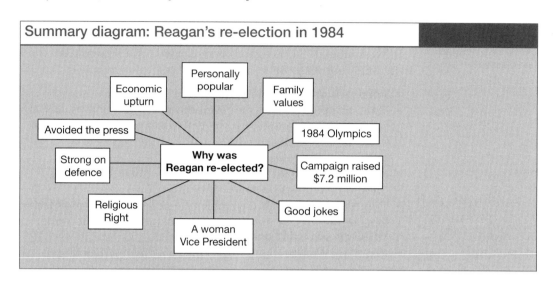

Summary diagram: Reagan's re-election in 1984

5 | Reagan's Second Term

(a) Problems with Congress

In 1984, Reagan was re-elected President with a landslide victory in the popular vote and the Republicans retained control of the Senate. However, Reagan never managed to repeat his 1981 successes with Congress. Why?

(i) Lame-duck syndrome

Congress knew the second term would be Reagan's last (the 22nd Amendment limited any President to two terms of office). Republicans no longer felt obliged to support Reagan, who would soon acquired the inevitable **'lame-duck' President** status that afflicts most presidents in their second term. The Democrats were more confident and enthusiastic about opposing him, especially when they regained the Senate in the congressional mid-term elections (1986).

(ii) No movement to the right

In 1981, Congress was convinced that the President was in tune with public opinion, and that those who disagreed with him were likely to lose their seats. By 1985, the congressional elections of 1982 and 1984 had made clear that although the President was personally highly popular, there was no large-scale movement towards the right and the Republican Party.

(iii) No movement anywhere

In 1980, Reagan had offered the country a change of direction. However, there were no specific policy proposals in his 1984 campaign, which one contemporary described as a 'feelgood campaign, wrapped around the glow of economic recovery, low inflation … and the campaign slogan IT'S MORNING AGAIN IN AMERICA'. Although Reagan claimed, 'You ain't seen nothing yet', the country had already seen the best of him.

Key question
How successful was Reagan's second term?

Key question
Why and how did Reagan have problems with Congress in his second term?

Reagan re-elected by near-record margin: November 1984 | Key date

'Lame-duck' President
When a President nears of the end of his second term, Congress and country, knowing that he is to lose power, look to his likely successor. Then it is hard for that President to achieve much. | Key term

Unlike 1981, Reagan lacked focus. His budget quickly got stuck in Capitol Hill, he failed to obtain congressional approval for aid to the Contras in Nicaragua, and he made a massive error with the **Bitburg** affair. Major staff changes had deprived the administration of momentum.

(iv) The President's weakened team
Meese, Baker and Deaver
Reagan told *Fortune* magazine, 'I believe that you surround yourself with the best people you can find, delegate authority and don't interfere.' That worked well in his first term, but not in his second, when the quality of his senior staff deteriorated sharply.

In Reagan's first term, Meese (see page 107), Chief of Staff James Baker and Michael Deaver had been a formidable trio. Deaver was a superb image creator, Baker ensured both press and Congress stayed friendly. Their effectiveness was essential to a President who delegated so much, and who occasionally needed saving from his own gaffes.

In the second term, Meese wanted to be attorney general, Deaver left the administration, and Baker exchanged jobs with Donald Regan. Meese was an inappropriate choice for attorney general: his deputy resigned in 1988, telling the President that, although he would do anything Reagan wanted, 'including going up and down the halls of the White House with a broom in my behind', he would not work with Meese, whom he considered to be without ethical standards. Donald Regan too presented problems.

Donald Regan
New chief of staff Regan lacked political experience. Recruited from a top Wall Street post, he was a notably loyal treasury secretary in Reagan's first term. Similar in age, class origins and

Key terms

Bitburg
German Chancellor Helmut Kohl asked Reagan to attend a wreath-laying ceremony at the military cemetery in Bitburg, West Germany, in May 1985. There was an outcry in the USA when it was revealed that 49 Nazis and members of Hitler's military police were buried there, but Reagan went ahead.

Antsy
Uneasy, fidgety.

Reagan as a team leader
One aide described Reagan as 'a genuinely nice man', yet found 'a kind of barrier between him and the rest of the world … You can't get inside of him.' Another said, 'He is on the one level the easiest person to work for, always or usually genial, pleasant … but if anyone relies on Reagan for emotional support, he's making a big mistake.' Journalist Lou Cannon emphasised how many Reagan aides felt this distance and lack of support, and often gave up their posts, usually going on to write rather uncomplimentary things about him.

Although they all said they loved him, Reagan's own children frequently told of how trying to get too close made their father '**antsy**' (Ronald Reagan Jr). Daughter Patti said, 'I never knew who he was, I could never get through to him.' Son Michael never forgot how his father failed to recognise him in his graduation gown and said to him, 'My name is Ronald Reagan, what's yours?' 'Even I feel that barrier', admitted wife Nancy.

ethnic roots, Regan and Reagan got on particularly well. Regan was so dominant in the White House that he had to reassure people, 'I'm not power mad.' Even he admitted he lacked 'the politician's temperament'. He refused to cultivate the media or Congress, and left Reagan cruelly exposed, for example, he neither anticipated nor understood congressional and public hostility towards trading arms for hostages with Iran (see page 117).

Faction
The Iran crisis was also an example of the fatal role of faction in the White House: Secretary of Defence Caspar Weinberger and Secretary of State Schultz both disapproved the sale of arms to Iran but would not work together to stop Reagan getting into the biggest disaster of his presidency.

(v) Congress taking the lead
As the federal budget deficit soared, Congress passed the Balanced Budget and Emergency Deficits Control Act (December 1985), which enforced spending cuts. Congress also demanded a more active environmental policy, and although Reagan vetoed the renewal of the $18 billion Clean Water Act (he said it was too expensive), Congress overrode his veto of the 1987 Water Quality Control Act, which was almost identical.

However, although Reagan seemed to be a lame duck, he nevertheless worked successfully with Congress for a major tax reform in 1986.

(b) Major tax reform – 1986
(i) Attempting the impossible
Reagan considered the current tax coding excessively complex, unfair and full of loopholes: it helped certain industries (oil, gas, real estate and agriculture) and individuals (the rich) at the expense of everyone else. However, although it had long been almost universally agreed that tax reform was needed, reform seemed an impossible task. Voters and big business feared it would lead to tax increases.

The Democrat Speaker urged the House of Representatives to vote for Reagan's bill, calling it 'a vote for the working people of America over the … well-financed corporations.' While some Republicans were horrified by Reagan's bill (their party was traditionally the party of big business), others believed the bill would win the party new voters, and approved the clause that ensured the very wealthy could no longer be taxed as high as 50 per cent.

(ii) Achieving the impossible
The passage of the 1986 tax reform bill represented a very impressive joint effort by the **executive and legislative branches**. Its origins lay in a Democrat bill introduced in 1982. In May 1985, Reagan sent his version to Congress and crusaded for tax reform nationally, promising that the bill would not mean higher

---

Key dates

Congress enforced spending cuts: December 1985

Major tax reform: 1986

Key question
How did Reagan engineer major tax reform in 1986?

Key term

Executive and legislative branches
The federal government comprises three branches: the executive (the President), the legislative (Congress) and the judicial (the Supreme Court).

taxes. After a great struggle, particularly with Republicans (whom Reagan had lobbied hard), the bill passed in December 1985. 'What's that I heard about lame duckery?' asked Reagan.

(c) From success to failure?

During the first six years of his presidency, it could be argued that Reagan was an effective President, even if he did not always get his own way (for example, he had been forced to accept tax increases). However, this changed with the Iran-Contra affair in November 1986, and the autumn 1987 rejection of Robert Bork, Reagan's first choice for a US Supreme Court vacancy.

(d) Failure: Iran-Contra – 1986

(i) What was the Iran-Contra affair?

In November 1986 it was rumoured then admitted that the Reagan administration had covertly shipped arms to Iran in an attempt ('almost too absurd to comment on', according to Defence Secretary Caspar Weinberger) to get hostages held by pro-Iranian forces in Lebanon released. Defensive and ill at ease on TV for once, Reagan also had to confess that profits from the arms sales had been diverted to **Contra rebels** in Nicaragua.

Many Americans were shocked. Iran was supposed to be a great enemy (see page 90), and the Reagan administration had not kept Congress informed. The law said the President could not make major weapons sales or intervene in Central America without congressional knowledge and assent.

(ii) Results and significance of Iran-Contra

- The **Iran-Contra** affair triggered uproar in Congress, large-scale and hostile investigative journalism in the media, and a dramatic fall in Reagan's approval ratings, which plummeted from 64 to 44 per cent.
- Multiple investigations into Iran-Contra were highly critical of Reagan's foreign policy. The **Tower Commission** recorded that by violating its own embargo on arms sales to Iran, the United States raised questions as to whether US policy statements could be relied upon, and rewarded a regime that clearly supported terrorism and hostage taking.
- The Tower Commission criticised Reagan's delegatory management style as totally inadequate. He ignored experienced foreign policy professionals in the State Department and tended to give the most general guidance and to leave the details of implementation to his staff.
- The Tower Commission concluded that Reagan probably did not have prior knowledge of the diversion of funds for Contra aid. However, in Senate hearings in summer 1987 and then during Colonel Oliver North's trial in early 1989, it emerged that Reagan knew of and probably authorised the diversion of funds. Had this been known at the time of the Tower Commission, Reagan might have faced impeachment.

Key question
What was Iran-Contra and what was its significance?

Key dates

Iran-Contra scandal exposed: November 1986

Tower Commission criticised Reagan's delegatory management style: February 1987

Key terms

Contra rebels
Opponents of the left-wing Sandinista Nicaraguan government.

Iran-Contra
The 1986 scandal in which the Reagan administration covertly sold arms to Iran and diverted funds from the sale to help Contra rebels in Nicaragua.

Tower Commission
Reagan appointed a commission headed by Texas Republican Senator John Tower to investigate Iran-Contra. The report was published in February 1987.

Historians debate why Reagan committed and then lied about illegal actions that went against the advice of his Secretaries of Defence and State and against his own declared foreign policy, and would inevitably cause a furore when known.

One suggestion is that the faults in his governmental style were to blame. If one believes (and not everyone does) that the 76-year-old President was not ultimately in control, one could blame his tendency to forget what he had been told and had done, and his inattentiveness (partly explicable by his hearing difficulties). Members of the Tower Committee were shocked and amazed by Reagan when he testified before them. A Republican member said it was a 'waste of time' talking to him because, 'with Ronald Reagan, no one is there. The sad fact is we don't have a President.'

Another suggestion is that Reagan as usual stubbornly refused to believe he had been wrong. He blamed press muck-raking instead! Others suggested motives included security concerns, or sympathy for the hostages.

Reagan's actions achieved little. The Iranians decided that hostage-taking paid off and took more hostages. Furthermore, hardly any hostages were freed. Nicaragua's pro-Soviet government remained in power. Such was the disaster, that had it not been for a booming economy and for luck in other areas of foreign policy, Reagan might have ended his presidency in disgrace. As it was, his ratings plummeted.

(e) Failure: Robert Bork – 1987
(i) The importance of nominations to the federal judiciary

Reagan's power to nominate to the federal judiciary (nine US Supreme Court judges, 68 US Appeal Court judges and around 600 federal district court judges) was very important. Nominations to the Supreme Court mattered most. A conservative Supreme Court could make rulings in line with Reagan's political beliefs.

In June 1987, Supreme Court Justice Lewis Powell resigned. Powell was the swing vote in a court split between conservatives and liberals. If Reagan appointed a conservative, the Supreme Court could swing to a conservative position on social issues important to the Religious Right (see page 93). If Congress accepted Reagan's nominee, Robert Bork, American society could be changed.

(ii) Bork's background

Liberals loathed Bork. He had attacked some liberal Supreme Court decisions. He had defended a Connecticut law that would have denied contraceptives to married couples, opposed abortion and claimed women's rights were not included in the 14th Amendment. He had criticised the principle of racial equality.

Black organisations such as NAACP and women's organisations such as NOW (see page 13) mounted an exceptionally aggressive congressional lobby drive and played a big part in the congressional rejection of Bork.

Key question
Why did Supreme Court nominations matter so much?

Key question
Why did the Senate reject Bork?

Reagan, religion, family, sex and drugs

Creationism
A biblical account of the origins of the earth and the life that is on it.

Homemakers
Mothers who stay at home to look after their families, rather than going out to work.

AIDS
Acquired immunodeficiency syndrome is the result of a sexually transmitted disease. It is acquired through the exchange of bodily fluids, especially blood and semen. It strikes down the body's natural defence system, making it vulnerable to other diseases.

- Reagan rarely attended church, but appealed to the Religious Right by supporting school prayer and criticising the federal courts for not allowing **creationism** to be taught. He told an audience of evangelical ministers that he was 'born-again'.
- Despite his divorce in 1952 and his difficult relationships with two of his four children, Reagan was the apostle of the nuclear family. However, divorces were rocketing and fewer than 50 per cent of women were full-time **homemakers**.
- Reagan persuaded Congress to outlaw Medicare and Medicaid-funded abortions for poor women. He preferred 'chastity clinics' (advice centres) where they would be encouraged to avoid sex. Because **AIDS** struck male homosexuals and intravenous drug users, Middle America associated it with immorality. Even after his Hollywood actor friend Rock Hudson died of AIDS in 1985, Reagan refused to advocate the use of condoms or speak to Congress to get funding to help investigate and find cures for the disease. By the mid-1980s, AIDS had spread to blood banks and haemophiliacs; by 1990, 100,000 people had died from it.

  In 1986 the Supreme Court upheld a Georgia law that criminalised sodomy, and 24 other states and Washington DC had similar laws against what they called 'deviant sexual intercourse', even in private.
- Around 40 million Americans used illegal substances. Half the population under 45 had tried marijuana at least once. The poor could afford the new drug 'crack', an inexpensive cocaine derivative. Drugs were a means of temporary escape and/or social mobility (fortunes were made selling them) for Hispanics and African Americans in the ghettos. There were around 12,000 drug-related deaths annually (compared to 200,000 alcohol-related and 300,000 tobacco-related deaths).

  Stung by criticism of her extravagance ($25,000 on her inauguration dress and $200,000 of privately donated money on new White House china), First Lady Nancy Reagan turned to charity work. She launched an anti-drugs 'Just Say No' campaign, but generally her husband's administration concentrated on dealers and users rather than on rehabilitation or on the poverty that often underlay the problem. During Reagan's presidency, the federal government expenditure on a futile war on drugs was around $15 billion annually.

(iii) The Bork hearings

The Senate rejected Bork's nomination by 58 to 42, the largest ever defeat for a Supreme Court nominee, for several reasons. Liberal lobbying was highly effective. The public responded unfavourably to Bork's performance in the televised hearings (he tried to come across as flexible, which led to charges of 'confirmation conversion'). Bork's nomination would only have got through the Senate in the highly unlikely event of full Republican support and some Democrat defections.

Key date

Reagan's nomination of Robert Bork as Supreme Court justice failed: 1987

> **Was the Supreme Court moving right in the Reagan years?**
> After 1984, the Supreme Court upheld a raft of new state capital punishment statutes, permitted the introduction of illegally seized evidence, and eroded previous decisions requiring police to advise suspects of their rights.
>
> However, the Court refused to overturn ROE vs WADE (see page 69) and to dismantle the barrier (established in the American Constitution) between church and state.

(iv) The significance of the rejection of Bork

On the one hand, the rejection of Bork was a big setback for the Reagan administration. Bork was probably an unwise choice. Reagan and Attorney General Meese overestimated their strength and underestimated the public and congressional opposition this controversial candidate would encounter, particularly in President Reagan's 'lame-duck' stage. On the other hand, the defeat of a Supreme Court nomination was not unusual. Twenty per cent of twentieth-century nominations failed to get Senate approval. Furthermore, rejection of Bork was atypical, in that Reagan successfully appointed many conservative judges.

(v) Judicial strategy – success?

In general, Reagan's judicial strategy was highly successful. His successful selection of a great many conservative judges (three associate justices, a chief justice, 168 appeal Court judges and 211 federal district court judges) 'Reaganised' the judiciary, and helped compensate for his failure to win congressional approval for his conservative social agenda.

As Reagan recognised in 1986:

Key question
How successful was Reagan's judicial strategy?

> In many areas – abortion, crime, pornography, and others – progress will take place when the federal judiciary is made up of judges who believe in law and order and a strict interpretation of the Constitution. I'm pleased to be able to tell you that I've already appointed 284 federal judges, men and women who share the fundamental values that you and I so cherish, and that by the time we leave office, our administration will have appointed some 45 per cent of all federal judges.

In the end, Reagan appointed over 50 per cent of the federal judiciary. The election of George Bush as his successor (a result that many attributed largely to Reagan's popularity) ensured that by 1992, three-quarters of federal judges were conservative Reagan or Bush appointees.

Reagan's judicial strategy was exceptionally successful and any assessment of his effectiveness in imposing his agenda on the country must take into account his judicial appointments.

Key question
What was Reagan's role in ending the Cold War?

(f) Success – a new era in American–Soviet relations
(i) An incoherent foreign policy?
The media was amazed when Reagan, who had referred to the Soviet Union as the 'Evil Empire' early in his first term, then had increasingly friendly summits with Soviet leader Mikhail Gorbachev. Reagan explained his 'Evil Empire' phase was 'another time, another era'.

(ii) What was Reagan's role in ending the Cold War?
Strategic defence initiative (SDI)
In March 1983 Reagan launched his ('the whole thing was my idea') strategic defence initiative (SDI), which the press nicknamed 'Star Wars', after the movie. Some scientists derided the proposal, which envisioned shooting missiles out of the sky.

Soviet leader Mikhail Gorbachev (left) and President Reagan (right) at their first summit, Geneva, 1985. Why did presidents such as Reagan, Clinton and Bush concentrate upon peacemaking in their second terms?

The plan was developed secretly by a small group around the President and launched without any consultation with the State Department, the Defence Department, Congress or NATO allies. Reagan was once more (see page 118) committed to a policy that had no support from the federal bureaucracy, Congress or public opinion. This seems to disprove the claim that Reagan was not really in charge, but raises doubts about his consultative processes (see page 117) and his financial sense (by 1988, $12 billion had been spent on SDI, a system that could only be tested against a nuclear weapon).

Reagan in outer space
Reagan enjoyed science-fiction movies and talked so much about aliens invading the earth that behind his back, his exasperated national security adviser Colin Powell would roll his eyes and say, 'Here come the little green men again.'

While few Americans believed SDI would work, the Soviets took it very seriously. Some Americans believe that, along with Reagan's massive defence expenditure, SDI forced the Soviets to bankrupt themselves trying to keep up and/or helped convince them to negotiate with Reagan, which facilitated important arms limitation treaties and the end of the Cold War.

Reagan and Gorbachev

Gorbachev, worried about the Soviet economy, wanted peace. He and Reagan both wanted to halt the nuclear arms race. Their good working relationship effectively ended the Cold War and made Americans feel more secure.

Reagan's stories
Reagan was a great storyteller. Some of the stories were confused. He several times told the story of a heroic Second World War pilot as if it were true – but it was from a movie. He told of how he had seen Nazi concentration camps at the end of the Second World War, but he had never left the United States during the war.

'I never know where I'm going'
In late 1982, when asked if he would be visiting the new Vietnam Veterans Memorial, Reagan replied, 'I can't tell until somebody tells me. I never know where I'm going.'

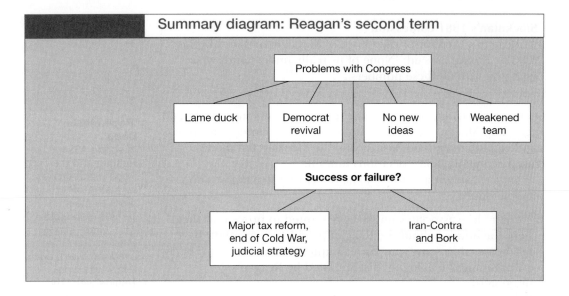

Summary diagram: Reagan's second term

6 | An 'Amiable Dunce'?

Clark Clifford, President Johnson's Secretary of Defence, concluded that Reagan was simply an 'amiable dunce'. The issue is much debated.

(a) Brainpower

Key question
How intelligent was Reagan?

When he became President, Reagan was nearly 70. Doubts about his intelligence were widespread. Some Congressmen, including Republicans, worried about him. Robert Michel, leader of the House Republicans, said, 'Sometimes I think, my gosh, he ought to be better posted. Where are his briefing papers?' Unsympathetic biographer Edmund Morris described him as an 'apparent airhead'. Equally unsympathetic journalist Lou Cannon focused on Reagan's reliance on 'scripts': for example, Reagan frequently read from notes when talking to Tip O'Neill.

> **'Born in the USA'**
> A top-selling album of the 1980s was Bruce Springsteen's 'Born in the USA'. The title song was an indictment of unemployed, working-class Americans born 'in a dead man's town' going 'to kill the yellow man' in Vietnam, but Reagan and others thought the song was a hymn to America.

When asked to help Reagan prepare for the televised presidential debates in 1980, David Stockman was 'shocked' by Reagan's 'woolly platitudes … his lack of agility was disquieting'. In his 1985 memoirs, Stockman called Reagan an economic illiterate, whose enthusiasm for supply-side theory (see page 107) derived from his having to pay 91 per cent tax while working in Hollywood. Stockman's view of Reagan's limited intellect was highly influential.

> **Stockman's 1981 confession**
> As Reagan's Director of the Office of Management and Budget (OMB), Stockman said: 'None of us really understands what's going on with all these numbers'.

On the other hand, some well-informed observers such as Donald Regan and Martin Anderson, who both worked closely with him, said Reagan understood basic economic theories and made crucial economic policy decisions himself.

What then might account for the belief that Reagan was an 'amiable dunce'?

- Former close associates might have wanted to prove that they were the brains behind the Reagan presidency, or might have felt betrayed in some way. For example, Stockman was probably a disillusioned ideologue, disappointed by Reagan's pragmatism.
- Perhaps Reagan only concentrated when fully engaged. He seemed to have a low boredom threshold: it was rumoured that he frequently nodded off at cabinet meetings, although that might have been due to his age and increased difficulty hearing. Some work clearly bored him. When Chief of Staff James Baker asked him in 1983 why he had not read the (short) briefing file for the world economic summit that day, Reagan replied that he had been watching *The Sound of Music* the night before.
- Possibly his poor eyesight made him fail to recognise his own son at his graduation ceremony and his sole black Cabinet officer at another public occasion.
- Perhaps there were problems during Reagan's presidency with the onset of Alzheimer's disease.
- Perhaps Reagan lacked the academic intelligence more usual in a President, but had different kinds of intelligence, such as interpersonal intelligence (he handled people well) and 'language intelligence' (he sometimes spoke incredibly well).
- Defence Secretary Caspar Weinberger directed the Pentagon to produce graphics and cartoons to make their pitch to the President. Reagan's national security adviser in 1986 soon realised that the best way to overcome Reagan's ignorance of the rest of the world was through Defence Department films. Reagan clearly needed to visualise things.

'Pope Meets Dope'
In spring 1984 Reagan and the Pope used Alaska as a stop-off in order to meet. T-shirts were sold with 'Great Minds Meet In The Great Land' on them, but a few wits wore T-shirts with 'The Pope Meets The Dope' on them.

Brazil or Bolivia?
At a 1982 state dinner in Brazil, Reagan toasted the President of Brazil and the 'people of Bolivia'.

A Reagan joke on being lazy
'It's true hard work never killed anybody, but I figure why take the chance?'

(b) Excessive delegation and indecision?
(i) Reagan did not know what he was doing

Many accused Reagan of excessive delegation and indecision. Stockman said Reagan 'gave no orders, no commands; asked for no information; expressed no urgency', while Secretary of the Treasury Donald Regan said:

Key question
Was Reagan guilty of excessive delegation and indecision?

> From first day to last at Treasury, I was flying by the seat of my pants. The President never told me what he believed or what he

wanted to accomplish in the field of economics. I had to figure these things out like any other American, by studying his speeches and reading newspapers.

(ii) Reagan knew what he was doing

Many sources suggest Reagan was more in control than is commonly thought. Martin Anderson said:

> He just sat back … and waited until important things were brought to him. And then he would act, quickly, decisively, usually, very wisely … He knew what he wanted to do and we knew what he wanted done. For five years before he was elected President he staked out clear positions on hundreds of policy issues, and on major issues he spelled out his proposals in some detail.

When asked to describe his own management style, Reagan said:

> you surround yourself with the best people you can find, delegate authority, and don't interfere as long as the overall policy that you've decided upon is being carried out … I encourage all the input I can get … And when I've heard all that … I make the decision.

Even liberal Arthur Schlesinger admitted:

> If the President can point the country and persuade the voters that it is the right direction in which to go, and if he can find reasonably competent subordinates to figure out the details, it does not matter so much politically that he himself hardly knows what is going on.

Education in the Reagan years – 'A Nation at Risk'
Reagan did not seem interested in education. His own Secretary of Education, Terrell Bell, commissioned a study, 'A Nation at Risk', which exposed the dreadful state of public education, with declining test scores and poorly equipped schools that had produced around 23 million functional illiterates. Conservatives blamed the permissive society, while liberals blamed the lack of federal funding and old-fashioned teaching methods.

Middle-class parents often opted out, sending their children to private schools, away from poor minorities and/or non-Christians.

When talking to a group of economic advisers in 1980, Reagan said:

> I'd like you to tell me what has to be done to restore the health of the economy. Don't worry about the politics of what has to be done. That's my job. I'll take care of that.

Perhaps it was sensible to concentrate upon setting the general direction of policy and act as a salesman for the policies, leaving details to others. This 'hands-off' style, which earned him the nickname **Teflon President**, helped him survive political disasters such as Iran-Contra.

(c) 'Far tougher' than his immediate predecessors

Key question
Was Reagan
exceptionally
determined?

Martin Anderson described the outwardly affable Reagan as 'one of the toughest men' he had ever known ('far tougher' than Carter, Ford and Nixon), who pursued his goals relentlessly. Donald Regan echoed that: 'he doesn't change his mind. Therefore he doesn't confuse Congress or the public as to what he stands for'. Stockman described how, late in the first term, when senior staff insisted upon defence cuts and a tax increase, Reagan refused to budge, saying, 'No, we have to keep faith with the people. Everywhere I go they say, 'Keep it up! Stick to your guns!' Well, isn't that what we came here to do?' When Baker persisted in advocating tax raises and cutting defence expenditure, Reagan got angry: 'If that's what you believe, then what in the hell are you doing here?'

Teflon President
When policies went wrong, the people believed Reagan was not too closely involved; the blame never stuck to him. (Teflon is a non-stick material used in saucepans, etc.)

Key term

The public responded well to Reagan's determination. For example, in 1981 the air traffic controllers union struck for higher wages. This violated a law against strikes by public employees. Reagan fired them all and called in the military to do the job while new controllers were trained. The public was impressed.

Summary diagram: An 'amiable dunce'?

- Brainpower?
- Excessive delegation and indecision?
- Tough and determined?

---

7 | The Reagan Legacy

(a) Economic problems for the future

Key question
What was Reagan's
legacy?

Japan buys Hollywood
This was the *Newsweek* cover story in 1989 after Sony bought Columbia Pictures. The US nevertheless remained an economic giant, with 5 per cent of the world's population producing 25 per cent of its goods in 1990.

Reagan joking about the deficit
'I'm not worried about the deficit. It's big enough to take care of itself' (1984).

Reagan left the United States with marked economic weaknesses: enormous sums owed to foreign investors, massive budget and trade deficits, and a huge national debt, which owed much to his huge defence expenditure.

Federal expenditure increased from $699.1 billion in 1980 to $859.3 billion in 1987; even non-defence expenditure increased. The budget deficit in constant dollars was over five times that of his predecessors.

(b) The reinvigoration of the economy

When Reagan took office, inflation was what most concerned the American public. In Carter's last year, inflation was 13.5 per cent, in Reagan's, 4.7 per cent. In 1980, unemployment was 7 per cent; in 1988, 5.2 per cent. Seven million new jobs were created. After the recession early in Reagan's first term, the United States experienced its longest ever period of economic growth in peacetime. At the end of Reagan's presidency, the public perceived his economic policies favourably.

(c) Less government

Reagan achieved a reduction in the size and role of the federal government. The reduction owed much to his cutting taxes and curtailing domestic programmes.

(i) The New Deal philosophy

In the half-century before Reagan's presidency, the big government philosophy of the New Deal-era dominated American politics. This philosophy favoured large-scale federal government intervention, for example, to help the poor with health, educational and equality issues. In 1964, Republican presidential candidate Barry Goldwater, avowed opponent of the New Deal, was crushingly defeated. Reagan was as radical a conservative as Goldwater, but a far more skilful political operator. Also, public opinion and times had changed.

(ii) Reagan's attacks on the New Deal philosophy

Some Americans thought that their country was on the way to becoming a **welfare state**, but that Reagan finally halted that process. Before him, no Republican dared 'assault the federal government as the last haven for help in solving social ills' (historian Louis Harris).

Unlike his Republican predecessors, Reagan was willing to challenge directly the assumptions upon which Roosevelt's New Deal was based. He failed to dismantle the New Deal, but he halted New Deal interventionism and began to reverse it.

(iii) Reagan's aims

In his inaugural address in 1981, Reagan said:

> Government is not the solution to our problem; government is the problem ... It is time to check and reverse the growth of government ... It is my intention to curb the size and influence of the federal establishment and to demand recognition of the distinction between the powers granted to the federal government and those reserved to the states or to the people.

Key question
Why and how did Reagan decrease the role of the federal government?

Key term

Welfare state
A nation in which the government ensures that, 'from the cradle to the grave', citizens are cushioned against poverty and ill-health.

(iv) Cuts in federal programmes

Reagan called for a 'new federalism', decreasing the size and scope of the federal government and returning regulatory authorities to the states. He managed to cut and eliminate federal programmes, although far less than he wished. Reagan failed to abolish the Department of Education, but reduced its staff by 25 per cent, and cut its programmes savagely. He also decreased education block grants to the states by 63 per cent. Civilian employment in the federal government actually rose under his watch by 3 per cent, due to his emphasis on building up the national defence (where civilian employment grew by 11.5 per cent).

In the 1980 campaign, Reagan had promised to do something about the 'welfare mess'. He said he would eliminate 'waste, fraud and abuse'. He reduced the level of benefits and the range of benefits for 'safety net' programmes such as Aid to Families with Dependent Children (13 million children lived below the poverty line in 1984). However, he left Social Security (senior citizens' pensions), Medicare, veterans' benefits, school lunches and Head Start (free breakfast for poor schoolchildren) basically intact. He had not dared do too much.

New York's Democratic governor, Mario Cuomo, said, 'At his worst, Reagan made the denial of compassion respectable.' When in a 1986 meeting Reagan said the unemployed just 'don't want to work', Tip O'Neill, who usually got on well with Reagan, lost it and accused a furious Reagan of talking 'a load of baloney':

> Don't give me that crap. The guy in Youngstown, Ohio, who's been laid off at the steel mill and has to make his mortgage payments – don't tell me he doesn't want to work. Those stories may work on your rich friends, but they don't work on the rest of us. I'm sick and tired of your attitude, Mr President, I thought you'd have grown in the five years you've been in office, but you're still repeating those same simplistic explanations.

The most famous proposed budget cut
In order to save federal money, the Department of Agriculture suggested that ketchup and pickle relish substitute part of the vegetable portion in federal-subsidised school lunches. The suggestion was ridiculed, then dropped.

(v) Deregulation

The consensus was that federal regulation was stifling capitalism and competition. Carter and Congress had begun the process of deregulation of the airline, trucking, railroad and financial industries. However, Reagan did not differentiate between stifling economic regulations and regulations that protected the environment or health and safety.

Reagan devolved some power to the states, and a certain amount of deregulation took place, although not as much as he

Key terms

Savings-and-loan
A kind of bank.

Uncle Sam
A cartoon-like drawing of a distinguished looking man with the US flag on his clothing became very famous. He was taken to represent the government of the nation.

'I KNOW WATT'S WRONG' – an environmentalist bumper sticker.

would have wished. In 1982, Reagan signed a bill that increased the amount of federal insurance available to **savings-and-loan** (S&L) depositors, and authorised S&Ls to engage in a wide range of risky investments. The administration paid no attention as the S&L industry leaders gambled and stole. In the late 1980s, many S&Ls collapsed, necessitating a $132 billion bailout from public funds – the costliest financial scandal in US history, all due to Reagan's lax oversight of federal agencies.

(vi) Deregulation and the environment

Reagan appointed individuals who did not believe in the regulatory function of government as heads of regulatory agencies, and slashed their budgets. This rendered the agencies incapable of enforcing regulations established by Congress.

> **A Reagan gaffe on the environment**
> When Reagan said trees and other vegetation caused air-pollution, students at Claremont College greeted him with a sign tacked to a tree: 'CHOP ME DOWN BEFORE I KILL AGAIN'.

Under Secretary of the Interior James G. Watt, the Interior Department opened federal lands to exploitation by coal and timber companies, blocked any creation of new protected wilderness areas, and made one million acres of offshore land available to oil companies for drilling. In 1983, Watt had to resign because he referred to a public commission as consisting of 'a black, a woman, two Jews and a cripple'. His policies were sustained by his predecessors.

Key question
Had the Reagan Revolution failed?

(vii) A new public philosophy

Reagan created a new public philosophy. Even Democrats came to accept Reagan's assumptions and stopped talking about more expenditure on social welfare. Liberal Democrats in Congress had to admit that major new domestic expenditures were out of the question, partly because of Reagan's creation of the new public philosophy and partly because he had left the federal budget in such a state. In the 1988 presidential election, the Democratic candidate, Michael Dukakis, did not talk about reversing Reagan's tax cuts.

The Democratic senator Ernest Hollings rejected liberal claims that the Reagan Revolution had failed. 'President Reagan dealt **Uncle Sam** a crippling blow': a debt-ridden federal treasury, a demoralised and discredited federal workforce, a crumbling public infrastructure, and an electorate effectively mobilised against necessary taxation.

Key question
Should Reagan be blamed for 'mortgaging the future'?

(d) Balancing the budget – failure

Although there were some reductions in federal expenditure, Reagan failed to balance the budget, due to tax cuts and defence expenditure ('defence is not a budget item', said Reagan).

Under Reagan, the national debt tripled to more than $2.6 trillion, but it could be argued that Congress shared responsibility for the budget deficit, because they were determined to defend domestic programmes (polls regularly revealed that the majority of Americans did not want to reduce spending on social programmes).

Democrat Walt Rostow called Reagan 'a good-time Charlie. Nothing bad is going to happen on my watch. Screw the future.'

(e) Social change
(i) President and Supreme Court vs Congress

Key question
Did society greatly change in the Reagan years?

Reagan's proposals regarding abortion, affirmative action, busing, pornography and school prayer got nowhere in Congress. However, Congress was circumvented by the administration's impressive judicial strategy. Reagan took careful steps to ensure that the federal judiciary would be packed at all levels with judges who shared his beliefs.

> **What's on TV?**
> Although President Reagan said there was too much sex and violence on TV, the most popular programmes included long-running soaps *Dallas* and *Dynasty* (which the BBC's Terry Wogan famously christened 'Dysentery'), which dealt with the families of fabulously wealthy businessmen. *The Cosby Show* and *Family Ties* were 'warmedies' (warm family comedies). The Korean War medical comedy-drama *MASH* had derided military authority in the 1970s, but the characters softened in the 1980s: 'Hot Lips' developed from a hard-drinking, highly sexed woman to a respected leader of the nurses.

(ii) Social programmes

Social programmes certainly suffered under Reagan. Left-wing critics bitterly compared Nancy Reagan's $25,000 wardrobe for the first inauguration with the 500,000 whose names Reagan deleted from the disability rolls. The gap between rich and poor widened, and the number of homeless increased from 200,000 to 400,000.

(iii) Ethnic minorities in the Reagan years
Signs that Reagan was illiberal on race

African Americans considered Reagan illiberal on race. He had opposed the 1965 Voting Rights Act, and in the 1970s had made much of a black Chicago 'welfare queen' obtaining excessive federal government aid. He had refused to address NAACP in 1981 because it would have interfered with his horse-riding plans. When he did address them in 1982, he upset them when he said federal aid had created 'a new kind of bondage [a reference to slavery]' for African Americans.

Reagan vetoed the 1988 Civil Rights Restoration Act, which undid a Supreme Court ruling (GROVE CITY COLLEGE vs

BELL, 1984) that limited anti-discrimination laws (Congress overrode his veto). Out of the 368 federal judges he appointed, only seven were black (15 were Hispanic, two were Asian, and the rest were mostly young, white males).

Reagan did nothing for the inner cities. Ghetto schools remained poor and segregated, and Reagan unhelpfully supported a constitutional amendment to outlaw busing. When Congress rejected that, his administration refused to press suits that would enforce busing. He also asked the Supreme Court to restore tax-exempt status to segregated private schools.

Black progress

There was some cause for celebration for ethnic minorities in the Reagan years. Reagan had a black Cabinet member (although he failed to recognise him at a meeting after six months in office). Chicago and Philadelphia elected black mayors. In 1983, despite Reagan's opposition, the third Monday in January was made into Martin Luther King Day, a national holiday. In 1984, King's old lieutenant Jesse Jackson made a serious run for the Democratic nomination. Bill Cosby and Oprah Winfrey had highly successful TV shows, Toni Morrison's books sold well. Reagan decided it would be politically unwise to attack affirmative action and Bork's nomination (see page 118) was rejected, which suggested blacks had increased political muscle.

Asian American progress and problems

In 1988, the bipartisan Japanese-American Redress Act (also known as the Civil Liberties Act) promised $20,000 reparations for the 60,000 Japanese Americans interned in the Second World War. On the other hand, in 1982, Chinese American Vincent Chin was clubbed to death in Detroit by two white car workers who thought he was Japanese and therefore to blame for layoffs in the car industry (increasingly dominated by Japanese imports). The killers' sentence was a mere three years' probation. Asian Americans were disgusted.

The 'subway vigilante'

In December 1984, four black youths demanded money from Bernhard Goetz in a New York City subway. He had previously been robbed and injured by blacks, so he drew out a gun and shot all four. None died, but one was brain-damaged and paralysed for life. In the 1987 trial, it emerged that all four had criminal records and they had screwdrivers (offensive weapons) in their pockets. The jury, on which there were only two blacks, accepted Goetz's self-defence plea and acquitted him of charges of attempted murder and assault. Convicted of illegally possessing a firearm, his prison sentence was only eight months. Goetz became a (white) hero.

(iv) Women in the Reagan years

There was much division among women in the Reagan years, whether over abortion (some were in favour, some against), sexual harassment, wife battering, or the fact that women only earned on average 72 per cent of what men earned in 1990 (it was only 62 per cent in 1980).

Equal Rights Amendment defeated: 1982

Key date

Anti-abortionists joined Operation Rescue (established 1988), a militant new organisation that used sit-ins to block access to abortion clinics: thousands were jailed in 1988–99. A few bombed clinics and killed medical practitioners. Increased social conservatism was evidenced in 1988, when federally funded family planning centres were forbidden to discuss abortion with patients, and the Supreme Court ruling BOWEN vs KENDRICK denied federal funding to pro-choice (pro-abortion) programmes. A great Religious Right victory was the defeat of the Equal Rights Amendment (ERA) in 1982.

'Women's Lib' went quieter in the 1980s. *Ms* magazine switched from feminism to celebrity coverage. Suits were out, frills and high hemlines came back: 'Girls want to be girls again', said one designer. Victoria's Secret stores were popular with their 'Intimate apparel [underwear] explosion'. *Newsweek* magazine lamented divorce rates and wondered whether working 'supermums' were damaging their kids.

(v) The Religious Right

Although Reagan said he wanted constitutional amendments to ban abortion and restore prayer in public schools, he could not get the necessary two-thirds majority in Congress and the Religious Right felt he did not try very hard on these issues. He failed to endorse the Family Protection Act, which called for the prohibition of abortion, the restoration of school prayer, tax breaks for wives and mothers who stayed at home, tuition tax credits for children attending private schools, single-sex sports at school, parental censorship of reading materials in schools, and the denial of teenage access to contraception unless parents were notified. Although he had Moral Majority founder Reverend Jerry Falwell (see page 93) bless the 1984 Republican National Convention, he did little else to please the Religious Right, perhaps because he knew that they would never vote Democrat.

(f) The revitalisation of the presidency

British historian Harold Laski wrote in *The American Presidency* (1940):

Key question
Had Reagan revitalised the presidency?

> The range of the President's functions is enormous. He is ceremonial head of the state. He is a vital source of legislative suggestion. He is the final source of all executive decision. He is the authoritative exponent of the nation's foreign policy. To combine all these with the continuous need to be at once the representative man of the nation and the leader of a political party is clearly a call upon the energies of a single man unsurpassed by any other political office in the world.

Reagan was brilliant at the ceremonial, tried quite successfully to effect the legislative reversal of the New Deal state, had some great foreign policy successes, represented and articulated the American Dream and helped revitalise the Republican Party.

In the 1970s, many commentators were discussing whether the United States was becoming ungovernable. Polls showed public confidence in political leaders at an all-time low. Congress appeared to be increasingly chaotic, political parties were greatly weakened, and after Nixon, Ford and Carter, it was felt that the presidency was not working well. Reagan revitalised the presidency and helped restore confidence in the American political system as a whole. Most people consider this one of Reagan's greatest achievements. On the other hand, polls showed that confidence in the Reagan presidency was badly damaged by the Iran-Contra scandal and it could be argued that the presidency did not seem revitalised under his successor, George Bush.

(g) The revitalisation of the Republican Party

Key question
Had Reagan revitalised his party?

Historians debate whether Reagan (unlike Carter) was an electoral asset to his party. He made a great contribution to the Republican Party revival in the 1980s. However, throughout Reagan's presidency, the Democrats retained control of the House of Representatives. They reasserted their domination in the Senate in 1986 and continued to hold a majority of state governorships and two-thirds of state legislative chambers. Thus Reagan's electoral success was personal rather than party based. He failed to carry significant numbers of Republican candidates into office 'on his coattails'. Even when he campaigned extensively on behalf of fellow Republicans, as in the mid-term elections of 1986, it had little effect: members of Congress got elected by pleasing and serving their constituents, not because their constituents liked the President.

On the other hand, Vice President George Bush's election to the White House in 1988 owed much to the continued popularity of Reagan. Polls showed that 80 per cent of voters who approved of Reagan supported Bush.

(h) Greater national security

Key question
Had Reagan improved national security?

Reagan had several foreign policy disasters. For example, the Iran-Contra disaster made him appear incompetent and without respect for the law. It made the USA look foolish and unreliable to the rest of the world.

On the other hand, Reagan's relations with the Soviet Union were far more successful and generally considered more important. He inaugurated a new era of cordial relations with the Soviets. It could be argued that this owed little to Reagan, and everything to Gorbachev and internal Soviet problems, but Reagan supporters argue that Reagan's massive defence expenditure was what brought the Soviet Union to the arms-control negotiating table.

Reagan on America
'The last best hope of man on earth.'

(i) How much credit does Reagan deserve?

Some of Reagan's achievements were due to others. The public had tired of big government and the New Deal and Great Society programmes before he took office. We have seen that Reagan's success owed much to his staff (see page 115), who fully exploited his formidable skills as the 'Great Communicator'.

On the other hand, a major reason for Reagan's success lay in his vision and commitment to a few simple beliefs. Long convinced of the need for minimal government, minimal taxation and opposition to Communism, he had a clear sense of direction. Democrat Arthur Schlesinger Jr believed Reagan represented 'the triumph of a man who earnestly believed in something … the proof of the power of conviction politics'. Reagan was an ideologue, but also a pragmatist. Unlike his predecessor, he compromised and gave way when necessary.

(j) 'We made a difference'

Reagan left the presidency with the highest popularity rating of any President since the polls began in the 1930s. Although one might disagree with or dislike his policies, he was often an exceptionally effective President. In 1981, even hostile critics were impressed by his successes in Congress, in bringing the bureaucracy under control and in reversing the acceptance of 'big

> **Key question**
> Were Reagan's achievements due to others?

> **Reagan on his administration**
> 'We meant to change a nation, and instead we changed the world.'

After seven Americans died on the space shuttle *Challenger* in January 1980, Reagan spoke to and moved the nation, saying, 'We will never forget.' Why do you suppose Reagan was such an effective speaker on this occasion?

government'. In foreign policy, he helped end the Cold War. In his final televised address to the nation in January 1989, Reagan thanked those who had supported the 'Reagan Revolution' and rightly asserted, 'We weren't just marking time, we made a difference'. His staff, changes in American public opinion and changes in the outside world also contributed, but most presidents fail to manage such meaningful public policy change (Nixon made a difference in foreign policy, but not in domestic policy, while Ford and Carter failed to make a difference either at home or abroad).

The 1980s

Cause for optimism?
- New York City's first African American mayor (David Dinkins in 1989).
- Scientific progress, for example, first reusable space shuttle (*Columbia*) (1981).
- Cigarette smoking decreased: 40 states restricted or banned it in public areas.
- Economic prosperity for many.
- Divorce rates and welfare take-ups stabilised.
- 'What I want to see above all is that this remains a country where someone should always get rich' (Reagan, 1983).
- Rap music and heavy metal articulated concerns of the poor and minorities.
- American popular culture (McDonald's, Coca-Cola, jeans, Hollywood films and rock-and-roll) was exported all over the world.
- Renewed patriotism, for example, D-Day anniversary.
- Vietnam War Memorial in Washington DC (1982) helped heal divisions.
- Cold War winding down; many countries became democracies.

Cause for pessimism?
- The rich got richer – the wealthiest 1 per cent possessed 8 per cent of the national income in 1980, 15 per cent by 1990. The average income of the poorest decreased by $1300 per annum.
- Massive federal budget deficit.
- Congress slashed the National Endowment for the Arts (NEA) budget, because the NEA supported the homoerotic work of photographer Robert Mapplethorpe.
- Increasing rates of teenage pregnancy.
- AIDS.
- Medicare offered partial insurance coverage for most of the elderly and Medicaid assisted many of the poor, but around 14 per cent of Americans lacked health insurance. The US was the only developed nation in the Western world without a system of universal health coverage.

- Reagan felt there was too much sex and violence on TV, but his deregulation had weakened the Federal Communications Commission (FCC).
- Prominent televangelist Jim Bakker was found guilty of massive fraud in relation to his multimillion-dollar religious empire. He was sentenced to 45 years in prison in 1989. Prominent televangelist Jimmy Swaggert admitted to using prostitutes and gave up his television ministry in 1988.
- President Reagan had little sympathy for conservation and the environment, saying 'a tree is a tree – how many more do you need to look at?'
- The space shuttle *Challenger* exploded, killing the crew; an investigation blamed corporate greed.
- The USA was disliked in many other countries. Terrorists targeted Americans, for example, a Libyan terrorist's bomb blew up Pan Am Flight 103 over Lockerbie, Scotland, killing 259 passengers and 11 people on the ground.
- Iran-Contra.

Summary diagram: The Reagan legacy

- Economic problems for the future
- A reinvigorated economy
- Less government
- Social change
- The revitalisation of the presidency, political system and party
- Greater national security

Which party controlled Congress?	
Congressional election year	**Party in charge of the Senate and the House of Representatives**
1968, 1970, 1972, 1974, 1976, 1978	Democrat control of both Senate and House of Representatives
1980, 1982, 1984	Republican Senate, Democratic House
1986, 1988, 1990, 1992	Democrat control of both
1994, 1996, 1998, 2000	Republican control of both

Study Guide: AS Question

In the style of Edexcel

How successful were President Reagan's economic policies?

(30 marks)

Exam tips

The cross-references are intended to take you straight to the material that will help you answer the question.

This question gives you the opportunity to explore an issue where there is much debate. There is still not overall agreement here. It all depends really on what weight you decide to give to the evidence of success and the evidence of failures or problems. Be careful to stay focused on the point of the question – do not get sidetracked into considering social or political issues – unless you make a directly relevant point that an economically successful policy had a problematic social impact which reduced its overall success. It will be easier to organise your answer if you remain focused on economic issues, and make it clear that you are going to apply solely economic criteria in evaluating success.

To show the success of Reagan's policies you could consider:

- His success in implementing a new direction in economic policy: reliance on 'supply-side economics' – reducing 'big government' and instituting tax cuts as a stimulus to the economy (pages 106–12, 116–17 and 127–30).
- Evidence of the reinvigoration of the economy during his period of office: the longest ever period of economic growth in peacetime.
- The fall in both unemployment and inflation suggesting a strong economy (pages 111 and 127).

To create a balanced argument you could consider the problems of the Reagan economic legacy:

- trade deficits (page 126)
- sums owed to foreign investors (page 126)
- a huge national debt (pages 126 and 129).

Were Reagan's economic policies a success in spite of the constant failure to balance the budget and the huge deficit which resulted from his defence spending? Remember that the defence programme itself would contribute to creating jobs and stimulating demand. Is it more important that his policies overall succeeded in creating more jobs and reducing inflation, or will you give more weight to the problems of the deficit?

---

5 President George H.W. Bush 1989–93

POINTS TO CONSIDER
The single-term presidency of George H.W. Bush is often seen as a rather unsuccessful interlude between two more famous presidents who served two terms. This chapter investigates whether the Bush years deserve to be considered a mere postscript or interlude, with sections on:

- How and why Bush won the 1988 election
- Ongoing social issues
- Foreign policy
- Why Bush lost the 1992 election

Key dates

1988	George Bush elected President
1989	US intervened in Panama
1990	Clean Air Act
1990–1	Kuwait liberated in Gulf War
1990–2	Recession
1992	Race riots in Los Angeles
	Bush defeated by Clinton in presidential election

1 | Background

(a) Youth and earlier career

The son of a Connecticut banker and Senator, Bush attended **prep school** then Yale. A fighter pilot in the navy during the Second World War, he moved to Texas and made a fortune from oil. He was twice elected to the House of Representatives for the Houston area (1966–71), but failed to get elected to the Senate in 1964 and 1970.

Bush was Ambassador to the United Nations (1971–2), chairman of the Republican National Committee (1973–4), Ambassador to China (1974–6) and head of the CIA (1976–7). In 1980 he failed to get the Republican nomination, but Reagan chose him as his running mate. After eight years as Reagan's Vice President, Bush stood for the presidency in 1988. He was such a discreet and loyal Vice President that many derided him as Reagan's 'errand boy', a wimp who would never be able to stand on his own two feet. Some Reagan loyalists felt he was a political chamelon, lacking strong opinions. Democrats publicly,

Prep school
Fee-paying school for the children of the wealthy élite.

Key term

Profile: George Herbert Walker Bush (1924–)

1924	– Born in Connecticut; father a banker and Senator; educated at private schools
1942–4	– Naval war hero in the Second World War
1945–8	– Yale University, then moved to Texas
1963–4	– Established oil corporations
1966	– Elected to the Texas House of Representatives as a Republican
1970	– Unsuccessful run for Senate
1971–2	– Nixon chose him as US ambassador to United Nations
1973	– Chairman of Republican National Committee
1974–9	– US ambassador to China
1976–7	– Reluctant head of CIA (he thought it would finish off his political career but accepted the job because 'one should serve his country and his President')
1980	– Unsuccessful bid for Republican nomination; he criticised Reagan's economic plans as '**voodoo economics**'; defeated by Reagan, who chose him as his running mate
1981–9	– Reagan's Vice President
1988	– Republican candidate for presidency; defeated Democrat Michael Dukakis by 54 per cent of the popular vote to 46 per cent
1989	– Ordered invasion of Panama
1990–1	– Liberated Kuwait after Iraq's invasion
1990–2	– Economic recession
1992	– Defeated by Democrat Bill Clinton in presidential election

Key term

Voodoo economics
When Bush gave this description to Reagan's economic policies, he meant that they would need some kind of magic to work effectively.

Bush was something of a caretaker President, elected primarily on the strength of his connection with the popular outgoing President Reagan. Reasonably successful in foreign policy (Panama and the Gulf War), he made little impact on domestic issues which, in a period of recession, cost him re-election.

Bush 41 and Bush 43
George Herbert Walker Bush was the 41st President of the United States. When his son George Walker Bush became the 43rd President, many labelled the father 'Bush 41'.

repeatedly and pointedly asked, 'Where was George?' during Iran-Contra and other Reagan-era scandals. On the other hand, no one could question his experience. He had even served as acting President for eight hours in 1985 while Reagan had surgery to remove a malignant colon polyp.

(b) The 1988 election

Initially, the Democrats favoured the Kennedy-style Gary Hart, until the *National Enquirer* published a photo of him with a female model (not his wife) sitting on his knee on his yacht, which he had named *The Monkey Business*. The Democrats next choice was Michael Dukakis, the liberal governor of Massachusetts, who initially led Bush in the polls.

Bush surprised people by his choice of Dan Quayle as his running mate. Quayle was a figure of fun in the Senate, where he had an abysmal attendance record and once read a speech given him by an aide that had nothing to do with the topic being debated. Even when it became known that Quayle had used family influence to avoid the draft in Vietnam (he served in the National Guard instead, as did George Bush Jr), Bush stood by him, perhaps because he wanted to be sure his Vice President would not upstage him, or because he thought Quayle's conservative championing of 'family values' would help the ticket with the Religious Right.

Bush won because:

- He had Reagan's endorsement and the general feeling was that Reagan had done well and that Bush had gained invaluable experience as his Vice President.
- His team publicised how Governor Dukakis had vetoed a bill compelling public schoolteachers to lead the **Pledge of Allegiance** each day. They had also made public how Dukakis had signed a weekend furlough (official leave) bill for convicted criminals, and produced advertisements telling how convicted Massachusetts murderer Willie Horton perpetrated a rape while on furlough. The Horton advertisements played on racism (Horton was black) and fear of crime.
- Dukakis concentrated on state business and did not campaign until it was too late. He was not always enthusiastic about running. He came across as aloof (voters were unimpressed by his emotionless response to the question as to whether he would support the death penalty if his wife were raped) and without a clear programme (the Democrats were divided about issues).
- Bush's promises ('Read my lips – no new taxes') went down well.
- The Republicans raised far more money for the campaign.
- Bush's son George Jr, who had kicked a serious drinking habit two years before ('It was goodbye Jack Daniels [whiskey], hello Jesus'), helped his father relate to the Christian Right.

Bush won 53 per cent of the popular vote, Dukakis 45.6 per cent. Voter turnout was the lowest since 1942, perhaps because neither candidate was inspiring.

(c) President-elect

In the three months between his election and inauguration, Bush chose his Cabinet. His son George W. Bush played an important part in this. The so-called 'Scrub Team' 'scrubbed' potential appointments to check that underneath their first loyalty was to Bush not Reagan. In these three months, Bush was conciliatory to the press and politicians: he gave more press conferences than Reagan had in his last two-and-a-half years. Black leader Jesse Jackson was delighted: 'Reagan had a closed-door policy for eight years. You couldn't get an audience with him.' There were many other signs that this President would be different, especially in his inauguration address.

Key question
Why choose Dan Quayle as a running mate?

Key date

George Bush elected President: November 1988

Key question
How and why did Bush win the 1988 presidential election?

Key term

Pledge of allegiance
Every morning, schoolchildren and their teachers stand before, and pledge allegiance to, the US flag.

(d) Bush's inaugural address

Bush's inaugural address was deemed critical of the Reagan years (as usual, the previous President and his wife sat nearby, and someone had to nudge Nancy Reagan because she looked so angry). Bush advocated bipartisanship, helping the homeless and bringing down the deficit, and pointed out that money and possessions (both of which he had in exceptional quantities) were not the most important things in life.

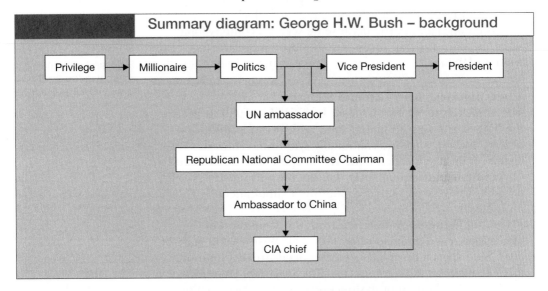

Summary diagram: George H.W. Bush – background

Privilege → Millionaire → Politics → Vice President → President

UN ambassador

Republican National Committee Chairman

Ambassador to China

CIA chief

2 | Comparing Bush with Reagan

Key question
How was Bush different from Reagan?

Bush's presidency was unlike Reagan's in many ways.

- According to his staff, Bush 'never accepted the need for an overarching vision. He is the embodiment of pragmatism'. That enabled one reporter to write an article entitled, 'A Ship Without a Rudder: The White House Appears to Lack Direction or Purpose'.
- Whereas the Reagan administration 'hit the ground running', one wit said that Bush 'hit the ground crawling'. Months after his accession to the presidency, Congress still had no clear idea of his foreign and domestic policy priorities.
- Both the above points owed much to the fact that, unlike Reagan, Bush faced a Democratic House and a Democratic Senate. Even some (conservative) Republicans were suspicious of him.
- It was hard for Bush to have any great ideas or programmes when the federal budget deficit was $2.7 **trillion** and the interest on it $2 billion per annum.
- Bush lacked Reagan's skill before the cameras. One commentator said:

Key term

Trillion
One million million or a thousand billion.

> The guy knows he's no good on television. You get the impression he held his nose and did it during the campaign because he was convinced he had to. But now that's over, and he's back mumbling and babbling and cutting off his words in mid-sentence.

The Bush staff seemed to lack the awareness of the Reagan staff of the importance of television in politics. The Reagan administration was criticised for trying to manipulate the media, but the Bush administration 'doesn't care if the President gets on the evening news or not', according to one TV newscaster.

• Bush's staff did not test and monitor potential appointees as Reagan's staff had.

On the other hand, Bush was very popular in his first 18 months, partly because the international situation was pleasing (the Cold War was ending) and partly because he seemed compassionate toward the poor (he had promised 'to make kinder the face of the nation' in 1988).

A new American hero – Homer Simpson

The animated series *The Simpsons* first aired in 1989. It became the longest running animated show and sitcom in television history, and the most internationally syndicated show in history. It has been called both 'the deepest show on TV' and a 'corporate-manufactured show that openly and self-reflexively parodies the very consumer capitalism it simultaneously promotes.'

Viewing figures soon rocketed from the 13 million of the first season, even more so when President Bush's 1990 State of the Union speech bewailed, 'America needs to be a lot more like **The Waltons** and a lot less like *The Simpsons*.' He rejected the show's celebration of dysfunctionality and 'slacker culture' (Bart Simpson T-shirts saying 'Underachiever – And Proud of it, Man!' were selling well). A Simpsons' episode responded: in it, the family watched the televised Bush speech, and Bart says, 'Hey, we are like the Waltons, we are praying for the end of the [economic] Depression too.'

Was it all counterculture? Politicians, bosses and the news media are always portrayed as corrupt in *The Simpsons*, but the Simpsons' dreaded evangelical Christian neighbour Ned Flanders has been praised by many Christians and the characters frequently feature in church sermons.

> **Key term**
>
> **The Waltons**
> A popular, long-running (1972–81) TV series about an idealised family living through the Depression.

Season 1 – 1989–90

The first season of *The Simpsons* made fun of and/or attacked therapy, television addiction, war ('except World War II, the American Revolution and *Star Wars*'), schools stifling creativity, commercialisation, peer pressure, lynch-mob mentality, religious fanaticism, the dehumanisation of women, televised violence, Communism and French people. The environmentalist viewpoint was made at the start of every episode, when Homer accidentally takes radioactive material out of the nuclear power plant. As well as an unsafe nuclear power plant, the Simpsons' hometown, Springfield, has a toxic waste dump ('Just hide the waste where no one will find it').

On the other hand, Season 1 was also a hymn to the value of family and family values.

Summary diagram: Comparing Bush with Reagan		

Bush		Reagan
✗	Vision	✓
✗	Hit the ground running	✓
✓	Democratic Congress	✗
✗	Increased deficits	✓
✗	Good with media	✓
✗	Monitoring potential appointees	✓

Key question
What did Bush do to
help education and
the environment?

3 | 'The Vision Thing' – Education and the Environment

Bush tended to dismiss what he called 'the vision thing', but in the 1988 campaign he seemed to suggest that he had a vision to be the 'environment President' and to help improve education.

(a) The environment

After a great environmental disaster in Alaska (the *Exxon Valdez* fuel tanker ran aground under a drunken captain, and its crude oil spoilt 800 miles of coastline and affected 6000 square miles of ocean), Bush earned praise for the administration's clean-up operations. He urged clean-ups of toxic waste dumps, but when voters in California and New York defeated tax initiatives to pay for clean-ups, the administration backed off. While Bush acknowledged that there was an environmental problem and that it was the government's duty to act, his administration rejected the idea of the 'greenhouse effect' and global warming that came from burning fuels and creating a carbon dioxide build-up in the upper atmosphere. He did nothing to restrict the use of petrol.

Key date

Clean Air Act: 1990

The *Exxon Valdez* tragedy helped the passage of the Clean Air Act (1990), which required city governments to reduce smog and harmful emissions from cars and to try to control the 'acid rain' that fell on the Northeast and Midwest where industries burned coal high in sulphur content. The acid rain decreased, but mostly because so many coal-burning industrial plants were closing down. The act 'shows George Bush at his policy-making best and was clearly the administration's most significant victory in the domestic sphere' (historian J.R. Greene). Bush also issued executive orders that protected or extended parks and wildlife refuges.

(b) Education

The 1983 publication *A Nation at Risk* (see page 125) stirred up debates about national educational standards. In 1989, Bush held an 'Education Summit' for state governors, and in 1991 he asked Congress to approve his plan for 'America 2000'. The plan encouraged states to test vigorously in the fourth and eighth grades (nine and 13 year olds), and set out detailed standards in core subjects. Bush also wanted vouchers to help children go to private schools. Liberals disliked these ideas, advocating instead more federal expenditure. Fiscally conservative and worried about the deficit, Bush did not want to spend on education, so America 2000 got nowhere in Congress. However, he had really publicised the problem and a 'big government' solution was favoured by Congress in 1994.

More of *The Simpsons*

The second series continued to deal with highly topical 1990s issues – educational success and failure, popular culture, the influence of TV and cartoon violence, the horror of nuclear power ('Keep those mutants coming, Homer', says Bart), ambulance-chasing lawyers, hospital queues, women's lib and women's lives, the morality of theft from big business, and $125 running shoes. Most interesting for the student of politics, is when the villainous capitalist owner of the dangerous nuclear power station, Mr Burns, decides to enter politics. 'Do you know how much it costs to run for office?', asks Homer rhetorically. 'More than any honest man can afford.' At that point Homer and Mr Burns realise that Mr Burns is the ideal political candidate! Mr Burns runs the 'finest campaign that money can buy', employing a make-up artist, speechwriter, spin doctor, joke writer, personal trainer, muckraker, character assassin and mud-slinger ('Excellent – this is exactly the kind of trickery I'm paying for'). When Mr Burns says, 'Visual aids help so much', 'I will lower taxes', and condemns 'those bureaucrats down there in the state capital', he begins to sound suspiciously like Ronald Reagan.

Summary diagram: 'The vision thing' – education and the environment

Environment	Problems	What Bush did	Did it help?
	Exxon Valdez	Cleaned up	Yes
	Toxic waste dumps	Urged clean up	No
	Global warming	Said something should be done	Not much
	Smog emissions	Clean Air Act 1990	Yes
Education	Low national standards	Summit	No
		America 2000	No

Key question
Who won – Bush or
Congress?

4 | Bush vs Congress

(a) A draw?

Bush and Congress sometimes had a productive relationship. For example, although as a presidential candidate Bush had rejected the idea that the federal government should ever bail out the savings and loan (S&L) industry (see page 129), as President, he asked Congress to do so. He also co-operated with Congress on the budget.

(b) Congress?

Bush's first clash with the Democratic Congress was over his nomination of John Tower as Secretary of Defence. Congress made much of Tower's affection for alcohol and rejected the nomination – the first time Congress had rejected a cabinet appointment since 1957.

(i) The budget deficit

The budget deficit was a major issue in the 1988 presidential campaign. Bush's target was to balance the budget within five years by ensuring that expenditure on domestic programmes with the exception of Social Security did not grow faster than inflation. He had repeatedly promised ('read my lips') that he would not introduce new taxes (one congressional wit describe this as 'deja voodoo', see page 139) and would work to curtail domestic expenditure. By 1990, however, Bush finally agreed with Congress that there had to be higher taxes, although not before the President shut down the federal government for three days, which infuriated the public (tourist attractions were closed down, and there were fears that payment of federal employees' salaries and federal benefits might suffer). Conservative Republicans led by Newt Gingrich (see page 172) opposed the tax hike, which damaged the Republicans in the 1990 and 1992 elections.

(ii) Legislation

The Democratic Congress had some successes: it doubled the appropriations for **Head Start**. In the face of great business opposition to the cost, it passed the Disabilities Act to protect disabled workers, who had not been protected by the 1964 Civil Rights Act. President Bush strongly supported the Disability Act, perhaps because his dyslexic son, George W. Bush, had been discriminated against at school. Congress also passed a bill that gave workers the right to 12 weeks' (maximum) unpaid leave to handle family emergencies, and a bill that increased the money for welfare recipients needing day-care. Bush twice vetoed family and medical leave acts and also a civil rights bill to counter racial discrimination in employment (the civil rights bill was a major issue in the 1990 congressional elections, where Republican Senator Jesse Helms gained re-election by appealing to white hostility to racial quotas in the job market). Bush vetoed but then compromised with Congress on the minimum wage law (1989).

Key term

Head Start
A federal government programme to help economically disadvantaged pre-schoolers, providing educational, health, social and other services.

Almost one-quarter of the bills he vetoed were designed to make abortion easier, including abortions for victims of rape or incest (August 1989).

Summary diagram: Bush vs Congress	
Co-operation	**Failure to get along**
S&L	Tower
Budget	Government shut down
Disability Act	Frequent vetoes
Minimum wage	

5 | Social Themes: The New Right, The Supreme Court, Sex, Drugs and Race

← Key question
Was Bush's America increasingly conservative?

(a) Flag burning

The New Right hoped that Reagan's conservative appointments would result in judicial decisions in line with their beliefs. They were disappointed by the 1989 Supreme Court TEXAS vs JOHNSON decision that ruled that the First Amendment (which guaranteed free speech) protected protesters who burned the American flag. Bush denounced the decision and called for a constitutional amendment against flag burning, but the Supreme Court struck down an October 1989 act of Congress outlawing desecration of the flag. A proposed constitutional amendment was rejected in Congress in June 1990. However, on affirmative action and abortion, the Supreme Court increasingly frightened liberals.

(b) Abortion

The New Right were pleased by a 1989 Supreme Court decision, WEBSTER vs REPRODUCTIVE SERVICES of MISSOURI, which ruled that states could deny women access to public abortion facilities. Chief Justice Rehnquist said, 'Nothing in the Constitution requires states to enter or remain in the business of performing abortions.' Conservatives hoped that many states would follow this Missouri example, but only three did so. WEBSTER did not manage to overturn ROE vs WADE. The latter was reaffirmed by a 1992 Supreme Court decision. Disappointed that the Supreme Court had not overturned ROE, the Bush administration declared support for an anti-abortion constitutional amendment. However, no Democratic Congress would agree to that.

Like the vast majority of experienced politicians, Bush sensed that both nation and parties were divided on this issue, so he kept quiet, even though he had said 'abortion is murder' in his campaign (earlier in his career he had been pro-choice but had changed his stance to please conservative Republicans). The Moral Majority (see page 93) were disappointed when, following Justice William Brennan's retirement from the Supreme Court,

Bush nominated David Souter, whose views on abortion were unknown. Souter refused to discuss them at his confirmation hearings, to the relief of the Senate, which promptly approved the nomination.

(c) Feminism

In mid-1991, Bush selected African American Clarence Thomas as the replacement for retiring African American Supreme Court Justice Thurgood Marshall. Thomas grew up impoverished in the segregated South, then went to Yale Law School. He worked as a congressional aide, then headed the Equal Employment Opportunities Commission (EEOC) under Reagan. Reagan appointed him to the US Court of Appeals, where he sat for only 16 months before Bush nominated him to the Supreme Court. Thomas had expressed public doubts about a woman's right to abortion, rejected a minimum wage, and questioned whether busing, **quotas** and affirmative action (through which he attended Yale) were the right methods to achieve racial equality. Bush had cleverly nominated an African American conservative: anyone who criticised or rejected him would be open to charges of racism.

Thomas's confirmation hearings became big news when Anita Hill, a black Oklahoma University law professor, testified that Thomas liked pornographic movies, discussed his sexual prowess with female aides and had sexually harassed her when they worked for the EEOC. Republican committee members subjected Hill to a brutal cross-examination. Thomas described the hearings as 'high-tech lynching for uppity blacks'. The Senate confirmed him by 52 to 48.

The feminist movement had gone quiet. In 1975, even pioneer feminist Betty Friedan had abandoned NOW, criticising it as anti-male, anti-family, anti-feminine and preoccupied with gay and lesbian issues. However, Hill's ordeal mobilised women on the issue of sexual harassment: many campaigned for laws and regulations, particularly on college campuses, to protect women, and unprecedented numbers stood for local, state and national office in 1992, pointing out that the 98 per cent male Senate had brushed aside Hill's accusations.

(d) Homosexuals

Back in 1977, homosexuals had failed to prevent the repeal of an ordinance protecting gay rights in Miami. That accelerated gay rights activism. ACT-UP (AIDS Coalition to Unleash Power) organised a half million strong parade in New York City in 1987, demanding more research into AIDS and equal rights. By 1992, ACT-UP got $2 billion from Congress for research, more than was spent on cancer, which killed 22 times as many people.

(e) Drugs

Bush had promised in his election campaign to make drug abuse his top domestic priority. He appointed a dynamic 'drugs czar',

Key term

Quotas
The setting aside of a number of places for ethnic minorities or other disadvantaged groups.

Key question
What was the impact of Bush's drugs policy?

Protesters meet in President Bush's holiday town of Kennebunkport, Maine, demanding more funds for AIDS research in 1991.

President Bush addresses the nation on his drug policy (September 1989), clutching the bag of crack (see page 149) that had been bought for him to display.

and gave several billion dollars to the Drug Enforcement Agency, which worked on employee drug testing, increased border controls and subsidising police in other countries such as Colombia.

The problem was huge: in 1989, 375,000 babies were born addicted to cocaine or heroin. In January 1990 former civil rights activist Marion Barry, Mayor of Washington DC, was arrested for possessing and smoking crack cocaine. The Bush administration emulated the Reagan administration's concentration upon law enforcement, and was equally unsuccessful.

The whole issue of drugs led President Bush into a massive public relations blunder. As part of his 1992 TV speech on drugs, Bush ('I haven't seen crack … I bet a whole lot of people haven't') decided to show the nation some crack that police had confiscated. However, the crack he showed had actually been bought (for $2400) for use in his speech by a federal drug enforcement agent. The agent had lured a drug dealer to Lafayette Park, adjacent to the White House ('where the fuck is the White House?' the dealer asked), so the President would be able to say drugs were available near to the White House.

(f) Rodney King and race
(i) Bush and race

Key question
Did Bush help ethnic minorities?

Despite curbing college aid to black students, Bush was remarkably popular amongst middle-class blacks, thanks to high-profile appointments such as Colin Powell as head of the JCS (see page 54), and because of astute symbolic gestures, such as celebrating Christmas at a black church in 1989 and publicly courting Jesse Jackson. However, Bush did nothing to help working-class ghetto inhabitants.

(ii) Rodney King

Minorities in urban Los Angeles suffered from poverty, family break-ups, poor schools, violent gangs, drug dealers, unemployment and racial tension. Blacks resented Latinos and Asian Americans as job competitors and the predominantly white police force as racist. Acute racial tensions were illustrated by the Rodney King case.

Key date

Race riots in Los Angeles: 1992

In 1991, Los Angeles police chased Rodney King, a black, speeding motorist for eight miles. He finally stopped, got out of his car, but resisted arrest. Four white policemen beat him up, which a local resident filmed on his home video camera. The police were charged, but put on trial in white, conservative Simi Valley. When the police were found not guilty, Los Angeles blacks rioted, looted and burned. Fifty-five people died, 2300 were injured, and $1 billion dollars worth of property was damaged. Blacks dragged a white truck driver from his cabin and beat him up – on camera again. These 1992 riots in Los Angeles prompted rioting in Atlanta, Birmingham, Chicago and Seattle.

Summary diagram: Social themes

Flag burning	Allowed
Abortion	Allowed, but harder to access
Feminism	Re-activated
Gays	Activated
Drugs	Increasing problem
Racial divisions	Still bitter

6 | Foreign Policy

(a) The Cold War

Bush was fortunate in that his presidency coincided with the end of the Cold War. His administration watched as the USSR and its East European empire imploded, thus ending a great security threat to the United States.

Key question
Was Bush's foreign policy a vote winner?

(b) Central America 1989

Partly motivated by accusations that he was a wimp in foreign policy, Bush intervened in tiny, impoverished Panama, which was ruled by a brutal military dictator, General Manuel Noriega (who used a cut-out labelled 'Bush' for shooting target practice). Bush approved 'Operation Just Cause', landing 27,000 marines in Panama. They were ordered to seize the strategically vital Panama Canal, protect US citizens and stop the drug traffic. Noriega surrendered. The American public felt this was a job well done, although the rest of the world was unimpressed by yet another US intervention in another country.

US intervened in
Panama: 1989

Key date

(c) The Gulf War

In August 1990, Iraqi dictator Saddam Hussein sent around 100,000 troops into tiny, neighbouring oil-rich Kuwait. Bush, his resolve supposedly stiffened by British Prime Minister Margaret Thatcher ('Remember George, this is no time to go wobbly'), assembled an international coalition to restore the status quo.

Key question
Why did Bush intervene in Kuwait?

(i) Bush's motives

Bush's motives in Kuwait were:

- If aggression went unpunished, it might continue. Saddam Hussein's troops were massing on the Saudi Arabian border.
- Saudi Arabia and Kuwait were US allies, so US credibility was at stake if they were threatened.

- Saddam Hussein, sympathetic to the impoverished Palestinian minority in Israel, talked frequently of organising a holy war against the US ally, Israel.
- Saddam had used chemical weapons (poison gas) against the Kurdish minority in Iraq, and was rumoured to be developing nuclear weapons.
- If Saddam kept Kuwait, he would control a quarter of the world's current oil supplies and could therefore determine the price of oil, and hold the United States and its allies' economies to ransom.

(ii) Desert Storm

Although Americans were divided about the wisdom of it ('Hell no, we won't go – we won't fight for **Texaco**'), with congressional assent and much international approval and aid, Bush sent 700,000 US forces to the area. 'Operation Desert Storm' liberated Kuwait by February 1991. Only 136 Americans had died (many from **friendly fire**).

(iii) Not finishing the job

Although Bush's closest advisers unanimously wanted to end the war as soon as possible, there was pressure on Bush to 'finish the job', especially when retreating Iraqi troops set fire to 650 Kuwait oil wells (these took nine months to extinguish) and perpetrated atrocities on Kuwaitis. Bush feared involvement in an Iraqi civil war and did not want to weaken Iraq to the advantage of Iran, so he stood by as Saddam massacred his opponents. Defence Secretary Dick Cheney said it would be too difficult to effect reform and democracy in Iraq (he changed his mind by 2003).

Bush's popularity temporarily skyrocketed. 'By God, we've kicked the Vietnam syndrome once and for all', he said. He had demonstrated US military might, followed clear and limited political and military objectives, and kept Congress onside and the US press controlled.

Key date

Kuwait liberated in Gulf War: 1990–1

Key terms

Texaco
A US oil company.

Friendly fire
When members of the armed forces are accidentally killed by their own side.

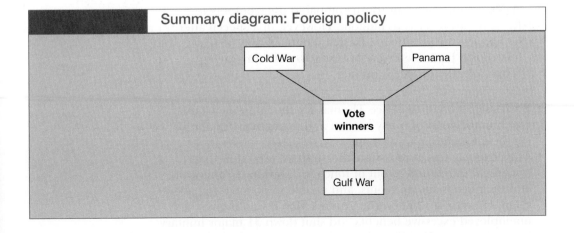

Summary diagram: Foreign policy

Cold War — Panama — Vote winners — Gulf War

7 | The 1992 Election

The Gulf War victory sent Bush's popularity soaring, but within a year he was grounded by a major economic downturn and the popular belief that he did not know or care much about domestic affairs.

The recession began in July 1990 and lasted until 1992. **AT&T** fired 100,000 workers, General Motors 74,000, and Pan Am and Eastern Airlines collapsed, losing 48,000 jobs. By 1992, the economy had lost two million jobs. Nineteen states were technically in a depression. Much of this was due to the legacy of the Reagan years – the massive federal deficit, the savings and loan bailout (which cost taxpayers billions), the ever-increasing trade imbalance and the lack of an industrial policy.

So, despite foreign policy triumphs, George Bush was defeated by Clinton in the 1992 election because:

Key question
Why was Bush defeated by Bill Clinton in the 1992 election?

Key dates

Recession: 1990–2

Bush defeated by Clinton in presidential election: 1992

Key term

AT&T
The US equivalent of BT.

- Key figures in the Bush administration had health problems. Brilliant Republican National Committee chairman Lee Atwater had been the strategic genius of the 1988 election. His March 1990 terminal cancer diagnosis removed an irreplaceable aide. Then, in May 1991, the 66-year-old President, jogging at Camp David, suffered severe shortness of breath. He was diagnosed with Graves' disease, characterised by irregular heartbeats and an overactive thyroid (popular First Lady Barbara Bush also contracted Graves' disease at the same time, and the Bush's dog Millie came down with a canine equivalent of this autoimmune disease, triggering a debate as to whether the White House was a healthy environment in which to live). The news about the President's health caused people to question his stamina, especially after he contracted a severe case of intestinal influenza on a January 1992 state visit to Japan, during which he vomited over Japan's prime minister (footage of this was replayed all over the world).

> **A Bush joke**
> While he was President, Bush compared unfavourably to Reagan with regards to humour. However, in a speech after he had left the presidency, Bush announced that he had invited the Japanese Prime Minister to visit him, saying, 'This time, the dinner is on me.'

- Bush's selection of Clarence Thomas for the Supreme Court cost him the votes of many women and made many doubt his competence and political sense.
- The economy was in recession and Bush seemed slow to get organised, uninterested, out of touch with ordinary Americans and their economic problems, and unable to do anything about them. He vetoed a bill on the grounds that it would give the unemployed excessive benefits and shut down 31 major military bases, depriving 70,000 of their jobs in 20 states, including electorally crucial California. When Bush pushed the North

American Free Trade Agreement (NAFTA) through Congress in May 1992, his opponents won support when they said it would cost Americans jobs. In contrast, the chief strategist of the Democratic candidate, Bill Clinton, posted signs saying 'It's the Economy, Stupid!' throughout Clinton's campaign headquarters (the economy began to recover in 1992 but that was too late for Bush's electoral prospects).

- Bush's tax hike and his soft-pedalling on the New Right social agenda (Bush said he would not mind having a gay cabinet member) triggered a right-wing challenge from within the Republican Party: self-styled 'pit bull of the right' Pat Buchanan said 'King George' (Bush) was no conservative, but 'the biggest spender in American history'. In response to Buchanan's impressive performance in the Republican primaries, Bush's team allowed him to dominate the National Convention. This was criticised by Presidents Nixon and Reagan. It seemed as if Bush could not even control his own party.

Buchanan's war

In the 1992 Republican National Convention, Buchanan spoke for the New Right. He attacked 'radical feminism', 'abortion on demand', and 'homosexual rights', saying:

> There is a religious war going on in this country. It is a cultural war as critical to the kind of nation we shall be as the Cold War itself. This war is for the soul of America.

- Bush's 1992 campaign was poorly run, unlike his brilliant 1988 one. Bush seemed to offer no vision and underestimated his own unpopularity. He missed his brilliant chief of staff John Sununu, whom he had fired because of unethical behaviour (taking an airforce jet to Boston for his dental appointment). Critical of the team's election performance, Marlin Fitzwater said, 'The President should have fired us all'.

- Bush's relationship with the press soured after they called him a 'wimp' for being slow to react to Noriega in Panama (see page 150). 'When the **Berlin Wall** fell', said Bush, 'I half expected to see a headline, WALL FALLS, THREE BORDER GUARDS LOSE JOBS: CLINTON BLAMES BUSH.' The press was kinder to Clinton. The Bush team waited in vain for the media to tell how Clinton was reportedly sleeping with a reporter on his campaign plane.

- Unlike Bush, Bill Clinton was a tireless, enthusiastic and brilliant campaigner. Voters liked Clinton's self-effacement (he joked on TV about his abysmal convention speech). Clinton's fund-raising team was probably the best ever. His campaign team produced an exceptionally effective documentary on Clinton's life, *The Man From Hope*, which emphasised Clinton's rise from poverty and his message of hope, playing on the name of his Arkansas hometown, Hope. The campaign team christened their man the 'Comeback Kid', after effective ripostes to the 'Slick Willie' (see below) campaign.

Key term

Berlin wall
The wall divided Communist East Berlin from pro-western West Berlin.

- While Bush lacked a viable social (he was considered slow to respond to the 1992 Los Angeles race riots) and economic programme, and waged a negative campaign, Clinton concentrated on the domestic issues, which impressed voters. Clinton kept off foreign policy issues, knowing Bush was far stronger there.
- Women voters liked Bill Clinton. He was pro-choice, his wife was clearly going to be important if he was elected, and women considered him even more attractive than Ronald Reagan. The Republicans made much of 'Slick Willie', the draft dodger who had smoked marijuana in his youth but claimed 'I didn't inhale', with a reputation for womanising. However, Clinton fought back and wife Hillary stood by him.
- As a Southerner, Clinton won back some voters from the Republicans in the South. He was the only presidential candidate who visited Florida after it had been devastated by Hurricane Andrew.
- Clinton reassured people of his centrist position on crime when he stopped campaigning to return to Arkansas (he was governor) to approve the execution of a mentally retarded black prisoner.
- Bush performed badly in the presidential debates. The cameras caught him looking at his watch, as if he were bored with the proceedings. When he subsequently said of Clinton and his running mate Al Gore, 'My dog Millie knows more about foreign policy than those two bozos', he looked childish.

Key figure: Ross Perot

Ross Perot's data processing company computerised Social Security and Medicare in the 1960s and 1970s, making him a millionaire. He criticised the President, Congress and political parties for focusing on their own political futures and pork-barrel projects. In a February 1992 televised call-in talk-show, he was asked whether he would consider running for the presidency. He said he would, with enough support. He got two million calls urging him to stand. In July 1992, he was almost as popular as Bush and Clinton. Republicans attacked his pro-choice, pro-gun-control and anti-Gulf War stance. 'I'm not having fun any more', he said, and quit the race. Bitter criticism from disappointed supporters got him back in the race, but he had lost credibility.

- **Ross Perot** (see the box) gained 19.7 million votes (19 per cent of the total) and around 70 per cent of them would have voted for Bush.
- The nation seemed to be swinging back to the left, electing a Democratic President by 43 per cent to 38 per cent of the popular vote, and a Democratic Congress.

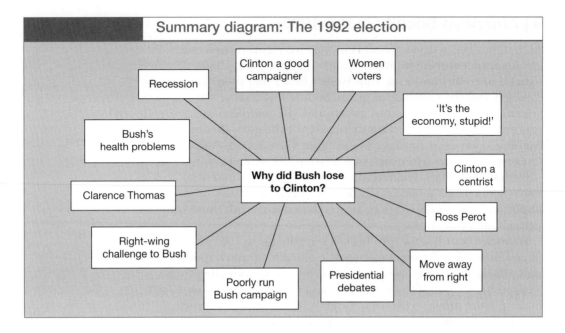

Summary diagram: The 1992 election

Recession — Clinton a good campaigner — Women voters — 'It's the economy, stupid!' — Bush's health problems — Clarence Thomas — **Why did Bush lose to Clinton?** — Clinton a centrist — Ross Perot — Right-wing challenge to Bush — Poorly run Bush campaign — Presidential debates — Move away from right

8 | Bush – The Verdict

'I hope history will show I did some things right', said Bush as he left the White House for the last time. He claimed that his major accomplishments were the fall of Communism, victory in the Gulf War, 'cleaning up' the S&L crisis and the environment (the Clean Air Act), helping the disabled (the Americans with Disabilities Act) and controlling federal government expenditure.

Michael Beschloss and Strobe Talbott (*At the Highest Levels: The Inside Story of the End of the Cold War*, 1993) praised Bush's cautious policies toward Mikhail Gorbachev as ultimately successful.

However, in *The Post-modern Presidency: Bush Meets the World*, Richard Rose said Bush was not a leader, simply a 'guardian', doing 'a limited number of things that are the obligations of the Oval Office and refraining from actions that expand the role of government'. A guardian President such as Bush is 'a player, but not in charge'.

Most historians judge Bush's Presidency a failure. However, in *The Presidency of George Bush* (2000), biographer J.R. Greene, perhaps because he considered Bush a genuinely nice person, defended him, for example, over the lack of the 'vision thing', pointing out that visions can be mere words and therefore disillusioning, as some of Reagan's were.

Summary diagram: Bush – the verdict

✓ Won the Cold War	✗ Guardian president
✓ Won the Gulf War	✗ No vision
✓ Cleaned up S&L	✗ Lacked empathy in recession
✓ Clean Air Act	
✓ Disabilities Act	

9 | American Society in the 1980s

Although social activism (feminism, the civil rights movement, gay liberation and environmentalism) continued, the 1980s seemed to confirm novelist Tom Wolfe's belief that there was a new, self-absorbed narcissism (a 'me decade'). Rejecting the volunteerism of their parents' generation, the middle classes concentrated upon perfecting themselves at the gym, dieting or running. They read Jim Fixx's bestselling *The Complete Book of Running*, until the writer died of a heart attack while running.

Ehrhard Seminars Training (EST) led the 'human potential movement'. Their seminars taught self-esteem and the importance of 'power relationships' (relationships with those who helped one's career or ego).

Financier Ivan Boesky told Berkeley graduates in 1986 that 'greed is healthy' (he was subsequently jailed for fraud). Young upwardly mobile urban professionals (*Time* magazine called them 'yuppies') rejected community ideals and concentrated upon making more money. Historian Randall B. Woods lists yuppie characteristics: BMW car, designer casual gear, gourmet food, high-tech sound equipment, jogging, high-fibre diet and natural-fibre clothes. Along with the yuppies, there were buppies (black urban professionals), dinks (dual income families with no kids) and grumpies (grim, ruthless, upwardly mobile young professionals).

Under Reagan, the very rich grew richer. Corporate raiders such as Ross Perot and real-estate tycoons such as Donald Trump benefited from lower taxes and Reagan's abandonment of anti-trust statues and regulations. Unregulated speculators proceeded knowing that the federal government (the US taxpayer) would bail out dubious banks.

The materialistic 1980s were very different from the socially conscious 1960s. Actress and activist 'Hanoi Jane' Fonda, who had visited North Vietnam to protest against US involvement in the war in 1972, now made millions from her workout videos, although she did say she was giving the money to good causes. Madonna sang that she was a 'Material Girl'. A Berkeley study concluded that 'American individualism may have grown cancerous' and 'maybe threatening the survival of freedom itself … The citizen has been swallowed up in economic man.'

Summary diagram: American society in the 1980s

Another 'me decade'

Self-esteem movement

'Greed is healthy'

Study Guide: AS Question

In the style of Edexcel

How far do you agree with the description of President George H.W. Bush's domestic record as a failure?   (30 marks)

Exam tips

The cross-references are intended to take you straight to the material that will help you to answer the question.

This question asks you for an assessment of what George H.W. Bush achieved. You will need to be clear about how you are going to measure failure. Did he achieve what he set out do? Did he not try to do enough?

What issues will you consider? You only have a limited time to write your response so selection is important. You could take his own key aims set out at the beginning of the presidency, plus major issues which developed during his term.

For his own aims you could ask:

- How far did he succeed as the 'environment President' (pages 143 and 155)?
- How far did his domestic record succeed in 'making kinder the face of the nation' (pages 142, 145–6 and 155)? What was his record on reducing disadvantage and helping the poor (pages 145 and 149)?
- How far did his plans for education succeed (pages 143–4)?
- How far did he succeed in reducing the budget deficit (page 145)?

Two major issues that developed during his term of office were the race riots of 1992 and the economic recession of 1990–2:

- How far were his race relations measures merely symbolic gestures which did little to reduce the existing inequalities and deprivation (pages 149 and 154)?
- Bush inherited economic problems from the Reagan years (pages 126 and 129), but how far were his attempts to deal with recession mistaken (page 153)?

What is your overall assessment? Was his record one of complete failure (see page 155)? Were there some achievements in the face of a Congress dominated by political opponents (page 141) and the legacy of a huge financial deficit (page 141)?

6 President Clinton 1993–2001

POINTS TO CONSIDER

Exceptionally intelligent, with an encyclopaedic knowledge of policy questions, Bill Clinton charmed many whom he met, and doggedly pursued his frequently admirable goals. 'He was, without question, the most talented politician of his generation', according to journalist Joe Klein. Yet in some ways, he was also the most disappointing politician of his generation. This chapter explores that contrast with sections on:

- Bill Clinton's background
- The reasons for his election in 1992, and his re-election in 1996
- Clinton's first term
- Clinton's second term and the Monica Lewinsky scandal
- Clinton's foreign policy

Key dates

1989　Governor Clinton became chairman of the Democratic Leadership Council

1992　Clinton defeated George Bush in presidential election

1993　Clinton's budget narrowly passed by Congress
NAFTA approved

1994　The First Lady's universal health care plan rejected by Congress
Republicans took control of both houses of Congress

1995　Federal government shutdown after dispute between President and Congress over budget
Newt Gingrich's *The Contract with America*

1996　Clinton re-elected President

1998　Monica Lewinsky sex scandal

1999　Attempted impeachment of Clinton

2000　Vice President Gore defeated by George W. Bush in presidential election

1 | Bill Clinton – Background

Profile: William Jefferson 'Bill' Clinton (1946–)

1946 – Born to a lower middle-class family in Hope, Arkansas
1968 – Graduated from Georgetown University (Washington DC) with a degree in international affairs
1970 – Rhodes scholar in Oxford, England
1972 – Directed presidential campaign for George McGovern in Texas
1973 – Graduated from Yale Law School; joined law faculty at University of Arkansas
1974 – Unsuccessfully ran for the House of Representatives
1976 – Directed presidential campaign of Jimmy Carter in Arkansas; elected Attorney General of Arkansas
1978 – Elected governor of Arkansas (youngest US governor for 40 years)
1980 – Defeated in gubernatorial election
1982 – Thrice re-elected as governor by substantial majorities
1992 – Defeated President Bush in presidential election
1993 – Narrow congressional approval for legislation to reduce federal government budget deficit by increased taxes on wealthy and modest cuts in government programmes; obtained congressional approval of NAFTA
1994 – Clinton health care plan died in Congress; Democrats lost control of both houses of Congress for the first time since 1954, so Clinton accommodated some of the Republican agenda
1996 – Re-elected, defeating Republican Bob Dole
1998 – Monica Lewinsky sex scandal
1999 – Republican Congress tried to impeach him
2000 – Clinton's Vice President Al Gore defeated by George W. Bush in presidential election

Clinton was admirable (to liberals) and important in that his presidency helped ensure the continuation of the US welfare state (which was greatly threatened by the Republicans). He also helped restore the US economy (particularly through turning the federal budget deficit into a huge surplus). Partisan Republicans tried to ruin his presidency by exploitation of his sexual escapades, but, while distracted, he remained popular with the American public.

> **Key question**
> Does Clinton's background help explain his presidency?

(a) Family

Clinton's mother, according to Joe Klein:

> was the sort of woman whom proper folks tend to scorn, particularly in the South: a ton of makeup, almost comically applied; a white streak down the middle of her dyed black hair (some of the locals called her 'skunk woman'); a passion for the racetrack, for nightlife … and for the wrong sort of men.

Clinton's stepfather, Roger, was an alcoholic: once Clinton smashed through the bedroom door to stop him abusing his mother. Clinton's brother Roger was busted for cocaine while Clinton was governor of Arkansas, and the two brothers and their mother went into family therapy after this. Clinton was the first American President to admit that he had participated in a form of psychotherapy. When asked about his brother's addiction, Bill confessed, 'Well, there are different sorts of addictions.' Perhaps he meant politics, perhaps sex.

Despite this unpromising background, Clinton acquired the education necessary to give him the chance to fulfil his adolescent dream of becoming President. After graduating from Georgetown University (he supported himself by working for a senator), he won a Rhodes Scholarship to Oxford, then obtained a Yale law degree. He persuaded fellow Yale student Hillary Rodham to return with him to Arkansas and to be his wife.

(b) Governor Clinton
In 1979, 32-year-old Bill Clinton became the youngest governor in the United States. He remained governor of Arkansas until 1992, apart from a two-year period when Arkansas voters rejected him. As governor, he reformed Arkansas' inadequate educational system and encouraged the growth of industry throughout the state through favourable tax policies.

(c) Bill Clinton and the changing Democratic Party
(i) Old Democrats

Key question
What sort of Democrat was Bill Clinton?

Klein characterised the Democratic Party in the 1980s as suffering from 'intellectual sclerosis', refusing to look critically at the rapidly rising crime rate and successive generations mired in poverty and characterised by out-of-wedlock births and welfare dependency. Klein considered the Democratic Party to be in thrall to special interest groups such as environmentalists, feminists, minorities and trade unionists, all of whom were more concerned with their cause than with winning elections. At a time when government had lost credibility, the Democrats proudly and stubbornly remained the party of government, in which public employees' unions (especially the teachers) were very influential.

Key date
Governor Clinton became chairman of the Democratic Leadership Council: 1989

However, these Old Democratic positions were being challenged by New Democrats, who in 1985 set up the **Democratic Leadership Council**, a moderate, predominantly Southern response to the increasingly left-looking and electorally unsuccessful trajectory of the Democratic Party. The organisation emphasised fiscal conservatism, responsible social behaviour and a more assertive American stance in the world. In 1989, Governor Clinton became chairman of the DLC.

Key term
Democratic Leadership Council
A 1980s' association of centrist Democrats who believed the party had to move away from the left in order to be electable.

(ii) New Democrats
One issue that clearly illustrated the difference between Old and New Democrats was day-care. Hillary Clinton and congressional Old Democrats wanted state-supervised day-care centres for the working poor across the nation, which conservatives derided as

Key question
What was the difference between an Old Democrat and a New Democrat?

'government baby-sitting'. Bill Clinton favoured a middle way, tax credits that would go directly to poor people in need of day-care. A DLC think-tank member said:

> The two things we learned in the 1980s were entirely contradictory. Socialism doesn't work, and [yet] the most ideological President of the twentieth century, Ronald Reagan, couldn't put an end to the welfare state. He couldn't even put a dent in it.

Some called the DLC or New Democrat answer to this conundrum a 'Third Way' (between the federal government activism of Franklin Roosevelt and the alternative anti-governmentalism of Ronald Reagan). The DLC wanted to create a welfare state in which government was necessary but unobtrusive, utilising marketplace efficiency (for example, with competition and accountability).

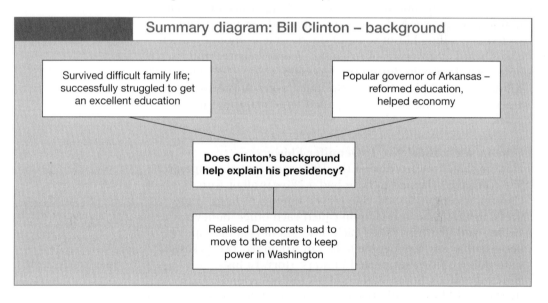

Summary diagram: Bill Clinton – background

Survived difficult family life; successfully struggled to get an excellent education

Popular governor of Arkansas – reformed education, helped economy

Does Clinton's background help explain his presidency?

Realised Democrats had to move to the centre to keep power in Washington

Key question
Why was Clinton such an appealing candidate?

2 | The 1992 Presidential Election

Clinton was a tireless, brilliant campaigner – handsome, charismatic and an excellent speaker. He knew that to get elected he would have to present himself as a centrist, a New Democrat, not an Old Democrat who believed in big government, which caused high taxes. His messages and policies appealed to the electorate. He said government was not the problem; it simply had to be more efficient. He wanted to 'end welfare as we know it', so that it would 'cease to be a way of life': benefits should be terminable and tied to work. He promised a new health care system, based on universal coverage, and tax relief for the middle classes. Old Democrats were soft on crime, so Clinton approved the execution of a mentally retarded black man in Arkansas during the presidential campaign. He carefully balanced liberalism and conservatism when he was pro gay rights but against gay marriage, pro affirmative action but against racial quotas. He took care to seem more concerned with the 'forgotten' middle class than the poor.

Clinton earned the nickname 'Slick Willie' when he managed to emerge apparently unscathed from two scandals that surfaced during the campaign. Just before the New Hampshire primary, the news broke that Clinton had had a long-term affair with an Arkansas nightclub singer called Gennifer Flowers. That did not seem to hurt his chances, but he was in more trouble when he was caught lying about his determination to avoid the draft during the Vietnam War. His poll numbers fell, but soon recovered.

Clinton seemed to empathise with everyone he met. In the second presidential debate (October 1992) an African American woman asked the candidates how the national debt had affected their lives. If it had not, she asked, how could they expect to find a cure for the economic problems of ordinary people? Bush did not understand the question and kept looking at his watch, but Clinton moved towards the woman and asked her how it had affected her, telling her of some of the terrible economic stories he had heard as governor of Arkansas. People believed Bill Clinton felt their pain during the recession.

Clinton won 43 per cent of the popular votes to Bush's 38 per cent, and the Democrats gained large majorities in both houses.

Key date

Clinton defeated Bush in presidential election: 1992

Clinton sex scandal No. 1: Gennifer Flowers
Flowers came forward during the 1992 presidential campaign. She (correctly) claimed to have had a 12-year affair with Clinton, which he denied. She played tape recordings to the press, in which she and Clinton called each other 'honey'. Hillary said that they called each other 'honey' in the tapes because that was how people talked in Arkansas. Two Arkansas state police officers supported Flowers' story. In his autobiography, Clinton reiterated his testimony under oath that he and Flowers only had sex once. In 1995, Flowers published her memoirs. Later, she posed nude for *Penthouse*.

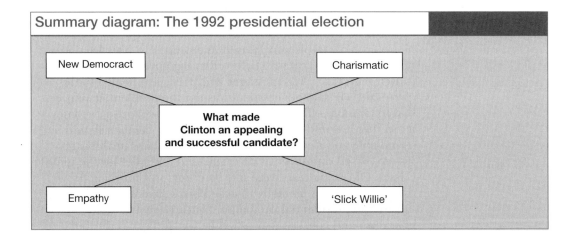

Summary diagram: The 1992 presidential election

New Democract — Charismatic

What made Clinton an appealing and successful candidate?

Empathy — 'Slick Willie'

Key question
Was Clinton's first
term a success?

3 | President Clinton's First Term

Subsequently, Clinton admitted that he made many mistakes early in his presidency, but one of his strengths as a politician was that he learned from mistakes.

Key question
Old Democrat or New
Democrat?

(a) Old Democrats and New Democrats in 1993

(i) Moving left from New Democrat to Old Democrat

Having been elected as a New Democrat, Clinton then unwisely seemed to revert to an Old Democrat, when he focused upon obscure liberal causes such as homosexuals in the military, particularly emphasised health care (see page 166), and surrounded himself with high-profile Old Democrats. It was unclear whether he was a closet liberal, a pragmatist who knew that he had to keep the party faithful happy, or responding to pressures from his wife or fundraisers.

While many voters feared that Clinton was just another Old Democrat, New Democrats were also disillusioned with him, believing he had merely used their agenda to win office. With the exception of Vice President Al Gore, he had no prominent New Democrat adviser. New Democrats resented Clinton's political consultant Dick Morris, who had helped him win the governorship of Arkansas but had also helped prominent right-wing Republicans such as Trent Lott.

(ii) Homosexuals in the military

Homosexuals constituted around 5 per cent of the total population, so allowing them to serve openly in the military was no great vote winner. It upset the JCS and veterans in particular. So Clinton compromised, with a 'don't ask, don't tell' policy (recruiters could not ask about an individual's sexual orientation, and homosexuals could be in the military so long as they kept quiet about their sexuality). The compromise pleased no one.

(iii) Abortion

Clinton's championing of abortion rights was more popular. He quickly signed executive orders reversing President Bush's policies (Bush had forbidden doctors working in federally funded clinics to give advice on abortion, stopped military hospitals performing abortions, and cut off US funding to United Nation's agencies that tried to decrease the population of impoverished countries). A 1993 Supreme Court decision rejected a Louisiana state law that prohibited the vast majority of abortions, and polls showed that a majority of Americans were pro-choice, although extremism flourished. For example, pro-life activists shot a Florida gynaecologist outside an abortion clinic.

(iv) Law and order

American TV and films continued to glorify violence in the 1990s. American society was indeed violent. Drug lords and gangs engaged in ritualised warfare in the ghettos. Middle-class youths throughout America bought guns for protection and/or status.

The gun control issue had long polarised Americans. Advocates of gun control emphasised rising levels of violent crime, the use of guns by teens and even subteens, and the gun culture that lacked respect for human life. Opponents said it was the constitutional right of all citizens to bear arms, it was criminals not guns that committed crimes, and law-abiding Americans had the right to defend themselves.

Gun control dominated the headlines in 1993, in which year nine tourists were shot dead in separate incidents in Florida, and four federal agents died during a raid on the headquarters of a religious sect in Waco, Texas. Seventy-two sect members killed themselves after a 51-day siege by the federal authorities. During that siege, which raised questions as to whether the President had acted wisely, Clinton criticised the National Rifle Association (it opposed gun control). Congress shared his concerns and several measures were passed, for example, the sale of guns to juveniles was prohibited and 100,000 extra police officers were recruited. On law and order, Clinton seemed to be a New Democrat.

(b) President vs Congress: the budget battle of 1993
(i) The federal government deficit

Key question
Who won in 1993: Clinton or Congress?

Upon becoming President, Clinton was informed by the Government Accounting Office that the budget deficit would be even greater than expected. Clinton had to delay many of the programmes he had promised (such as middle-class tax cuts) and continue Bush's policy of 'caps' on all domestic programmes other than Social Security and Medicare. Clinton aimed to reduce the federal deficit by raising taxes on high earners and corporations, and by cutting the defence budget for the first time in half a century.

(ii) Problems with the Republicans in Congress over the budget

The Republicans did not grant Clinton the traditional presidential honeymoon. They quickly made it clear that they would be unhelpful over the budget, although Clinton subsequently admitted that he could have made more effort to improve relations with Republican leaders Senator Bob Dole and Congressman Bob Michel (both moderates and open to compromise).

Key dates

Clinton's budget narrowly passed by Congress: 1993

NAFTA approved: 1993

(iii) Problems with the Democrats in Congress

Although the Democrats had a 257 to 177 majority in the House, Clinton's budget passed by only one vote. The Senate was equally awkward. Congressional Democrats resented Clinton's campaign promises to reform congressional staff and campaign finance. They also opposed his support for the North American Free Trade Agreement (**NAFTA**) negotiated by his predecessor. While Clinton argued that NAFTA would increase American white-collar jobs, most Democrats believed blue-collar jobs would disappear from the United States to Mexico, where labour costs were far cheaper.

Key term

NAFTA
The North American Free Trade Agreement provided for the gradual elimination of tariffs and other trade barriers between the USA, Canada and Mexico.

President Clinton signing NAFTA, with former presidents Gerald Ford (far left), Jimmy Carter (behind Clinton) and George Bush (right of Carter), and Vice President Al Gore (far right) looking on. Why do you suppose these former presidents supported Clinton here?

(iv) A weak President?

Clinton looked weak in 1993. He struggled to get his budget through Congress, then abandoned a new energy tax, having persuaded many reluctant House Democrats to vote for it. It was felt that Clinton had no 'core values'. On the other hand, in his first year, he managed to cut taxes for 15 million poorer families and to raise them upon wealthy individuals and corporations in order to start cutting the federal deficit.

(c) President vs press

While Clinton was doing a great deal of admirable and serious work, the media tended to trivialise his administration from the outset. In his first term, the media made a great deal of the disorganisation of the White House (Clinton certainly held many inconclusive meetings, and was usually behind schedule).

The First Lady tried to keep reporters out of the White House altogether. Her suggestion that they be moved across the road increased press hostility. The press enjoyed spreading the rumour that the First Lady had tossed a lamp at the President.

Why did the press oppose Clinton? One Republican told him it was because they liked wielding power. Historian James Patterson said it was because he tried to manipulate them. Clinton admitted his inexperience led to early errors that made good material for the press, such as '**Nannygate**', which raised questions about Clinton's competence.

Key question
Why were relations between Clinton and the press so bad?

Key term

Nannygate
Two of Clinton's nominees for attorney general were forced to step down when it was revealed that one hired an illegal immigrant as a nanny and another had not paid the relevant Social Security tax.

(d) Hillary Clinton and health insurance

Perhaps the biggest error of Clinton's first term was the failed health insurance plan.

Key question
Why did the Clintons' health insurance plan fail?

(i) The problem with health care

Workers and companies paid out billions in private medical insurance, but 35 million Americans (14 per cent of the population) had no medical insurance at all, and another 20 million had inadequate coverage. Most of the two latter groups were poor or unemployed.

(ii) The Clinton plans

There has been much speculation about the state of the Clintons' marriage. Some believe that along with political partnership, there was genuine love and friendship, which, combined with Mrs Clinton's undoubted abilities (when Clinton's team was working on his 1992 Democratic National Convention acceptance speech, it was Mrs Clinton who came up with the impressive line, 'I still believe in a place called Hope') help explain Bill Clinton's decision to allow the First Lady to work on health insurance. He hoped this would be the most important legacy of his administration. It turned out to be its greatest failure. The administration was unwisely stubborn in handling the health issue, and many blamed Hillary Clinton for failing to compromise.

Hillary Clinton's health plan (presented to the public in September 1993) envisaged universal coverage: all employers would be required to provide health insurance for employees. Small business owners hated this, as did their Republican friends in Congress. Her plan was perhaps unwise, an Old Democrat rather than a New Democrat solution.

(iii) The Clinton errors

Hillary Clinton's Health Care Task Force produced a 1300-page bill that revolutionised one-seventh of the US economy and entailed countless new rules and regulations. Aides admitted that it was 'impossibly complicated … most people in the White House couldn't understand what was in the plan. If they couldn't explain it to us, they weren't going to explain it to the Congress.' Bill Clinton's legislative strategists were no help: they were struggling to get the budget passed.

Bill Clinton subsequently admitted to two great errors. The task force should have just produced generalisations and then passed them to specialists to draft the bill. Also, it would have been better to give health care tax credits to those who needed them (mostly the working poor, as the poorest were covered by Medicaid). However, the latter was impossible without a tax increase.

Clinton claimed that Bob Dole had initially agreed to co-operate, but then agreed with Newt Gingrich (see page 172) that the measure must be opposed, lest the Democrats triumph in the next elections. Dole claimed that he was willing to compromise, 'but we had no input', as 'Mrs Clinton didn't want to give up very much', which aroused increasing Republican opposition. Perhaps the simple truth was that Americans with good health insurance did not want to pay for those without.

In January 1994 Clinton himself probably killed off the health insurance scheme altogether by a tactless gesture in his State of the Union address. He pulled a pen from his pocket, waved it around, and said he would veto any health care bill that did not provide universal coverage.

Key question
Why did the Democrats do so badly in 1994?

Key dates

First Lady's universal health care plan rejected by Congress: 1994

Republicans took control of both houses of Congress: 1994

Federal government shut down after dispute between President and Congress over budget: 1995

(e) Democratic disasters in the congressional mid-terms

The health insurance fiasco affected the 1994 congressional mid-term elections, after which the Republicans took control of the House of Representatives for the first time in 40 years. They also won the Senate. Some historians attributed this Republican landslide to voter disillusionment with Bill Clinton. He seemed to be an Old Democrat after all: he concentrated upon gays in the military instead of middle-class concerns, and had proposed a ridiculously complex big government programme on health insurance.

Historian Randall B. Woods talks of a 'revolt of the middle class' in these elections. While the rich grew richer (earning 27 per cent more than in 1979), middle-class incomes had decreased by 4 per cent. Therefore, middle-class voters opted for conservative Republican candidates who promised to limit immigrants' access to federal benefits (for which middle-class voters resented paying taxes).

Key question
How did Clinton master Congress?

(f) Mastering Congress

Despite his early failures, Clinton soon mastered the legislative process. He learned to dominate the Republicans in the budget negotiations, in which he obtained many of his most important social programmes while still keeping the budget balanced.

When in 1995 the Republicans refused to compromise on the budget, Clinton twice shut down the federal government because of lack of funds. Many voters considered the Republicans to be obstructing Clinton for partisan advantage. Furthermore, the Republicans had been insisting upon budget cuts in social programmes. Polls showed that the American public opposed such cuts. Clinton successfully branded the Republicans as opponents of Social Security and Medicare, to which the middle classes were particularly attached. The Republicans finally accepted his budget.

Clinton was never powerless. He had the veto and enough Democrats in Congress to sustain it. He learned that it was easier to stop change than to create it, so he waited quietly, let the Republicans try to enact measures, and then used the veto.

The Lincoln Memorial in Washington DC, shut down because of the federal government's closure.

(g) Welfare reform

(i) The welfare problem

African Americans liked Bill Clinton. Black novelist Toni Morrison christened him the first black American President. In a 1993 speech before a group of black ministers in Memphis, Tennessee, Clinton focused on ghetto problems, including the number of African Americans on welfare. Clinton said if Martin Luther King were still alive, he would say:

> I've fought for freedom, but not for the freedom of [black] people to kill each other with reckless abandon, not for the freedom of [black] children to have children, and the [black] fathers of the children to walk away and abandon them as if they don't amount to anything … That is not what I lived and died for.

Most voters resented welfare costs. However, welfare reform was a difficult issue for a Democrat: theirs was the party that traditionally cared for the poor.

A proposed welfare reform bill ended Aid for Families with Dependent Children (AFDC), which had given cash aid to low-income families (mostly headed by single mothers). The bill required able-bodied welfare recipients to work after two years and terminated all welfare payments after five years. When a Department of Health and Human Services' official predicted that one million children might be without food or shelter if the bill were passed, most of the President's staff and his wife opposed the bill.

Key question
Did Clinton succeed on welfare reform?

The Million Man March, in Washington DC in 1995, was designed to urge the federal government to be more helpful to African Americans, and to increase black community activism. Women were excluded from the march, as it was organised by Black Muslims. Why did protestors so often march, and on Washington?

(ii) The Welfare Reform Act

The final version of the bill, as passed by the Republican-dominated Congress, had 'gratuitously brutal provisions' (Klein). It denied benefits to immigrants who were not yet citizens, limited eligibility for Medicaid and food stamps for those who did not find work, and eliminated the lifetime guarantee of government support to poor mothers.

(iii) Old Democrats vs Clinton

Clinton felt that he dared not veto the bill for a third time, after having promised to 'end welfare as we know it', because it might cost him the next election. This infuriated Old Democrats. One of Clinton's old friends resigned from the administration, saying:

> I was, and remain, disappointed with the President for several reasons. First, his tendency to pick on people who don't have the political power to oppose him, especially on the crime and welfare reform issues. Second, his personal behaviour. And the glitz factor – all that fundraising, the Hollywood business.

(iv) Did Clinton's welfare reform work?

On the other hand, there were those who felt the welfare reform worked well. Welfare rolls were halved, although the booming economy helped that. Clinton made work pay. In 1986, a single mother who left welfare for work could expect to make about

$1900 more than she was getting from the government and lose her health benefits. In 1999, she earned $7000 more and kept her health benefits. People responded to the incentives. The workforce participation rate amongst the poorest women rocketed from 35 per cent of 55 per cent within three years. Clinton had removed the disincentive to marriage that had been an unintended consequence of the old welfare system, which had only given benefits to single mothers. The number of children living with single parents dropped by 8 per cent within five years of the bill's passage, while the percentage of black children raised by married parents rose from 34.8 per cent to 38.9 per cent.

(h) Conclusions on Clinton's first term

Klein talks of a chaotic and frequently inept first term performance, epitomised by the 'failed and foolish' health insurance fiasco. Clinton later conceded:

> We didn't know enough about how the system worked. It can only digest so much at once. We did the big economic plan and NAFTA in 1993. But trying to push through health care at that point was a mistake … I should have done welfare reform before we tried health care. If we had done welfare reform and the crime bill in 1994, the Democrats might have had something to run on in the fall … But I think in the beginning, for the first two years, I was pushing a lot of rocks uphill. I was obsessed … I was trying to get as much done as quickly as I could and also trying to learn on the job, learn how to get the White House functioning.

Also, it was soon clear that Clinton would always be dogged by scandals, sometimes deservedly. For example, as soon as he became President, he fired most of the White House travel office staff (allegedly for incompetence, but probably because most were Republicans) and put his cousin in charge of the office. The press uproar over 'travelgate' made Clinton re-hire the staff, and give his cousin another job.

However, Clinton learned a great deal in his first term. He got his way over budget negotiations with a hostile and frequently extremist (see page 171) Republican Congress. He had several minor successes, for example, the Family and Medical Leave Act, which his predecessor had twice vetoed (see page 145), the

---

Supreme Court conservatism
Under Chief Justice Rehnquist, the Supreme Court became increasingly conservative. For example, in 1995, MISSOURI vs JENKINS hampered school desegregation, ADARAND CONSTRUCTORS INC vs PENA opposed quotas, and US vs LOPEZ overturned the 1990 act that made it a federal offence to bring guns into a school zone (Rehnquist said this was a matter for states, not the federal government).

restoration of abortion in federally funded clinics, two successful presidential nominations for the Supreme Court and some limited restrictions on the sale of weapons. All his first term gambles (higher taxes, budget discipline, welfare reform, freer trade) were paying off. Stimulated by federal government care over the deficit, the US economy was booming.

Clinton had demonstrated his strengths as a politician, and thus ensured his re-election, despite the Republican opposition and hatred he aroused.

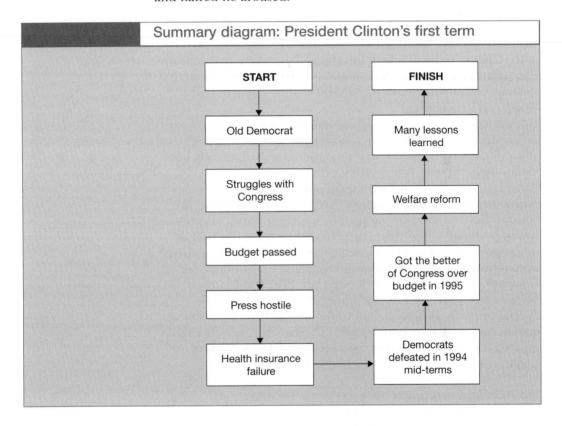

Summary diagram: President Clinton's first term

START → Old Democrat → Struggles with Congress → Budget passed → Press hostile → Health insurance failure → Democrats defeated in 1994 mid-terms → Got the better of Congress over budget in 1995 → Welfare reform → Many lessons learned → FINISH

Key question
Why did the Republicans ferociously oppose Clinton?

4 | Republican Opposition and Extremism

Clinton's presidency was characterised by relentless and sometimes vicious Republican opposition.

(a) Why kill Bill?

Although Clinton had decisively defeated George Bush in 1992 and Bob Dole in 1996, the Republicans, according to Dole, had 'a pretty hard-right group in the party who were just never going to accept him'. That group had allies in the press, which always inclined towards a greater interest in scandal than substance, and seemed obsessed with Clinton's personal failings. Indeed, his presidency marked 'an unprecedented escalation in the levels of partisan enmity and journalistic fecklessness in Washington' (Klein).

Why was Clinton so hated? He himself believed that it was because the Republicans felt they were the natural and legitimate party of power. However, Yale historian Stephen Skowronek categorised Clinton (along with Nixon) as a 'Third Way' President in the sense that he tended to appropriate his opponents' agenda and get a moderated version of it passed, and pointed out that such presidents are often mistrusted by their own party and detested by the opposition, but they are nevertheless often quite successful.

(b) 'American politics had turned rancid' (Joe Klein)

Historian Gordon Wood noted a difference in American politics in the Clinton years. While political scandals, severe partisanship and vitriolic rhetoric were not new, this period was unique in that so many prominent figures faced legal action. 'Politics', said Wood, was 'criminalised'.

It was not simply the Republican reaction to Bill Clinton. According to Klein (*The Natural*, 2002), the 'utterly noxious atmosphere' that Clinton found in Washington had actually been gathering for at least two decades, ever since Watergate. 'American politics had turned rancid', with 'endless legal procedures' against public figures. Klein blamed extremists in both parties who were encouraged by a happily voracious press. In this poisoned atmosphere, two House Speakers, Jim Wright (see page 174) and Newt Gingrich (see pages 175–6), were driven from office, while three Republican Supreme Court nominees – Douglas Ginsberg, Robert Bork (see page 118) and Clarence Thomas (see page 153) – came under often partisan attack. Special prosecutors investigated Clinton himself, along with five members of his Cabinet, and several Cabinet-level nominees were rejected 'for reasons trivial or incomprehensible'. According to Klein:

> partisan legal harassment had become a major industry in Washington, providing crude entertainment, and satisfying careers for thousands of short-sighted practitioners. All this in a nation's capital that was, by most accounts, far less corrupt than it had ever been … The Clinton era is likely to be remembered more for the ferocity of its prosecutions than for the severity of its crimes – and if there was one politician who personified that ferocity more than any other, it was Newt Gingrich of Georgia.

(c) Newt Gingrich
(i) Youth

Key question
Why was Newt Gingrich important?

Pennsylvania-born Newt Gingrich, like Bill Clinton, was (just about) lower middle class, the product of a broken home, and managed to avoid service in Vietnam.

(ii) Gingrich enters politics

Gingrich entered the House of Representatives in 1979 (representing Georgia). A college professor (he had a PhD in history) and political activist, he was obsessed by war. He called politics 'war without blood'. His friend, Congressman Vin Weber, confessed:

> I don't think you can underestimate the generational aspect of this situation. Our generation came in and we had absolutely no respect for any of the traditions – not the speakership, not the presidency, not bipartisanship. We thought the parliamentary language was stuffy and silly. We thought hypocrisy was the only sin. Bob Michel's [see page 164] generation – they wanted to make life less political for the returning [Second World War] veterans. We wanted to politicise everything.

(iii) Rise to fame

In May 1984, in an unprecedented action, the normally charming Speaker of the House, Tip O'Neill, left the Speaker's chair, walked into the centre of the chamber, and shouted at Newt Gingrich. Why?

O'Neill found it hard to cope with this new generation of disrespectful **baby boomer** politicians, especially these more partisan and ideological Republicans. The introduction of televised debates had made Congress more theatrical. With an eye on TV audiences across the country, Gingrich had apparently questioned the patriotism of several named Democrats in a virtually empty House. House rules said that the camera must be fixed on the orator. With the camera focused on him, Gingrich challenged the Democrats to defend their votes against defence spending. The audience did not know that the Democrats in question did not respond because they were not there. O'Neill decided to allow cameras to pan the empty chamber. When Gingrich protested this 'unilateral' decision, O'Neill marched to the microphone, and yelled:

> You deliberately stood in the well of this House and took on these members when you knew they weren't here. It is un-American! It's the lowest thing I've heard in my 32 years here.

Republican Representative Trent Lott of Mississippi demanded that O'Neill's words be condemned as they violated House rules that prohibited derogatory remarks about fellow members. An O'Neill protégé who had taken the Speaker's chair reluctantly agreed.

The Republicans had spent 30 years as a downtrodden minority in the House. Proud and delighted, they gave Gingrich a standing ovation. One Gingrich ally (he had a lot of support from Southern Republicans) described this as 'the opening shot in the war':

> The Democrats were arrogant to the point of corruption, and Newt's idea was to expose the arrogance and corruption for what it was. It was a guerrilla war, and I don't think we could have won the House in 1994 without those sort of tactics. But the victory came at a price, and the price was a loss of civility.

Key term

Baby boomer
An American born in the post-Second World War population boom (when the soldiers returned home).

(iv) Gingrich vs O'Neill – round 2

In 1985, the House of Representatives was asked to investigate a close congressional race in Indiana. O'Neill chose a three-member commission, consisting of two Democrats and one Republican. Not surprisingly, the Democrats voted in favour of the Democratic candidate. The Republicans walked out of the House chamber in protest. A Gingrich ally said:

> That was Newt's second big victory. People began to think, 'Well, if the Democrats are going to be like that, maybe Newt's right. We might as well blow up the place.'

Gingrich felt unbeatable. In 1987, he brought ethics charges against O'Neill's successor, Jim Wright. The charges were 'flimsy' (Klein), but when the House Ethics Committee appointed a Special Counsel to investigate Wright, the investigations went on and on, until the exhausted Wright felt he had to resign (1989).

(v) Gingrich vs George Bush

Gingrich even took on his fellow Republican, President George Bush. When Bush broke his 'no new taxes' pledge in 1990, cutting a budget deal with the Democrats, Gingrich led the Republican revolt that forced a renegotiation of the deal.

By the start of 1994, as leader of the new Republican majority in Congress, Speaker Gingrich was ready to focus upon Bill Clinton. Gingrich had drawn up ***The Contract with America***, which he hoped would help bring about a Republican victory in the off-year elections. It certainly helped turn them into a referendum on the 'liberal' Clinton administration. The Republicans were brilliantly successful in 1994, capturing the Senate for the first time since 1980 and the House for the first time since 1954.

Key term

The Contract with America
The right-wing, 10-point governing doctrine of Newt Gingrich's Republican followers in 1995.

The Contract with America
The Contract with America promised:

- Tax cuts for the middle class.
- Reductions in the federal bureaucracy.
- The elimination of 'non-essential' social programmes.
- 'Effective death penalty provisions'.
- An emphasis upon American family values.
- 'Reasonable limits on punitive damages' and reform of product-liability laws 'to stem the endless tide of litigation'.
- A constitutional amendment requiring the federal government to present a balanced budget each year.
- Term limits for political office holders (Republicans changed their minds on this after their 1994 electoral landslide).
- Increased defence expenditure to strengthen national defence.

Newt Gingrich holding the Republican Contract, 1994. Why do you suppose Gingrich put his priorities in the form of a contract?

Key date

Newt Gingrich's *The Contract with America*: 1995

(vi) Gingrich vs Clinton

When, in winter 1995, the House of Representatives quickly passed most of Newt Gingrich's 10-point governing doctrine, *The Contract with America*, it seemed that Speaker Gingrich was the most important politician in America. In April 1995, when President Clinton held a rare prime-time press conference, amazingly, only one TV network broadcast it and one reporter questioned his relevance in the policy process underway in the Republican Congress.

(vii) The fall of Gingrich – 1998

Gingrich's meteoric rise was paralleled by a meteoric fall, because:

- His abrasive arrogance alienated voters. For example, riding home in Air Force One from a state funeral abroad, he complained to the press that he had been given a seat in the back of the plane, and had not had a chance to speak with Clinton. His mother was unhelpful. After Mrs Gingrich had publicly called the First Lady a bitch, she and her son had been graciously invited to the White House to meet the Clintons, who then came out best from the incident.

- Many began to turn against *The Contract with America* when they realised that some federal programmes that particularly affected them were likely to be hit. Some realised that the proposed cuts in federal programmes would still be insufficient to finance increased defence expenditure and tax cuts.
- Clinton cleverly showed up the Republican ideologues and partisanship by moving to the middle ground and co-opting some Republican programmes. For example, he pushed a crime bill through Congress (see page 164). He worked with House Speaker Gingrich and Senate Majority leader Bob Dole on the welfare reform bill. Clinton also decreased the federal workforce by 230,000, which helped cut the federal deficit by 60 per cent. When he clashed with Congress over the 1996 budget, voters blamed the two federal government shutdowns in late 1995 on Republican partisanship.
- Gingrich's role in the impeachment proceedings against the President (see page 183) alienated voters, especially when, like the President, he was revealed as having had an affair with a young aide.

(d) Increased political partisanship
(i) Pre-1960s coalitions

Key question
Why had the parties become so much more partisan?

Before the 1960s, the South was solidly Democratic and both political parties were broad coalitions. The Democrats included conservative Southerners and urban Northerners, and while both groups supported an activist federal government in economic matters, they agreed on little else.

Meanwhile, the Republicans represented both Wall Street and Main Street, both the Eastern élite and the Western middle class. Those Republican groups agreed on the desirability of limited government, but on little else.

(ii) Collapse of the coalitions
Then, in the 1960s, the solid South shattered over civil rights (because Northern Democrats supported desegregation). White Southerners became Republicans. Both parties became more ideologically rigid, and debate became more abrasive and partisan. The Democratic majority in Congress became far less tolerant of the Republican minority. Mutual respect decreased, and the Republicans, in the minority, suffered.

(iii) Activist groups
After the Vietnam War, there was a whole generation trained in activism, some of whom were looking for something to do. They got involved in the explosion of 'public interest' activist groups in the early 1970s. They put a great deal of pressure on the Democrats and the Republicans, making them both more extreme.

These interest groups would often provide money for candidates' advertising, which led to more vicious television campaigns. In 1980, the National Conservative Political Action Committee ran a 'scurrilous' (Joe Klein) television campaign against six liberal senators, four of whom were defeated. That returned control of the Senate to Republicans for the first time in 26 years. 'It makes it a lot harder to work together', said one Republican who left Congress in disgust in 1992. 'A lot harder to do anything.'

(e) How to kill Bill – legal weapons

By the time Clinton came to the presidency, each party was using high-powered legal weapons to stalk the other party. The weapons were the product of governmental reforms that resulted from the Watergate scandal. The reforms definitely curtailed some outrageous practices, but powerful new ethics weaponry such as the **independent counsel** was too easy to appropriate for trivial, partisan political use.

Under the independent counsel act of 1979, the first to be investigated were Carter's chief of staff and his campaign manager, for alleged cocaine use. No charges were filed in either case. In the Reagan presidency, the Democrats investigated several leading Reaganites, only one of whom (Michael Deaver) pleaded guilty to an unrelated infraction. The independent counsel weapon was used against Clinton.

(f) How to kill Bill – smear tactics

When, in 1987, liberal activists successfully fought against the nomination of Robert Bork to the Supreme Court (see page 118), they used the tactics of consumer rights activist **Ralph Nader**, one of whose protégés said, 'One of the first things Nader taught me was to demonise the opposition'. Another new and notable feature of the Bork campaign was media invasion of Bork's privacy, in the hopes of getting some 'dirt' on him. A few months before, *Miami Herald* reporters had hidden in the bushes outside the town house of Democratic presidential candidate Gary Hart, hoping to catch him with a woman other than his wife.

By the time Clinton became President, the press had become 'an essential, omnivorous, and obnoxious component in the machinery of scandal' (journalist Joe Klein). A new generation of reporters wanted to be the new Woodward and Bernstein (see page 51). However, unlike Woodward and Bernstein, their research was careless, and they fixed on the personal lives of politicians such as Clinton and Gingrich. Their purpose was no longer to find things out, but to bring politicians down. There was, says Klein, 'a gleeful, voyeuristic quality to much of the reporting; politicians were now, routinely, presumed guilty'.

'The media love hate', according to Representative Barney Frank of Massachusetts, a homosexual whose private life was exposed in 1989. Statistics confirmed the negative trend in political reporting. In the 1960 election, 75 per cent of the references to the candidates were positive, in 1988, only 40 per cent. Furthermore, stories emphasising conflict between politicians increased 300 per cent from the early 1970s to the late 1980s.

Key term

Independent counsel
Also known as the special counsel; under a 1979 act, the wrongdoing of powerful figures in an administration (including the President) could be investigated by an independent counsel.

Key question
How did Clinton's opponents attack him?

Key figure

Ralph Nader (1934–)
As a consumer advocate and critic of governmental corruption, he stood for President in 1996 and 2000 on the Green Party ticket, and in 2004 as an independent. Many believe the votes that he took from Al Gore in 2000 gave the presidency to George W. Bush.

(g) The great right-wing conspiracy

The First Lady believed ex-journalist Sidney Blumenthal when he said that there was a 'great right-wing conspiracy' against the Clintons (Blumenthal now denies that it ever existed).

Key question
Was there any great right-wing conspiracy?

(i) The death of Vince Foster

Several publications seemed out to get Clinton from the first. Hillary Clinton's friend Vince Foster, who committed suicide in July 1993, felt hounded by the *Wall Street Journal*, which always insisted the Clintons were corrupt. Foster's death reinforced the Clintons' belief that the press was out to get them, and the press belief that there was something rotten at the heart of the Clinton administration. Special investigators simply concluded that Foster had taken his own life.

(ii) Clinton sex scandal No. 2: Paula Jones

In 1994, a conservative magazine, the *American Spectator*, quoted former Arkansas state troopers on the sex lives of the Clintons. The investigation had been funded by conservative billionaire Richard Mellon Scaife. Conservatives encouraged one of Clinton's supposed conquests, Paula Jones, to tell how the governor of Arkansas had approached her in an inappropriate manner and how she had steadfastly refused him. The trooper who originally told the story had a different version, in which Jones visited Clinton's hotel room and emerged wreathed in smiles, offering to be the governor's girlfriend forevermore.

> **Paula Jones**
> In 1994, Paula Jones sued Bill Clinton for sexual harassment committed in 1991 (Jones had kept quiet until a 1994 story in the *American Spectator* mentioned a 'Paula', after which she filed suit). Jones claimed that she could and would identify the President's genitals, which caused a great deal of media speculation. The case reached the Supreme Court in 1997 (see page 182). Jones said Clinton had exposed himself to her, after she rejected his advances. Her lawyers called in other Clinton girlfriends, including Monica Lewinsky (see page 181). Like Gennifer Flowers, Paula Jones posed nude for *Penthouse*. In 2002 she participated in a public boxing match.

(iii) Whitewater

The press made a great deal of the **Whitewater** land deal, but years of dedicated investigation, at the cost of $50 million in public funds for special prosecutors, found no evidence of criminality in the Clintons' business deals while in Arkansas.

Most of the charges against Clinton were insubstantial, but his response to them was a furious, self-defeating defiance that damaged his administration. One aide blamed this on Hillary, citing a conversation when the President said:

Whitewater
The name by which some of the Clintons' property deals while in Arkansas were known.

Key term

'I don't have a problem with giving them what we have [information on Whitewater],' he said, almost apologetically, his mind elsewhere … 'But Hillary …' Saying her name flipped a switch in his head. Suddenly, his eyes lit up and two years worth of venom spewed out of his mouth. You could easily tell when Clinton was making Hillary's argument … '*No* President has ever been treated the way I've been treated.'

(iv) Kenneth Starr

In January 1994 Clinton made what he subsequently believed to be a great error when he asked Attorney General Janet Reno to appoint a special counsel to investigate Whitewater. After Congress renewed the special counsel act (see page 177), the three federal judges whom the act said should appoint the counsel, replaced the original moderate Republican investigator with Kenneth Starr, Bush's solicitor general, and an adviser to Paula Jones' legal team. Clinton explained why he asked for an investigation by special counsel:

I did it because I was exhausted, because I had just buried my mother, and because I had people in the White House who couldn't stand the heat and they suggested that I do it, that I had to do it. I knew there was nothing to it, it was just a lie … Why did this thing hang on? There was nothing in those private papers … And if you notice, when Starr got a hold of this, he immediately abandoned it and went on to other stuff.

That 'other stuff' was Bill Clinton's sex life, which dominated Clinton's second term.

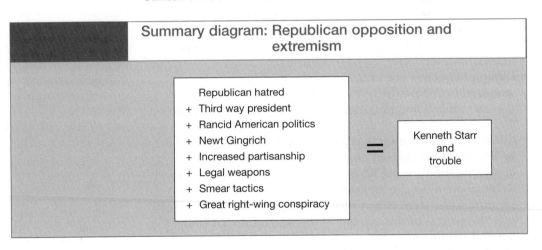

Summary diagram: Republican opposition and extremism

Republican hatred
+ Third way president
+ Rancid American politics
+ Newt Gingrich
+ Increased partisanship
+ Legal weapons
+ Smear tactics
+ Great right-wing conspiracy

= Kenneth Starr and trouble

5 | The 1996 Presidential Election

In April 1995, pollsters told Clinton that voters were unimpressed with him, apart from his signing (Bush had refused) of the Family and Medical Leave Act. Voters felt he was feckless, disorganised, a closet liberal, and weak in the face of the Washington establishment. His approval ratings slipped to 39 per cent in April 1995.

After the health care fiasco, and the disappointing 1994 election results for the Democrats, Clinton lacked credibility. However, he cautiously, quietly and cleverly rallied and impressively won the second term. How?

- Clinton was a brilliant public speaker, probably even better than Reagan. In April 1995, a powerful truck bomb destroyed a federal building in Oklahoma City, killing 63 people. The right-wing extremist behind it was retaliating for the lethal federal assaults on a cult in Waco, Texas, two years before. Clinton's ratings improved after his moving speech at the memorial service for the dead.
- In his 1996 re-election campaign, Clinton pleased Old Democrats by supporting affirmative action, and New Democrats by advocating welfare reform. He and Vice President Gore had effectively conciliated both Democrat factions. Clinton also managed to satisfy conservatives by favouring quota modifications ('mend it don't end it,' he said).
- The economy was booming, with inflation, interest rates and unemployment at their lowest since 1968.
- Clinton fund-raised brilliantly, for example, effectively selling overnight stays at the White House Lincoln bedroom.
- On pollster Dick Morris' advice, Clinton concentrated upon the **'triangulation strategy'**.
- Clinton emerged triumphant from the acrimonious budget negotiations for 1996 (see page 170).
- Clinton frequently outmanoeuvred the Republicans. He managed to appear conservative (thus appropriating their ground) while doing nothing, as when he criticised violence on TV.
- Clinton impressed middle-class voters when, in August 1996, he honoured his election pledge to 'end welfare as we know it', by signing the Personal Responsibility and Work Opportunity Reconciliation Act (he had vetoed two earlier conservative measures) (see page 169). Conservatives and liberals disagreed over the success of this act, but its passage improved Clinton's popularity ratings.
- The Republican candidate, 73-year-old Senator Bob Dole, was weakened by other Republican candidates in the primaries. Dole seemed too old, lacked charisma and, unlike Clinton, did not seem to enjoy campaigning.
- Voters were not convinced that Dole's proposed tax cuts, balanced budget and increased defence expenditure added up.

Key question
Why was Clinton re-elected in 1996?

Key date
Clinton re-elected President: 1996

Key term
Triangulation strategy
Clinton presented himself as a moderate, standing between the liberals and conservatives.

- In order to appease conservatives, Dole had come out against abortion, which perhaps explained why women voters favoured Clinton by 54 per cent to 38 per cent (Dole won 44 per cent to 41 per cent of male votes).
- The Republicans had decided that they would have to get something done in Congress if they were not to be defeated in the congressional elections. So, ironically, the Republicans found themselves passing welfare reform, increasing the minimum wage and extending health insurance to workers who lost or left their jobs, all of which helped Clinton win some votes.

Clinton won 50 per cent of the popular vote, Dole 41 per cent, but the Republicans retained control of both houses of Congress.

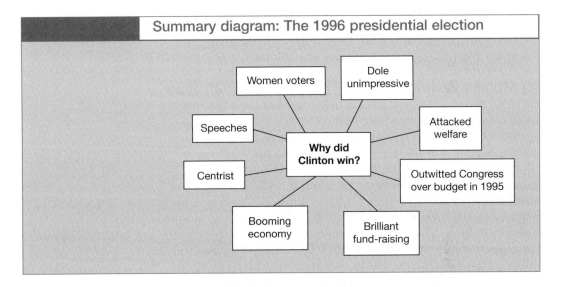

Summary diagram: The 1996 presidential election

Why did Clinton win?
- Women voters
- Dole unimpressive
- Speeches
- Attacked welfare
- Centrist
- Outwitted Congress over budget in 1995
- Booming economy
- Brilliant fund-raising

6 | The Monica Lewinsky Affair

Key question
How did the Monica Lewinsky affair develop into a constitutional crisis?

Key date
Monica Lewinsky sex scandal: 1998

(a) Investigations into Whitewater and the Paula Jones civil suit

By January 1998, when the Lewinsky scandal broke, Clinton was already involved in investigations into his conduct. The first was that by Kenneth Starr, the independent counsel who had begun investigating the Whitewater affair in mid-1994 (see page 178). The second was the civil suit that Paula Jones (see page 178) had filed in May 1994, alleging that Governor Clinton of Arkansas had sexually harassed her in a Little Rock hotel room in 1991. Jones' lawyers sought to prove Clinton's womanising ways by testimony from other women, including Monica Lewinsky.

(b) Monica Lewinsky and Bill Clinton

In July 1995, 21-year-old Monica Lewinsky secured an internship in the White House, thanks to the influence of a family friend who was a generous donor to the Democratic Party. Between

November 1995 and December 1997, she and Bill Clinton met privately, 10 times, in the White House. In nine of those meetings, she performed oral sex acts upon the President. He inserted a cigar into her vagina. Their meetings took place either in the small private study just off the Oval Office or in the windowless hallway outside the study. Lewinsky said the President called her frequently, 15 times for phone sex.

President Clinton's lawyers fought these two investigations, taking the Jones one to the Supreme Court in May 1997. Although the Supreme Court unanimously rejected Clinton's claims that the Constitution protected him from civil suits such as Jones' while President, many Americans agreed with Clinton's argument that a busy President needed to be exempt from time-consuming and potentially frivolous litigation relating to pre-presidential events. In 1998, a federal judge finally threw out Jones' case for lack of evidence that she had been coerced or suffered job discrimination, but by that time, the Monica Lewinsky affair dominated the nation's headlines.

(c) Monica Lewinsky, Linda Tripp and Kenneth Starr

In 1996, 49-year-old Linda Tripp befriended Monica Lewinsky (both were now working at the Pentagon). It seems that Tripp resented being moved from the White House to the Pentagon, and (encouraged by Starr, who had expanded his Whitewater investigation to include the Jones case) saw an opportunity to get back at the Clinton administration, when it became clear to her that Lewinsky had had a sexual relationship with the President. In September 1997, Tripp began secret recordings of conversations with Lewinsky, in which the latter told of her affair. Tripp gave the tapes to Paula Jones' legal team. When Lewinsky submitted an affidavit (in which she denied having an affair with Clinton) in the Jones case (January 1998), Starr asked Attorney General Janet

Monica Lewinsky (wearing the beret) and President Clinton at a political rally. The Lewinsky scandal raised the question: are a President's romantic liaisons anyone's business but his own?

Reno if he could broaden his inquiries. Starr got the go-ahead. He hoped to prove Clinton had conspired to obstruct justice by encouraging Lewinsky to commit perjury in her affidavit.

(d) 'Monicagate'
(i) Clinton's denial

Meanwhile, the Drudge Report, an Internet site, exposed the Lewinsky affair, and on 21 January 1998, the *Washington Post* published the story. For the next 13 months, 'Monicagate' was front-page news. Clinton denied the affair to his wife, his staff, and on TV, on 26 January: 'I did not have sexual relations with that woman, Ms Lewinsky. I never told anybody to lie.' Hillary Clinton vigorously supported her husband, blaming the 'vast right-wing conspiracy'.

Starr, a deeply religious and conservative Republican, granted Lewinsky immunity from prosecution (she had committed perjury in her affidavit) in exchange for her telling a federal grand jury about the affair. Starr produced a semen-stained navy blue dress she had worn in a meeting with the President. DNA tests proved the semen was Clinton's, in August 1998.

(ii) The Clinton confession

In a White House interrogation on 17 August, Clinton admitted the 'inappropriate' relationship with Lewinsky to Starr's aides, and, hours later, did the same on TV. His TV apology was rather ineffective. It was neither heartfelt nor emotional, combative rather than contrite, and his appeal for the nation to get back to normal business did not rally public opinion or isolate Starr. Clinton's 21 September televised claim that oral sex was not sex was unconvincing. For the moment, this great communicator was struggling to communicate.

Meanwhile, the President accomplished little in early 1998, although some felt he was engaging in dangerous overseas adventures (see page 186) to distract the nation from this scandal.

(e) Impeachment
(i) Kenneth Starr's report

Starr moved for the impeachment of the President. In September 1998, he sent a report to the House of Representatives that said nothing about Whitewater (the original topic of his inquiry) but said a great deal about Clinton's sex life. Starr's report charged the President with perjury (a felony) for denying under oath that he had had sexual relations with Lewinsky, and with obstruction of justice (another felony), as when he had encouraged Lewinsky to submit a false affidavit.

(ii) Differing reactions

The press was highly critical of Clinton's behaviour, but his job approval ratings remained very high. Nevertheless, House Republicans voted (October 1998) to proceed with an impeachment inquiry. They hoped this would give them a boost in the **off-year elections**, but it did not. Indeed, this was the first

---

Jay Leno, host of the popular *The Tonight Show*, joked, 'The President has complained about powerful forces threatening to bring down his administration. I think that they are called hormones.'

Key term

Off-year elections
Also called congressional mid-term elections. Elections in the middle of a President's four-year term.

off-year election since 1954 in which the party holding the White House had increased its numbers in the House of Representatives. Because of that and the revelation that he too had been having an affair with a young congressional aide, Newt Gingrich (see page 176) resigned as House Speaker. His designated successor was also revealed to be an adulterer and, like Gingrich, he promised to leave Congress in January 1999. It was also revealed that Congressman Henry Hyde of Illinois, the Republican chairman of the Judiciary Committee, who was to preside over the impeachment hearings, had himself had an adulterous liaison 40 years before.

(iii) Congressional votes on impeachment

Undeterred, in January 1999 the House voted, on largely partisan lines, to impeach the President on grounds of perjury, obstruction of justice and abuse of power. However, conviction in the Senate would require a two-thirds majority, which the Republicans lacked, so the outcome there was never in doubt. On 12 February 1999, the Senate rejected the perjury charge 55 to 45, with 10 Republicans joining the 45 Democrats. On the obstruction of justice, only five Republicans joined the Democrats.

(f) Postscript

Although Clinton had survived, Starr's Whitewater investigation resulted in 14 successful prosecutions relating to fraud and tax evasion (none of it by the Clintons) by summer 1999. Also, the judge who had dismissed the Paula Jones case ruled that Clinton had given 'false, misleading, and evasive answers that were designed to obstruct the judicial process'; Clinton was held in contempt and ordered to pay Jones' lawyers $90,000. On his last day in office, Clinton admitted giving false testimony concerning his relations with Lewinsky. He was fined $25,000, and his law licence was suspended for five years. In return, he received immunity from prosecution for perjury or obstruction of justice. In March 2002, Starr's successor produced the final report on the Whitewater investigation. It said there was insufficient evidence that the Clintons had been guilty of any crimes relating to Whitewater. The investigation had cost Americans taxpayers $60 million.

> **Key date**
>
> Attempted impeachment of Clinton: 1999

(g) The results, significance and impact of 'Monicagate' upon domestic politics

(i) 'Monicagate' and the American public

> **Key question**
> How did 'Monicagate' reflect and affect domestic politics?

While 60 per cent of Americans disapproved of his personal conduct, Clinton's job approval ratings were consistently and exceptionally high during the scandal (always over 60 per cent and even over 70 per cent in early 1999). He left office with the highest sustained job approval ratings of any President since Kennedy. Why?

Joe Klein offered two explanations for the contrast between the intensity of outrage in Washington and the reaction of the general public, who, although fascinated by the sordid details, felt that this was not something for which a President should be impeached. First, Klein felt that Washington had so disgusted the public for nearly a quarter of a century with its self-destructive partisanship, that the public could no longer be shocked by anything that politicians did. Second, Klein suggested that Clinton simply encapsulated all the flaws of his baby boomer generation, who could not find it in their hearts to condemn him, because he was so like them in his sexual and material excesses and his apparent emphasis on style over substance. A third suggestion was that when the Paula Jones civil suit was dismissed in April 1998 on grounds of insufficient evidence, the public decided Clinton had been getting a raw deal. A fourth suggestion was that the American public disliked Starr. He seemed sanctimonious and vindictive, with a prudish attitude that had turned a sex scandal into a constitutional crisis. A fifth and most convincing suggestion is that the US economy was booming. Voters were happy.

(ii) Congress and the Constitution

Within Congress, both parties remained confrontational and partisan. Republicans felt Clinton's perjury and obstruction of justice really met the constitutional definition of 'high crimes and misdemeanours', while Democrats disagreed and felt Republicans had set a dangerous precedent for some future Congress to simply get rid of a President they did not like.

There was great debate about the independent counsel. The independent counsel law (1978) was designed, in the aftermath of Watergate, to allow unbiased investigations into presidential, vice presidential or high-ranking administration officials' wrongdoing, because the nation's highest ranking legal official, the attorney general, was a presidential appointee and could not be considered impartial. The 1978 law let the attorney general ask a three-judge panel to name a special prosecutor, whose powers, as Starr proved, were considerable – and, thanks to him, increasingly unpopular.

Some observers emphasised the faults in the US Constitution, where the checks and balances slowed processes such as the impeachment to an unprofitable crawl, and where the separation of powers encouraged adversarial relationships between the executive and the legislature. Some felt the presidency had been damaged, but others felt that Congress would be more careful before it tried impeachment again.

(iii) The Democratic Party

The Democratic Party had often been ill at ease with Clinton, but they really rallied to him during the Monica Lewinsky scandal. 'What kept us close to the President was the Republicans', said one Democratic senator. 'Their extreme nastiness pushed Democrats into Bill Clinton's arms, even those who didn't like him very much.' Only a few weeks before, Democrats in the House had nearly rebelled against him, because of his willingness to compromise with conservatives in the budget negotiations of 1997 and on welfare reform and free trade.

(iv) The Republican Party

The Republicans suffered for their partisanship during the Monica Lewinsky affair. They lost five seats in the 1998 congressional elections, which was very rare for a mid-term election during a President's sixth year. Newt Gingrich resigned as Speaker after the elections, because he had been having an extramarital affair. His successor also resigned after rumours of similar behaviour.

(v) The press

The press also suffered. A Harris poll revealed that journalists were held in the lowest public esteem of any professional group, lower even than lawyers.

(vi) Culture wars and popular culture

'Monicagate' was one of several great cultural conflicts since the 1960s. In this particular conflict, more liberal (some would say permissive) public attitudes had prevailed. 'Monicagate' demonstrated the insatiable public demand for sensationalism. In March 1999, Lewinsky's television interview set record-breaking viewing figures of 70 million (advertisers paid record amounts for the commercial breaks – there were advertisements for Victoria's Secret lingerie, a special toothbrush and a stain remover).

(vii) Clinton and his presidency

According to historian James Patterson, 'Monicagate' had greatly damaged Clinton's presidency, leaving his reputation in tatters and destroying any opportunity to advance liberal goals or to lead a serious and productive discussion of public issues, including terrorism. Joe Klein, on the other hand, while recognising Clinton's moral failings, also emphasises his great achievements (see page 191).

(viii) Vice President Gore and the 2002 presidential election

The scandal poisoned relations between Vice President Gore and Clinton, so that when Gore ran for the presidency in 2000, he refused Clinton's help and insufficiently emphasised the achievements of their administration. This helped cost him the presidency.

Key date

Vice President Gore defeated by George W. Bush in presidential election: 2002

(ix) The impact of 'Monicagate' on foreign policy

Bombings

Key question
How did 'Monicagate' affect foreign policy?

Many were (and are) convinced that Clinton used foreign policy to try to distract from the Monica Lewinsky affair. For example, in August 1998, three days after his grand jury testimony, Clinton approved a cruise-missile attack on a pharmaceuticals factory in Sudan and on a guerrilla camp in Afghanistan, both of which were said to have links with Osama bin Laden, the Saudi millionaire who, the White House claimed, had masterminded the terrorist bombings of US embassies in Kenya and Tanzania. The attacks were ineffective and raised suspicions that Clinton was trying to distract people from the Lewinsky scandal. It was uncertain that the pharmaceuticals factory had any link to Osama bin Laden and sending cruise missiles against a desert camp seemed like overkill.

Nevertheless, the distraction seemed to work. The cruise-missile attacks dominated the news for a couple of evenings, and the public and many Republicans supported the actions.

More bombings

When Clinton was about to be impeached by the House of Representatives, in December 1998, there was another and equally futile aerial bombardment of Iraq, where Saddam Hussein continued to deny United Nations inspectors access to suspected weapons sites.

Many think that these foreign policy actions were influenced by the President's personal difficulties. Even if that was not the case, the distraction of the Lewinsky affair surely impacted upon Clinton's ability to prepare for the actions. Interestingly, Clinton was subsequently criticised for not doing enough against bin Laden (see page 191).

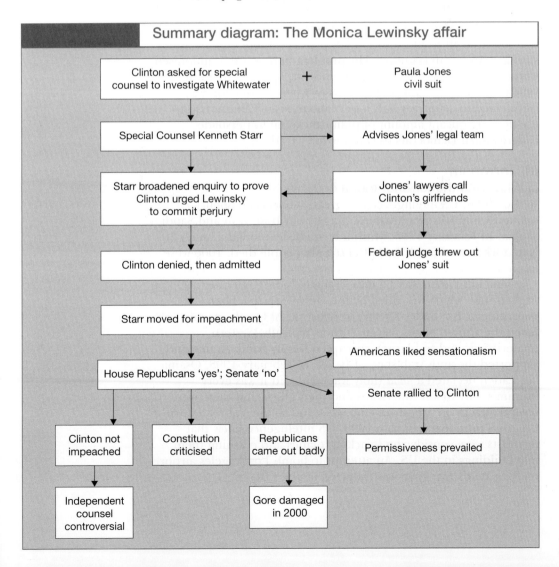

Summary diagram: The Monica Lewinsky affair

- Clinton asked for special counsel to investigate Whitewater
- \+
- Paula Jones civil suit
- Special Counsel Kenneth Starr → Advises Jones' legal team
- Starr broadened enquiry to prove Clinton urged Lewinsky to commit perjury ← Jones' lawyers call Clinton's girlfriends
- Clinton denied, then admitted
- Federal judge threw out Jones' suit
- Starr moved for impeachment
- House Republicans 'yes'; Senate 'no'
- Americans liked sensationalism
- Senate rallied to Clinton
- Clinton not impeached
- Constitution criticised
- Republicans came out badly
- Permissiveness prevailed
- Independent counsel controversial
- Gore damaged in 2000

7 | Foreign Policy

(a) Interventions in foreign civil wars

With the Cold War over, the great foreign policy questions facing Clinton usually revolved around whether or not to intervene in troubled areas. Sometimes his military intervention seemed to restore peace to an area (as in Bosnia in 1995), sometimes not (as in Somalia in 1993).

Key question
How successful was Clinton's foreign policy?

(b) Peacemaker

Clinton tried with some success to solve disputes in the former Yugoslavia, the Middle East, Africa and Northern Ireland. In the latter, he helped bring about a ceasefire between the warring religious factions.

(c) Trade

Perhaps Clinton's most important foreign policy legacy was that he raised economic issues to the same level of importance as strategic ones.

Clinton believed in the classical theory of free trade, convinced that lower tariffs would result in lower prices, more exports and a stronger American economy. His problem here was that unionised workers, who traditionally voted Democrat, opposed free trade, which would mean American job losses when production was transferred to countries with lower labour costs. Clinton had to use up a significant amount of political capital to persuade congressional Democrats to vote for freer trade.

(d) Terrorism

(i) What was the terrorist threat?

In the 1990s, US intelligence was greatly concerned about militantly anti-Western Muslims, many from Iraq, Iran and Saudi Arabia. In February 1993, Muslim terrorists exploded a bomb at New York City's World Trade Centre; six people died, 1000 were injured.

Osama bin Laden was a Saudi Arabian, hiding out after 1996 in Afghanistan, which was ruled by the anti-Western Taliban government. Bin Laden's terrorist network, Al Qaeda, particularly hated the United States, because it was typically Western (materialistic and secularist), corrupted its ally Saudi Arabia and supported the anti-Arab state of Israel. In February 1998, Osama bin Laden declared a *jihad* (holy war). He said it was every Muslim's duty to kill Americans and their allies, and there were several attacks on American embassies and soldiers abroad during Clinton's presidency. By late 1998, US intelligence knew that terrorists were considering hijacking planes and crashing them into buildings in the US. An attempt to bomb Los Angeles airport on New Year's Eve 1999 was thwarted by the FBI.

(ii) What did Clinton do about the terrorist threat?
Use of air power
Rather than risk American lives, Clinton used air power against
Iraq's Saddam Hussein (who continued to stockpile chemical and
biological weapons) and against the Afghan training camps of
Osama bin Laden in 1998. US military and intelligence experts
criticised the missions because they would only serve to
strengthen the reputations of those men in the Arab world and to
exacerbate their hatred of the United States.

Administration divisions
Divided as to what to do about terrorism, the administration
discussed the use of cyber-warfare against the financial assets of
terrorists, but it was feared that this might threaten the stability of
the international financial system. The FBI was furious that the
administration did not want to pressurise the Saudis to co-operate
more fully in investigations, but American diplomats in Saudi
Arabia and American oil companies argued against this option.
They claimed Osama bin Laden was not a serious threat.
   Clinton took terrorism very seriously: he obtained greatly
increased funding for counter-terrorism from Congress.

Hindsight
During Clinton's presidency, there was relatively little discussion
or criticism of his policy towards terrorism. After the terrorist
attacks on New York City of 11 September 2001, that changed
(see page 191).

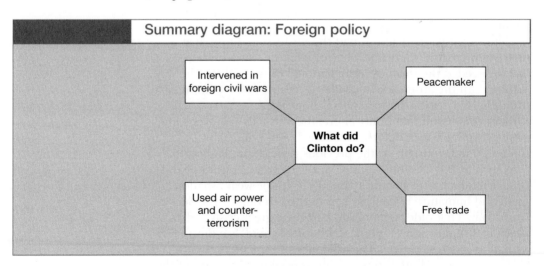

Summary diagram: Foreign policy

Intervened in foreign civil wars

Peacemaker

What did Clinton do?

Used air power and counter-terrorism

Free trade

Key question
Was Clinton a
successful President?

8 | Clinton's Presidency – Conclusions
(a) Moral failure
(i) Telling the truth
It became clear during the 1992 presidential election campaign
that Clinton did not always tell the truth ('I experimented with
marijuana a time or two. And I didn't like it, and didn't inhale,

and didn't try it again'). The President's dishonesty was confirmed in 'Monicagate'.

(ii) Unsavoury acquaintances

Clinton was always vulnerable when faced with sycophants, fund-raisers and favour-seekers. He gave them access, personal photos, coffees and overnight stays in the Lincoln Bedroom in the White House. He let them convince him to issue presidential pardons to their unsavoury acquaintances in the dying days of his presidency. Of the 177 pardons granted on his last night in office, the worst was to a disgraced financier called Marc Rich, who had fled the country and was on the FBI's 'Ten Most Wanted' list. Rich had evaded tens, perhaps hundreds, of millions of dollars in taxes. He had traded oil and perhaps even arms with US enemies. He had fled the country and renounced his citizenship. He contributed $450,000 to the Clinton Library, $100,000 to Hillary Clinton's Senate campaign and $1 million to the Democratic Party. His wife bought several thousand dollars' worth of furniture for the Clinton's new home in upstate New York, having visited the White House 96 times during the last two years of Clinton's presidency.

(iii) Bored baby boomers

Clinton was the first of the baby boomer (born after the Second World War) presidents and some historians suggest that perhaps he had faults typical of many of his generation: moral relativism and an addiction to marketing rather than substance (his administration spent more money on polling than all previous administrations combined).

Klein suggests that Clinton had the misfortune to serve at a time when greatness was not required, that he was a bit bored, that he needed the thrill of some national crisis, and that he was 'unlucky'. In the absence of a challenge that tested his impressive strengths, his distressing weaknesses flourished.

Klein contended that political greatness usually requires some great crisis. He concluded that all baby boom politicians compared unfavourably to the previous generation. He found men such as Bill Clinton, George W. Bush, Trent Lott and Newt Gingrich (along with Britain's Tony Blair) to be weak, shallow, small and immature in comparison to the veterans of the Second World War. That older generation had their great crisis with which to struggle and, 'I guess', said one of them, 'we didn't feel we had as much to prove'. The affluence of the late twentieth century also contributed to the unimpressive performance of the baby boomers.

(iv) Disgracing the office

Many people consider that Clinton's moral failings damaged and cheapened the presidency. Others feel that Republican partisanship publicised sexual behaviour that should have been allowed to remain private, even (and maybe especially) that of a President.

Key question
Should Clinton be
blamed for 9/11?

Key term

9/11
On 11 September
2002 (9/11/02),
terrorists took over
civilian aircraft,
flying two of them
into the World
Trade Center in
New York City.
Thousands were
killed.

(b) Terrorism

(i) Historians' criticisms of Clinton over terrorism

After the 11 September 2001 terrorist attacks upon the United States, there was a great deal of scrutiny of and disagreement over the way in which Clinton handled the terrorist threat. Most historians agree that Clinton paid too little attention to terrorism, thereby implying in varying degrees that he bore some responsibility for **9/11**.

(ii) The American public and terrorism in the Clinton years

In response to those who say that Clinton should have foreseen the danger of international terrorism and led the nation in a more aggressive and riskier war against it, some say it would have been hard to mobilise Americans in a war against terrorism, just as it was hard to mobilise them in the war against Communism in Vietnam. They point out that Clinton was making these decisions before what the majority of contemporaries considered the unimaginable events of 11 September 2001.

(iii) Traditional anti-Western feeling

There were many factors for which it is sometimes difficult, sometimes impossible to blame Clinton. The anti-Western feeling had a long history in the Middle East, and while most of Clinton's recent predecessors had done a considerable amount to increase it, he had not. His interventions in the former Yugoslavia had been on behalf of persecuted Muslims.

(iv) A free society and a new kind of war

The United States was traditionally an open nation, easy for would-be terrorists to enter and operate within. This terrorism was a new kind of war to the United States, accustomed to facing a single hostile nation, but not hostile internationalised groups acting, often independently, out of several states.

(v) Divided US government agencies

In the struggle against terrorism, efficient co-ordination and policy formulation was difficult because of the overlapping jurisdictions of the several US government agencies and departments that traditionally dealt with it. They failed to get along with each other, and also with Clinton, who perhaps deserves blame for failing to force them to co-ordinate and co-operate. However, when the terrorist threat increased during his second term, he was preoccupied with 'Monicagate'. It could be said that the pursuit by Kenneth Starr and the Republicans of Clinton's sex scandals distracted the President, Congress and the nation from far more important matters, such as terrorism.

Key question
Had Clinton any great
achievements?

(c) Great achievements?

When Clinton's presidency came to an end, the general feeling was somehow that his had been a talent squandered, that opportunities had been wasted. However, as Klein points out, he had achieved a great deal that helped the less wealthy, he had

tamed the Republican Congress, and left his successor huge
budget surpluses.

(i) Social programmes

Clinton worked slowly and effectively to make a reluctant
Republican Congress spend more money on programmes that
raised the incomes of the working poor. He accomplished this in
small steps, in each of the autumn budget negotiations, even
when supposedly paralysed by the impeachment proceedings in
1998–9 (see page 183). For example, he got Head Start funding
raised from $2.8 billion in 1993 to $6.3 billion in 2000, and
childcare supports grew from $4.5 billion to $12.6 billion.
Furthermore, he managed to gain Congressional approval for
several new and quite large social programmes (for example,
grants of $30 billion in tax credits for higher education, and
$24 billion for a children's health programme). This was truly a
Third Way, the New Democrat tendency to favour cash and tax
credits over the establishment of new federal bureaucracies.

Clinton's critics on both left and right were unimpressed: the
left wanted bigger social programmes, and the right wanted less
spending. The press did not even notice his achievements, yet
Clinton's was a government 'that had dramatically improved the
lives of millions of the poorest, hardest-working Americans' (Joe
Klein).

(ii) Economic prosperity

The economic prosperity during Clinton's presidency was not
accidental. It owed something to thousands of his decisions, and
to the beliefs that he pursued with vigour, even if it was politically
inexpedient (such as the free trade and welfare reform that other
Democrats opposed).

During his presidency unemployment rates plummeted,
inflation rates remained exceptionally low, middle-class incomes
increased by an amazing 35 per cent, home ownership rose to a
record high (particularly benefiting ethnic minorities) and there
was some welfare reform, including measures that helped the
'deserving' poor.

Because Clinton's smaller deficit policy was ultimately
successful, Klein fears it is too easy now to undervalue what a
courageous decision it was then. It would have been so much
easier to propose big tax cuts or traditional Democrat liberal
spending programmes. 'We had', said one adviser, 'staked
everything on the theory that lower deficits would lead to lower
interest rates, which would revive the economy – which, you have
to remember, was an *unproven* theory at that point'.

On the other hand, critics note that the US trade deficit
continued to rise.

(iii) The Third Way – government activism and the Democratic Party

According to Klein, Clinton's Third Way had rescued the Democratic Party from irrelevance and popularised the new philosophy of government that made public sector activism acceptable once more. Clinton persuaded many that a revival of government activism would be appropriate: 'We have found the Third Way. We have the smallest government in 35 years, but a more progressive one.' In contrast, historian James Patterson contended that Clinton failed to build up the party (indicating that his self-absorption was a major reason).

(iv) Defeating Newt Gingrich

Clinton subsequently said that he felt that 'two of the great achievements of my administration' were 'facing down the government shutdowns' and 'defending the Constitution' during the Monica Lewinsky affair. 'Those two things together essentially ended the most overt and extreme manifestations of the Gingrich revolution.'

(v) AmeriCorps

In his 1992 campaign, Clinton got the most applause when he proposed a higher calling for young people, a new form of national service (AmeriCorps). Clinton managed to squeeze a great deal of money out of the Republican Congress for AmeriCorps, which was so successful that George W. Bush chose to continue it. However, the legislation that set it up was watered down, and the opportunities for service were decreased after pressure from public employee unions. Clinton himself seemed to lose track of it after he came to office. Here, as in other areas, many people felt that the Clinton presidency was more about gestures ('spin') than about true leadership.

(vi) Vice President Gore: 'reinventing government' and the 'Green Team'

Reinventing government

Although for the most part Gore had not impressed as Vice President, he made a rare successful appearance on late-night TV in summer 1993, waving the 10 pages of regulations that had to be followed by any company wanting to sell the government an ashtray. 'Now, here's my favourite', said Gore. 'This is the specification for how you test it … [on] a maple plank. It has to be maple, 44.5 mm thick.' The ashtray then had to be hit with a steel punch 'point ground to a 60 per cent included angle' and a hammer. 'The specimen should break into a small number of irregularly shaped pieces, no greater than 35'. In order to be counted as regulation shards, the pieces had to be '6.4 mm or more, on any three of its adjacent edges'. Gore shattered the government ashtray on TV, and got rave reviews (for once). It was part of his 'reinventing government' programme. This project eventually had a significant, if underappreciated, impact on federal government. The federal workforce was eventually

Key question
What did Vice President Gore achieve?

reduced by about 350,000, and an estimated $157 billion saved; 16,000 pages of bureaucratic regulations were binned.

The 'Green Team'

The unsympathetic Bush/Quayle stance on the environment had played a part in Clinton's 1992 electoral victory so Clinton put Gore (who had published environmentalist works) at the head of his 'Green Team', to show things would be different. Gore promised the reversal of federal policy, the boosting of energy efficiency, the preservation of wetlands and the reduction of global warming – 'a worthy but empty promise' (Randall B. Woods). Little progress was made in any of these areas.

As the fuel crisis of the 1970s seemed only a bad memory (fuel prices were cheaper in real dollars than at any time since the Second World War), excessive fuel consumption continued. However, emissions were cut by one-third between 1970 and 2000. US manufacturers cut their toxic waste releases for the first time in 1993 (acid rain had been halved between 1970 and 2000), and they and the general public dramatically increased their rates of recycling (50 per cent for manufacturers, 17 per cent for households). On the other hand, overburdened sewerage systems remained a great problem. For example, overflows caused a temporary closure of around 2000 beaches in 1991 alone. Furthermore, the rate of hazardous waste spills was increasing, approaching 100,000 in the 1990s.

Global warming was the great environmental issue of the 1990s, for which the United States bore a great responsibility (producing 21 per cent of the world's greenhouse gas emissions). Clinton and Gore attended many meetings about this, at home and abroad, and enthusiastically supported the 1992 Energy Policy Act, which gave incentives for renewable energy, established efficiency standards for appliances, and experimented with alternative fuels in government vehicles.

At best, it could be said that under Clinton the United States gained more awareness of environmental problems and, for the most part, made small gains in caring for the environment, although the problems remained great.

Global warming
The release of carbon dioxide into the atmosphere (mostly due to burning fossil fuels) threatened to raise the average global temperature.

Key term

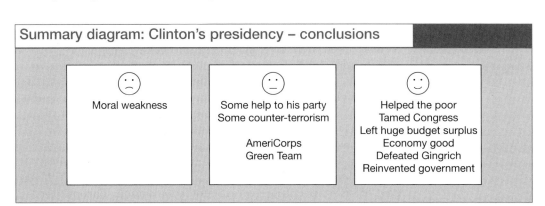

Summary diagram: Clinton's presidency – conclusions

☹	☐	☺
Moral weakness	Some help to his party Some counter-terrorism AmeriCorps Green Team	Helped the poor Tamed Congress Left huge budget surplus Economy good Defeated Gingrich Reinvented government

Study Guide: AS Question

In the style of Edexcel

How accurate is it to describe Bill Clinton as a successful President of the USA? (30 marks)

Exam tips

The cross-references are intended to take you straight to the material that will help you answer the question.

This is a question asking you to balance strengths and weaknesses, achievements and failures in order to come to an overall conclusion. Clearly 'Monicagate' overshadows the Clinton presidency, but take care not to devote too much time or space to it in your answer. And remember that you will only need to use information about it to support a point in your argument.

What were the successes? You could consider evidence of:

- successful management of Congress, for example in the budget negotiations (page 167)
- significant welfare and social reforms (pages 163, 168–170 and 192)
- economic prosperity – what contribution did Clinton's policies make to this (page 192)?
- huge budget surpluses at the end of his presidency.

And the failures or weaknesses? You could consider:

- the failure of the health insurance plan in the first term (pages 166–7)
- voter disappointment with his first term record, which contributed to Republican success in the congressional elections – how did that create difficulties for the President seeking to implement policies (page 167)?
- the public humiliation of Bill Clinton and his impeachment by Congress – is this important when considering his achievements as President (pages 174–9 and 181–4)?
- the extent to which the Lewinsky affair damaged the office of President (pages 184–7).

What overall conclusion you come to will depend on what weight you give to the points on both sides. Klein gives a favourable assessment of Clinton's political economic and social achievements, but note that there were critics of Clinton in each of the areas. This is a controversial debate which you can explore. On which side does the weight of evidence lie in your view?

It might be worth considering whether Clinton, like Reagan, deserves considerable credit for governing such a vast and divergent nation without making any massive political errors.

7 Sport and American Society

POINTS TO CONSIDER
Sport was important in fostering a sense of national identity and patriotism in Cold War America. Also, some of the great social themes of 1968–2001 (racism, sexism, consumerism and materialism) were reflected in and affected by sport. This chapter looks at those issues through sections on:

- Sport reflecting the 'American Way'
- The decrease of discrimination (racial and sexual) in sport
- The Olympics and the Cold War
- The interrelationship between sport and domestic politics

Key dates

1968	Black power protests at the Mexico Olympics
1973	The Battle of the Sexes in tennis
1980	Oakland Raiders moved to Los Angeles
1981	President Reagan praised sport
1988	Carl Lewis tested positive for drugs three times at the US Olympic trials, but still competed
	Civil Rights Restoration Act
1991	Magic Johnson tested positive for HIV
1992	'Shoe war' at the Olympics

1 | Sport Reflecting the 'American Way'

(a) Sport is good

Many Americans considered that sport reflected all that was good about the United States and the **'American Way'**. Sport and the American Way were characterised by the capacity for hard work, equal opportunities for advancement, and frequent success. Team games and team spirit correlated with good citizenship, and all sports strengthened character. Sport fostered a sense of community: the Mayor of Oakland said his city needed 'the pride and identity it gets from the Raiders', Oakland's football team. In a 1981 speech, President Reagan praised sport as the preparation and proving ground for subsequent business or political challenges.

Key question
In what ways was sport considered good?

'American Way'
By this, Americans meant what they perceived to be their national characteristics of democracy, equality of opportunity and hard work.

Key term

Key question
In what ways was sport considered bad?

Key dates

President Reagan praised sport: 1981

Oakland Raiders moved to Los Angeles: 1980

'Shoe war' at the Olympics: 1992

(b) Sport is bad

Sometimes it was argued that sport represented all that was good in the American character, sometimes that it represented all that was bad: excessive greed, commercialisation, violence, drug abuse and cheating.

(i) Commercialisation

'Greed', said the reptilian Gordon Gecko character in the 1987 movie *Wall Street*, 'is good. Greed is right. Greed works'. American society was preoccupied with making money, and sport increasingly reflected that from 1968 to 2001. Sport was shaped by an American society that was increasingly commercialised.

One of the clearest signs that sport was all about money was an acceleration of the trends whereby teams dumped their supporters and traditional homes and moved to another city to earn more money, as with the Oakland Raiders. As a *Los Angeles Times* 1980 editorial admitted, 'Sports business is rough-and-tumble competition business. Self-interest rules.' The newspaper wanted the Raiders to come to Los Angeles, 'to provide a sense of identity and some economic benefit'. Raiders owner Al Davis had not been able to get the city of Oakland to finance a stadium improvements, so he moved the team to Los Angeles. When he did not obtain the go-ahead from the **NFL**, it tried to stop the move, but the circuit court ruled in favour of Davis. Such deregulation was typical of the Reagan era (see page 128).

Key term

NFL
The National
Football League.

Corporate America wanted to exploit successful athletes. World-beating cyclist Lance Armstrong, who had miraculously overcome cancer, had over $5 million of endorsements in 2001, from, amongst others, Coca-Cola, Oakley sunglasses, Nike shoes and the US Postal Service.

Money caused problems with loyalties, as in the 1992 'shoe war' between Reebok, the official Barcelona Olympic Games sponsor, and Nike, whose stars such as Jordan refused to wear the official Olympic logo because it advertised Reebok. The Nike stars were persuaded to drape themselves in the American flag at the medals ceremonies, in order to hide the Reebok logo.

Not only was sport shaped by society: sport and sportsmen sometimes shaped society. The influence of athletes and advertisements was demonstrated when products like Air Jordan (see below) caused heartbreak and violence amongst poorer children. At $125, sneakers were expensive (see page 144), and responsible for a surprising number of muggings and murders.

(ii) Violence

Sporting 'tradition' was damaged by increasing violence in the 1970s. A Texas Ranger baseball player's punch sent his manager to hospital. In a 1978 football game, a New England Patriot bumped into an Oakland Raider, and suffered two fractured vertebrae, which left him a quadriplegic. The Oakland Raider wrote his autobiography *They Call Me Assassin*, two years later, and said he did not feel guilty or sad about his opponent's fate, because it was 'what the owners expect of me when they give me my pay cheque'.

From 1965 to 1975, the national violent crime rate doubled, and disorderly conduct by fans increased simultaneously. In 1976, New York Yankees fans ended a game against the Dodgers with a riot.

Sex and violence

In 1995–6, over 200 athletes, mostly football and basketball players, were arrested for sexually or physically abusing women. A National Institute of Mental Health Survey said that although athletes constituted only 3.3 per cent of the male university population, they made up 19 per cent of the students reported for sexual assault and 35 per cent of those accused of domestic violence.

African American boxer 'Iron Mike' Tyson became the youngest ever world heavyweight champion in 1986. Jailed in 1992–5 for raping an 18-year-old female beauty contestant in Indiana, he boasted that 'the best punch I ever threw' was in the face of his wife. In a 1997 boxing match, he bit off part of his opponent's ear. Such behaviour helped to sell tickets. His 2002 fight against Britain's Lennox Lewis set box office records.

(iii) Sport and cheating

Sport often had a negative impact on society, for example, with repeated drugs and cheating scandals.

Performance-enhancing drugs

The need to keep competitive was an important factor in increased use of performance-enhancing drugs. Also, drugs were more acceptable in society at large. It was estimated that one-third of the 1968 US Olympic team used steroids. By 1972, it was around 68 per cent. By 1988, some thought it was more like 99 per cent. Sport's governing bodies were reluctant to crack down: nine times Olympic gold-medal winner (sprinter and long jumper) Carl Lewis tested positive three times at the 1988 US Olympic trials, but was let off when he claimed it was accidental use.

> **Key date**
>
> Carl Lewis tested positive for drugs three times at US Olympic trials, but still competed: 1988

Recreational drug use

Sports reflected national life again when, in the 1980s, there was greatly increased recreational drug use. Recreational drug use was endemic in basketball, where most players were black, and an estimated 45–75 per cent of players used them. In a court case of a cocaine trafficker it was estimated that nearly half of major-league baseball players used cocaine in 1980. However, in the Reagan era 'war on drugs' (see page 119) the sports authorities cracked down hard and quite successfully on recreational drug use.

Other ways of cheating

Although some still claimed that honesty, fair play and tradition were characteristics of sports, the rise in investigative journalism during the 1970s led to much exposure of corruption (and violence) in sport, and players themselves spilt the beans to make money.

With so much money at stake, it is not surprising that there was continued cheating. In 1980 University of New Mexico coaches were found tampering with athletes' test scripts (so as to keep mediocre students who were good athletes).

The old tradition of 'sporting' behaviour often seemed lost, for example, in tennis. Two highly successful players, Jimmy Connors and John McEnroe, brought a new (some thought unfair) level of aggressive competitiveness to the game, which greatly increased popular participation in the game in the early 1980s.

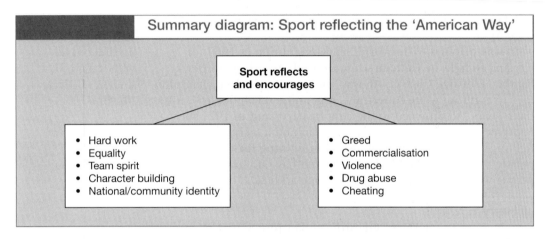

Summary diagram: Sport reflecting the 'American Way'

Sport reflects and encourages

- Hard work
- Equality
- Team spirit
- Character building
- National/community identity

- Greed
- Commercialisation
- Violence
- Drug abuse
- Cheating

2 | Sport and Race Relations

(a) Sport reflecting society – racism in the late 1960s and early 1970s

Some Southern college teams still resisted black membership, and black athletes were generally underrepresented on most college campuses. Out of 2236 athletics scholarships given in Southeastern universities in 1968, only 11 were awarded to black athletes. The first black basketball player in the Southern universities was greeted by opposing fans with, 'We're going to **lynch** you'. The University of Kentucky had **integrated** students in 1949, but its basketball team was all white until 1970: the coach considered black athletes naturally talented, but lacking the necessary self-control and intelligence to succeed. Coaches often threatened black students who dated white girls with expulsion. When brilliant long jumper Bob Beamon protested about the inequality at the University of Texas at El Paso, he lost his scholarship.

Even in the North, where the majority of Michigan State University's 22 football team starters were black, there were few black coaches or athletic councillors or black cheerleaders.

(i) Black athletes and keeping quiet

Black athletes felt great pressure from black radicals to 'make a statement', but there was equal economic pressure from the white

Key question
In what ways did sport reflect and impact upon race relations?

Key terms

Lynch
In this context, unlawful killing, usually by hanging, of African Americans that was common, particularly in the South, in the late nineteenth and early twentieth centuries.

Integrated
In this context, racially mixed.

community. Black college athletes, for example, were usually dependent upon white-funded sports scholarships for their college places, and those scholarships were likely to be withdrawn if a black athlete was deemed to be a troublemaker.

(b) Sport reflecting society – increased black assertiveness

(i) Muhammad Ali

Sportsmen were looked upon as reflecting broader social trends. Black athletes often personified racial aspirations and advance. This was particularly so in the case of Muhammad Ali, whose belief in black supremacy (he was a member of the racist **Nation of Islam**) reflected the contemporary black power movement (see page 5).

Ali was stripped of his world heavyweight title in 1967 for refusing to fight in Vietnam when drafted. According to Black Panther Eldridge Cleaver, Ali was 'the first "free" black champion ever to confront white America … a genuine revolutionary'. After three years, Ali returned to the ring in 1970, and in 1971 the Supreme Court overturned his conviction on a technicality. 'I'm fighting for me', said Ali, but also, 'I'm fighting for the black people on welfare, the black people who have no future, black people who are the wineheads and dope addicts.'

> **Key term**
>
> **Nation of Islam**
> Black separatist religion that considered all whites evil. Also known as Black Muslims.

(ii) Harry Edwards

Sociology professor Harry Edwards, of San Jose State College, California, established the United Black Students for Action to protest against discrimination in colleges. He echoed Malcolm X when he threatened to disrupt a football game 'by any means necessary', in order to draw attention to discrimination. He mobilised students across the United States, successfully organising a boycott of the 100th Anniversary Games of the New York Amateur Athletic Club, which refused equal access to blacks and Jews.

Increasing numbers of black athletes began to protest against bans on interracial dating, unequal housing opportunities, the lack of black coaches and support staff, and racist language from coaches and other players.

(iii) The 1968 Olympics and black power

When black athletes talked about refusing to participate in the 1968 Olympics in Mexico City, Cold War America stood to attention. These athletes were needed to beat the Soviets. A large US TV audience saw a famous black power demonstration: Tommie Smith and John Carlos, the gold and bronze medal winners in the 200 m, both raised a black-gloved fist when 'The Star-Spangled Banner' was played as they stood on the podium. Their aim was to draw attention to the inferior status of American blacks, and to their pride in their race. Smith and Carlos were thrown out of Mexico City and the US team.

> **Key date**
>
> Black power protest at Mexico Olympics: 1968

Not all black sportsmen were militants. Brilliant black football player O.J. Simpson (see page 212) denounced Smith and Carlos, saying that to him, black power meant economic power: 'it's the material things that count', he said, claiming that his wealth would 'give pride and hope to a lot of young blacks'.

(c) Sport affecting society – advances in the late 1960s

Sports impacted on American society in positive ways. The desire to win made many Southern schools integrate their football and basketball teams in the late 1960s and early 1970s.

(d) Sport reflecting society – multi-millionaire black sporting icons of the 1990s

O.J. Simpson (football) and Magic Johnson and Michael Jordan (basketball) made a fortune by advertising products. In 1992, Jordan earned over $21 million from endorsements, appearance fees and royalties. In one year alone $130 million worth of Nike's 'Air Jordan' shoes were sold. Florence Griffith-Joyner ('Flo-Jo') won much publicity with her world records in the 100 m and 200 m, and her bright fluorescent unitards and one-inch long nails painted in rainbow colours. Flo-Jo sold so many products that she became known as 'Cash-Flo'.

Several wealthy black athletes dominated their sport in the 1990s, including tennis-playing sisters Venus and Serena Williams and golfer Tiger Woods. As late as 1991, the Birmingham, Alabama, golf club where the PGA Championship was played had no black members. An early Nike advertisement had Woods deploring the fact that there were US golf courses from which he would be excluded, but after that, like Michael Jordan, he kept quiet about social issues.

(e) Sport reflecting society – brawn, brains and racism

Black athletes dominated team sports in the 1980s. In 1986, 63 per cent of top football players were black, 33 per cent of baseball players and 75 per cent of basketball players. Nevertheless, the belief that blacks could not cope with the 'thinking' positions, such as quarterback in football, persisted. Several TV commentators lost their job for perpetuating that myth. The first black baseball manager was appointed in 1975, but by 1999, there had still only been nine black managers and two general managers in **MLB**.

In a controversial 1997 publication, John Hoberman concluded that whites viewed blacks as natural athletes, and that this only served to reinforce white prejudices that blacks were physically aggressive and lacking in intellect. Hoberman lamented further the impact of sport upon African American society, pointing out that black schoolchildren neglected academic studies to concentrate upon sporting success: the successful black athletes had become an unproductive stereotype.

Key term

MLB
Major League Baseball.

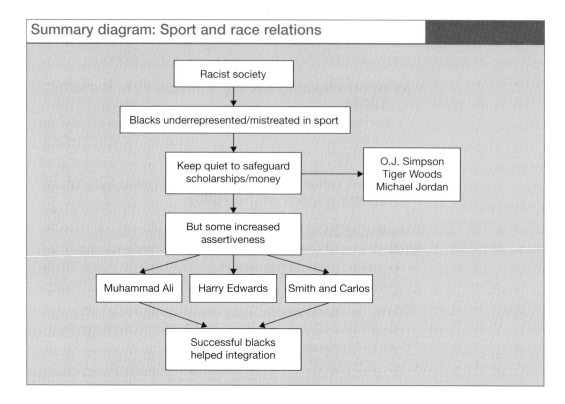

Summary diagram: Sport and race relations

3 | Women and Sport

(a) Sport not feminine

While it was acceptable for girls in feminine attire to stand on the sidelines and cheer their sporting men on, there was a long tradition that said that women belonged in the home not in sport, and that a competitive woman was not feminine.

A 1967 article proclaimed that 'the female breasts and other organs can be injured seriously by a sudden blow. The danger of scars, broken teeth or other results of injury are probably more of a psychological hazard for girls than for boys.'

(b) Increasingly competitive sportswomen

At college level, most women's sports were not competitive up to the 1960s, but 1969 saw the first national championships for women students. In 1967, a sole woman entered the Boston Marathon, having registered for it without giving her first name, in order to circumvent the AAU (American Athletics Union) rule that women could not enter any race longer than 2.5 miles. The marathon referee tried to throw her out, but her boyfriend and his friends formed a protective circle around her, enabling her to finish the race.

> Key question
> How and why did women gain greater equality in sport?

The Battle of the
Sexes in tennis: 1973

Tennis – the 'Battle of the Sexes'

Billie Jean King smiles as she is borne into the crowd for her tennis match against Bobby Riggs in 1973 at the Astrodome in Houston, Texas.

Billie Jean King won Wimbledon three times (1966–8). Her matches sometimes attracted audiences as large as male tennis players, but she earned far less: in 1970 she received $600 for winning the Italian championship, while the men's winner pocketed $3500. King therefore organised a lucrative women's tour, which enabled the women to threaten to boycott major tournaments such as the US Open, unless progress was made toward greater monetary equality. It was.

In 1973 the nation was riveted by the 'Battle of the Sexes' between Mrs King and 55-year-old Bobby Riggs. Riggs publicly proclaimed himself to be the world's No. 1 chauvinist, out of genuine conviction ('my goal is to keep our women at home taking care of the babies, where they belong') and/or because he saw a money-spinning opportunity. Riggs declared that women were naturally inferior to men, and that female tennis players were overpaid. King repeatedly rejected his challenges to play a match, but world No. 1 Margaret Court accepted. Court was thrashed 6–2, 6–1. Riggs, now a media superstar, repeatedly taunted King in the press, until she accepted his challenge at last. Bookmakers made Riggs the favourite. He said that while some women were excellent athletes, they were far more susceptible to pressure: 'I wonder whether she'll even show up. When the pressure mounts and she thinks around 50 million people are watching on TV, she'll fold.' The Houston Astrodome sold 30,000 tickets, the largest number ever to watch a tennis match. Cheerleaders danced on the sidelines, with midgets dressed as teddy bears. Bare-chested men carried King into the stadium on a litter, and she presented Riggs with a pig. Fifty million TV viewers watched

King beat Riggs 6–4, 6–3, 6–3, which at least proved that women could win under pressure.

King was representative of changing social forces. 'Almost every day', she sighed, 'someone comes up to me and says, "Hey, when are you going to have children? … why aren't you at home?" I say, "Why don't you ask [world No. 1] Rod Laver why he isn't at home?"' She brought gender equality to the forefront in tennis, and also helped make the sport less upper class (it had formerly been the preserve of the country club sets) and more mainstream.

(c) Society affecting sport – changing attitudes

The women's liberation movement and legal changes in the 1960s and 1970s were important agents for change in women's athletics. The 1964 Civil Rights Act included gender in the section prohibiting discrimination in employment. When the **Equal Employment Opportunities Commission (EEOC)** publicly refused to enforce those equality provisions for women, the National Organisation for Women (NOW) (see page 13) was set up in 1966 to promote legislative change and enforcement. The 1972 Education Amendments Act said that females deserved equal participatory opportunities in high school and college activities, and the Civil Rights Act provisions relating to gender equality were finally enforced in 1975, and re-affirmed in 1979.

There was a great gap to close. The leading athletic universities gave 5000 football scholarships to males in 1971, but only 50 scholarships in all sports to women. One Texas high school district was typical in that it gave $250,000 for boys' sports programmes, $970 for girls, and did not allow females access to local stadiums, athletic fields or gymnasiums.

Big money was involved. Male sportsmen attracted paying spectators, but sportswomen did not. However, the law directed change, and by 1980, women made up 30 per cent of college athletes, and obtained 16 per cent of the college sports budget (compared to 2 per cent in 1973).

(d) Politics affecting sport – changing attitudes again

President Reagan's opposition to big government impacted upon American sport. When he decreased the federal government's regulatory powers over sport, opportunities for women declined. Conservative court decisions undermined the Civil Rights Act provisions on female equal opportunities in college athletics.

Reagan's Republican Party emphasised traditional family values (see page 119), so feminism (see page 13) and talk of equal opportunities for women became less acceptable. In the Reaganite free-market economy (see page 107), women's athletics, which had less earning capacity than men's athletics, suffered.

Key question
Why were things changing for women?

Key term
Equal Employment Opportunities Commission (EEOC)
A federal agency established to deal with unequal employment opportunities for ethnic minorities.

Key question
How did the Reagan administration impact upon women's sports?

Key date
Civil Rights Restoration Act: 1988

When in 1988 Congress passed the Civil Rights Restoration Act (over Reagan's veto), anti-discrimination legislation became effective once more and female athletes' opportunities increased. Over 90,000 women participated in intercollegiate athletics in 1996, compared to under 30,000 in 1972.

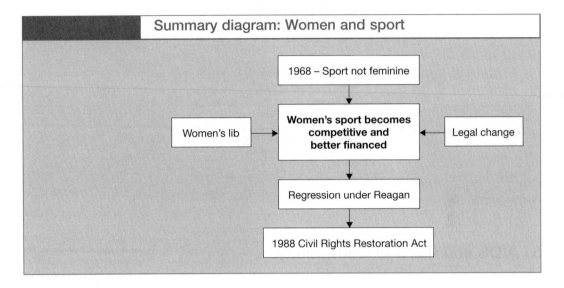

Summary diagram: Women and sport

Key question
Why did the Olympics matter so much to Americans?

4 | What Affects Sport? The Olympics and the Cold War

Society had an impact on sport, not only through contemporary financial, racial and gender preoccupations, but also through foreign policy concerns. During the Cold War (see page 2), the United States was desperate to beat the USSR in sport: here would be a concrete demonstration to the world that United States was better. The Olympics were for the most part the only time that American and Soviet athletes could compete against each other, so during the Olympics, sport was closely associated with patriotism. When the US defeated the highly fancied Soviet ice hockey team at the 1980 Winter Olympics in New York, it was 'as if the nation had been given a great present' (*New York Times*).

However, Cold War rivalry could also hurt sport. In 1980 President Carter orchestrated the US boycott of the 1980 summer games in Moscow, in protest against the Soviet invasion of Afghanistan.

Summary diagram: What affects sport? The Olympics and the Cold War

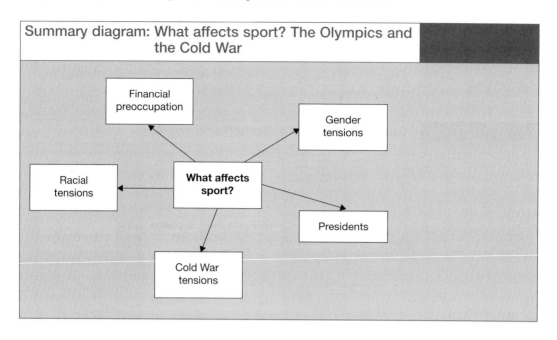

5 | AIDS and the Gay Community

In 1991, the news broke that Los Angeles Lakers footballer Magic Johnson had tested positive for **HIV** after unprotected sex with multiple partners. Over 100 newspapers covered Johnson's story, depicting him as a 'modern-day hero' (the Lakers' doctor) for speaking out. 'I confess', said the hero, 'that after I arrived in LA in 1979, I did my best to accommodate as many women as I could – most of them through unprotected sex'.

Lesbian tennis star Martina Navratilova complained that if a female athlete had confessed to such heroic athleticism in the bedroom, she would have been pilloried. Perhaps sports fans were simply homophobic and glad that Johnson was not gay: when a TV host asked him if he was, and Johnson said no, the audiences stood up and cheered long and loud.

Olympic diving gold medallist Greg Louganis had announced that he was gay in 1994. In 1995 he announced that he had AIDS. After his gold medals in the 1988 Olympics, *Newsweek* had christened him 'the classiest act of the games ... a Greek god beautifully rendered'. After the AIDS disclosure, *Newsweek* found him a 'troubling talent', describing him as a carrier of disease and a troubled individual.

While individuals such as these reflected the increase in numbers in cases of AIDS, tolerance of gays in sport did not reflect increasing tolerance of gays in the community. Perhaps sport was too closely associated with manliness or the 'American Way'.

Key question
How did sport reflect and react to AIDS and gays?

Magic Johnson tested positive for HIV: 1991 — *Key date*

HIV
Human immunodeficiency virus. The virus that causes AIDS. — *Key term*

Summary diagram: AIDS and homosexuals

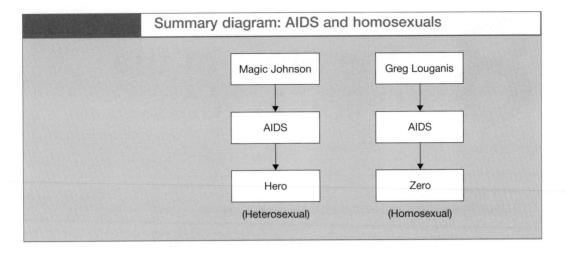

Study Guide: AS Question

In the style of Edexcel

How far do you agree that sport improved opportunities for black Americans in the USA in the period 1968–2001? (30 marks)

Exam tips

The cross-references are intended to take you straight to the material that will help you answer the question.

This question asks you to assess the wider impact of sport in American society. Did it open more doors for black Americans; did it open doors more widely? Did it have any effects which restricted opportunities? In answering this question you need to be clear about the links between sport and changes in opportunities.

To show improvement, you could consider:

- the role of black athletes, such as Muhammad Ali (page 200), personifying racial aspiration and advance
- black athletes exerting influence and protesting against inequality (pages 200–1)
- the increasing integration of football and basketball teams, even in Southern schools, in order to secure talented black athletes (pages 199–201).

To produce a counter-argument, you could consider:

- the persistence of attitudes which inhibited progress, for example the assumption that black footballers could not cope with 'thinking' positions (page 201)
- the continued stereotyping of black Americans as physically aggressive and lacking in intellect (pages 198–9 and 201)
- the influence on young black Americans to neglect academic studies in favour of sporting success (page 201).

You will need to make an overall decision. Had the successful black athlete become an unproductive stereotype (page 198) or an influence which broke down barriers?

8 The State of the Union in 2000

POINTS TO CONSIDER
This book has traced social and political developments in the United States after 1968. This chapter looks at society and politics in 2001, and considers the extent to which they had changed, through sections on:

• Multiculturalism
• Women
• Culture wars and 'decline'
• The strength of the US economy
• Politics in 2000

Having covered the period chronologically, the opportunity for the thematic approach is given.

Key dates

1994	California introduced 'three strikes and you're out'
1994–5	The O.J. Simpson affair
1996	Ebonics taught in Oakland
2000	Hispanic Americans overtook African Americans as the largest ethnic minority

1 | Multicultural America in 2000

By 2001, America was more multicultural than ever. However, African Americans and Hispanic Americans living in urban ghettos or depressed rural areas, and Native Americans on reservations, constituted an American 'underclass', incessantly fuelled by increased immigration (legal and illegal), particularly from neighbouring Mexico.

> **Key question**
> Was the United States happily multicultural?

(a) Immigration

In the year 2000, 29 million of the total US population of 281 million were foreign born (that was 10.4 per cent, compared to 4.7 per cent in 1970). Over 28 million immigrants had arrived in the United States between 1970 and 2000, by which date there was considerable tension about this influx.

> **Key date**
> Hispanic Americans overtook African Americans as the largest US ethnic minority: 2000

One-quarter of the legal arrivals during these years came from Mexico alone. In 2000, Latinos or Hispanic Americans (13.5 per cent of the early US population) overtook African

'Welcome to the United States.' A cartoon published in 2004 in *The New Yorker* magazine. What point is the cartoonist trying to make about immigration?

Americans (12.7 per cent of the population) as the nation's largest ethnic minority. The number of Asian Americans had been tiny in 1970, but they constituted 4 per cent of the population by 2000, in which year, over half of California's population was Asian American, Latino or African American. The 2000 census increased media talk of a 'complexion revolution' (Asian Americans and Latinos were considered 'people of color').

(i) Opponents of immigration

Some Americans opposed this large-scale immigration. African Americans complained that low-wage immigrants were taking their jobs, while labour leaders said immigrants who accepted low

A cartoon published in an American newspaper in 1997. What point is the cartoonist trying to make about the impact of affirmative action on universities?

pay drove down overall wage levels and increased poverty and income inequality in the United States. Opponents of immigration claimed that many immigrants worked for cash and paid no taxes, and that those on the welfare rolls were a burden to US taxpayers. They overcrowded US hospitals and classrooms. Some immigrants failed to **acculturate** because they frequently returned to their homelands, lived in ethnic enclaves, and continued to hear only their native tongue in frequent calls home and by watching non-English TV channels. Immigrants needed expensive bilingual education programmes, which also impeded acculturation. Latino participation in the 1992 African American riots in Los Angeles indicated that the United States was acquiring a large underclass of resentful, poorly assimilated people, who undermined national harmony. Some people resented the fact that the United States would soon be less than half white. Environmentalists worried about population growth.

> **Acculturate**
> Adapt to, adopt and accept the dominant culture of the country.
>
> *Key term*

> A Colorado bumper sticker's comment on Mexico and immigrants: 'DON'T CALIFORNICATE COLORADO'.

(ii) Supporters of immigration
Some Americans welcomed the immigrants, pointing out that the United States had always been a nation of immigrants and that they took jobs (maids, gardeners, crop pickers, dishwashers) vital to the US service-based economy, which other Americans would not do for such low wages. Most immigrants were hard-working and productive, and ambitious immigrants had energised the economy throughout American history. There was considerable sympathy for immigrants amongst liberals and recent immigrants, who claimed that these new entrants were just as eager to be acculturated as previous immigrants.

(b) African Americans in 2000
(i) Positive signs

> **Key question**
> Where did ethnic minorities stand in 2000?

Contemporaries disagreed as to whether divisions between blacks and whites were decreasing. By 2000, blacks were quite well represented in politics, government bureaucracies, police departments and the unions, and fully integrated in the armed forces. Affirmative action was solidly entrenched in major companies and universities (12 per cent of college students were black, a figure close to their percentage of the US population). The average black household income in 2000 was $30,400, compared to $24,000 (in constant dollars) in 1990. The average black household income had risen to 69 per cent of that of the average white household. Half of America's black population lived in neighbourhoods that were 50 per cent or more white, while interracial marriages were increasing. In 2000, there were over 350,000 black/white married couples (a 70 per cent increase over 1990). The number of blacks/whites cohabiting was estimated to be even higher. These statistics suggested an increasingly integrated society.

(ii) Less positive signs
On the other hand, black poverty and unemployment rates were twice those of whites. Two-thirds of black children had been on

the welfare rolls by the age of 18 years, and conservatives
bemoaned the cycle of dependency. Since California had taken
the lead in 1994, a backlash was eroding affirmative action
programmes. Despite the substantial black middle class,
9 per cent of the overall black population in 2000 lived in
overcrowded and impoverished central city ghettos. Not
surprisingly, black life expectancy in 2000 was lower than that of
whites (71.2 compared to 77.44 years).

(iii) Race and crime

The relationship between crime and race caused controversy. In
2000, 12 per cent of black males aged 20–34 (and 4 per cent of
Hispanics) were in jail, compared to only 1.2 per cent of similarly
aged white men. African Americans constituted 12.3 per cent of
the population, yet 46 per cent of prisoners (36 per cent of whom
were white, and 17.6 per cent Hispanics). The Justice Department
estimated that 28 per cent of black men would serve time during
their lifetime. Minorities and white liberals interpreted the
statistics as proof of racism and police oppression. During the
1990s, lawyers came out with the 'critical race' theory, which
claimed that white racism ensured that blacks remained
chronically disadvantaged and therefore justified black
lawbreaking. Conservative Americans believed the statistics
confirmed that blacks, and to a lesser extent Hispanics, were
more prone to criminal behaviour than whites.

Many black ghetto dwellers turned to crime, drugs and gang
turf wars because their poor education gave them few economic
opportunities. The year 1988 had been the peak for the
desegregation of public schools that had been mandated in the
Supreme Court decision BROWN in 1954. In 1988, 43 per cent
of black students in the South attended public schools that were
over 50 per cent white. However, by the year 2000, that
percentage had dropped to 30, about the same as in the early
1970s. In the residentially segregated Northern and Midwestern
ghettos, segregated schools were even more common than in the
South. The typical ghetto school was poorly funded and much of
the money allocated to ghetto schools was taken up by
particularly expensive programmes, such as special and bilingual
education. The conservative Supreme Court would do nothing to
promote integrated schools. Even in the integrated schools,
'tracking' (placing white students in college-preparation classes
and blacks in less demanding courses) had increased.

(c) Other ethnic minorities

(i) Hispanic Americans, Asian Americans and Native Americans

In 2000, Hispanics constituted the nation's largest minority. Over
14 million of them were Mexican Americans living in the
Southwest. Both Los Angeles and Miami were one-third Hispanic.
One-third of Puerto Ricans and one-fifth of Mexican Americans
lived below the poverty line. Hispanics were slowly increasing
their political participation. They married outside their ethnic

Black celebrities: O.J. Simpson

While whites admired black celebrities such as TV talk-show superstar Oprah Winfrey and actor Will Smith, the most infamous black celebrity in 2000 was still O.J. Simpson.

T-shirts on sale outside the O.J. Simpson trial court in Los Angeles, July 1994.

The murder

Former football star, film actor and TV sports announcer O.J. Simpson was arrested, charged with having stabbed to death his divorced (white) wife and her (white) boyfriend in 1994. After the bodies were discovered, the police issued warrants for Simpson's arrest, but he failed to turn himself in as promised.

Key question
What was the significance of O.J. Simpson?

The O.J. Simpson affair: 1994–5

Key date

The chase

Television cameramen in helicopters filmed the police chasing Simpson's vehicle. Over 100 million TV viewers (viewing figures comparable to Kennedy's assassination and the 1969 moonwalk) watched. Normal programmes were suspended. Police cars, red lights flashing, followed the vehicle for more than 50 miles over a period of two hours. Television commentators encouraged viewers to wonder whether the vehicle would crash, or whether Simpson would kill himself (he was said to be armed and suicidal in the car) or whether there would be a shootout. Simpson finally surrendered to the police.

The trial

O.J.'s nationally televised trial lasted nine months. More TV hours were devoted to his trial than to the forthcoming presidential election, the terrorist bombing that killed 168 people in Oklahoma City and the civil war in Bosnia put together. This was 'infotainment', sex and violence on the 'news'.

Simpson's lawyers played the 'race card' before a jury consisting of nine blacks, two whites and one Latino, claiming that a racially prejudiced criminal justice system had inspired the charges. The jury found O.J. Simpson not guilty.

In what ways was the O.J. Simpson affair significant?
- It demonstrated the American obsession with celebrities.
- It showed the commercialisation that often accompanied sensational events involving celebrities, sex and violence. For example, the *National Inquirer* paid the deceased woman's father $100,000 for her diary.
- The trial suggested that justice could be bought. Many thought that without his attorneys (whom few other Americans could have afforded) Simpson would have been found guilty (he had a history of battering his former wife, who had often called the police).
- Most significantly, the case polarised the USA along racial lines, just as the arrest of Rodney King had (see page 149). Generally, blacks believed Simpson was innocent, whites did not.

group more often than blacks, and their relations with the white majority were less strained (the most contentious issue was the estimated 12 million illegal aliens, mostly from Mexico).

Along with long established Chinese and Japanese communities (especially on the West Coast), there were newer immigrant groups of Asian Americans from places such as Korea, Vietnam and the Indian subcontinent. The average Asian American income remained above the national average.

There were 2.5 million (1 per cent of the US population) Native Americans in 2000. They had become increasingly keen to identify themselves as such, perhaps in order to share in the great profits generated by casinos on Indian reservations. Native American income, although only half the national average in 2000, had improved by one-third during the 1990s. However, Native Americans still suffered high rates of disease, poverty and alcoholism in 2000.

(ii) Minorities and education

Previously disadvantaged groups wanted their cultures taught, understood and valued more, so they demanded the adjustment of education to reflect their increased power and assertiveness. In cities such as Miami and Los Angeles, Hispanics called for bilingualism. In 1996, the Oakland city school board temporarily ordered the teaching of **ebonics**, but after the national outcry and a great deal of mockery, this ceased.

> **Key date**
> Ebonics taught in Oakland: 1996

> **Key term**
> **Ebonics**
> Black ghetto English.

By 2000 most colleges had well-established African American studies programmes. Latinos were beginning to make similar progress. Young radicals from all ethnic groups, tired of studying 'dead white European males', denounced 'élites' in history and literature. Some courses had become dominated by the underprivileged, whether American or foreign. When in 1988 prestigious Stanford University dropped a compulsory core course on Western culture, conservatives were in uproar, while the Stanford faculty rejoiced at the 'birth of multiculturalism' in their curriculum. There was even greater uproar in 1994–5, over proposed national standards in teaching American history. The standards emphasised the importance of evils such as slavery, the Ku Klux Klan and McCarthyism, and conservatives felt there was insufficient emphasis on great patriots such as the Founding Fathers. One Republican senator said Americans were faced with a choice between learning about George Washington or Bart Simpson (see page 142).

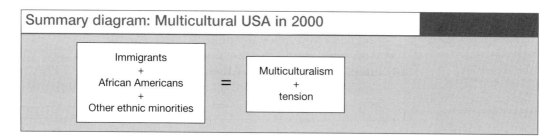

Summary diagram: Multicultural USA in 2000

Immigrants + African Americans + Other ethnic minorities = Multiculturalism + tension

2 | Women in 2000

> **Key question**
> Was there equality in the workplace by 2000?

In 2000, women held nearly 50 per cent of executive and managerial positions (compared to 32 per cent in 1983). Although underrepresented in the professions in 2000 (only 20 per cent of doctors and lawyers were women), they constituted around 50 per cent of students entering classes at law and medical schools. The number of women in the House of Representatives (62 in 2000, compared to 28 in 1991) and in the Senate (13, compared to three in 1991) remained depressingly low. These figures reflected both sexism and the desire of some women to interrupt their careers to give time to homemaking.

Many employers had become far more flexible over leave, especially after the 1993 Family and Medical Leave Act, but combining work and homemaking remained problematic, so many feminists focused upon issues such as better childcare facilities in the workplace. Work became increasingly essential as the rising divorce rate and number of single mothers made many women the heads of households in 2000.

Full-time female workers' earnings were only 76 per cent of men's in 2000, but that was an improvement upon the 62.5 per cent of 1979. Significantly, the incomes of childless young women were virtually the same as those of comparable males.

Toleration of sexual harassment in the workplace had decreased. Inspired by sympathetic Congressional legislation and Supreme Court rulings, groups such as NOW (see page 13) filed many successful lawsuits on behalf of sexual harassment plaintiffs. On the other hand, after a municipal courthouse employee claimed that the exhibition of an impressionist painting of a nude constituted sexual harassment, and won her case, a backlash set in. By 2000, 58 per cent of men and 53 per cent of women agreed, 'We have gone too far in making common interactions between employees into cases of sexual harassment.'

Summary diagram: Women in 2000

Category	Equality?
Top jobs	→ Not quite
Professions	→ Not quite
Politics	→ Nowhere near
Earnings	→ 76%
Sexual harassment	→ Yes

Key question
Were Americans deeply divided in 2000?

3 | 'One Nation, Two Cultures'?

(a) Liberals vs conservatives

Conservative radio talk shows
In the mid-1990s, around 20 million people listened to Rush Limbaugh, the most popular of the angry conservative radio talk-show hosts. Listeners loved it when he spoke of 'feminazi' and 'environmentalist wackos'.

In 2000, many Americans were reading Gertrude Himmelfarb's *One Nation, Two Cultures*, in which she echoed previous authors such as Robert Bork (see page 118) and claimed that culture wars were dividing the nation in half.

Cultural differences between conservatives and liberals were related to regional and class divisions. Cultural conservatism was particularly appealing to white working-class Americans in the

Pro- and anti-abortionists demonstrating near the White House in 1992. Why did these people demonstrate in this particular location?

South and the Plains and Rocky Mountain states, while liberal ideas appealed to better educated people on the East and West coasts and in the cities. While conservatives claimed 'liberalism has corrupted our culture', liberals complained that the Religious Right was increasingly aggressive in its wars against abortion, gay rights and other matters.

Religious conservatives remained a significant cultural force in 2000, with around 400 Christian radio stations. Although defeated on history textbooks (which had become multicultural and included figures such as Malcolm X), conservatives continued their fight against the teaching of evolution and sex education in schools. The power of conservative Christians was such that presidential candidates such as George W. Bush in 2000 paid great attention to them. In some areas, particularly in the Sun Belt states, conservative Christians affected electoral outcomes. However, many religious conservatives felt frustrated that none of their major goals (stopping abortion and pornography, starting prayer in public schools) had been achieved. Himmelfarb lamented that the United States was less religious than in the 1950s and 1960s: only 58 per cent of Americans in 2000 believed that religion was important in their lives, compared to 75 per cent in 1950.

Conservatives lamented the decline of family values. By 2000, 69 per cent of all black babies and 27 per cent of white babies were being born out of wedlock. The overall percentage of such births in 2000 was a record 33, up from 27 in 1990. Abortion rates remained at a ratio of roughly one for every three live births in 2000. Rising female employment, high divorce rates, later age marriages, greater sexual freedom and cohabitation all combined to make the traditional family less 'normal'.

Liberals were also dissatisfied with American society. Many of them decried excessive American materialism, rising inequality and a self-centred individualism that damaged the American tradition of co-operative community involvement.

(b) Popular culture

Popular culture was obsessed with sex. Two-thirds of all television shows aired during prime time (7–11 pm) had some sexual content. The popular *Jerry Springer Show* featured guests with sensational stories, such as the woman who described her five-year marriage to a horse, and the man who told of his romance with his dog. Fights between guests were common on the show.

The 'decline' of TV was much debated. On the one hand, it was pointed out that what a popular 1977 book called *The Plug-In Drug*, had never really purveyed much of cultural value since it began in the 1950s. On the other hand, there were still many quality television programmes, such as the critically praised political series *The West Wing* and hospital drama *ER*, and quality movies, for example, computer-generated and animated films such as *Jurassic Park* (1993) and *Toy Story* (1995) and serious films such as *Schindler's List* (1993).

The cultural impact of computers was also debated. The *Washington Post* called the Internet 'digital Ritalin [a calming drug] for the attention deficit generation', a 'weapon of mass distraction'. On the other hand, admirers emphasised that the Internet opened up new worlds of knowledge and communication.

Other important elements of popular culture included sport (see Chapter 7) and music. Young people had long used music to reject the older generation. By 2000, grunge (see picture) was on the way out, but African American rap music, which had developed in New York City in the 1970s, was mainstream. Rap lyrics, such as those of Eminem, were often criticised as obscene, violent and misogynistic. Gangsta rap glorified criminal gang violence and, like many elements of popular culture, was disliked by some Americans.

Key terms

Gas-guzzling
A motor vehicle using a great deal of gas (the American word for petrol).

SUVs
Suburban utility vehicles are bulky, with around eight passenger seats and low mileage per gallon.

Key question
Were Americans excessively materialistic?

(c) Capitalism, consumerism, materialism and the environment

Liberals and some conservatives lamented American consumerism and materialism. It was estimated that during 2000 any nine-year-old child would have seen 20,000 TV commercials. Americans were obsessed by brand names and 'must-have' items such as **gas-guzzling SUVs**.

Liberals stressed that the environment was greatly damaged by American materialism, attacking the world's chief 'throw-away society' (the US consumed 25 per cent of the world's energy and produced 25 per cent of its greenhouse gases, while possessing only 6 per cent of the world's population).

(d) A more violent society?

Songs, TV and movies were full of violence. Even the news was dominated by violence: 'If it bleeds, it leads'. However, crime rates were falling. Suggested explanations included a decline since the 1970s in the percentage of young people in the US population, and/or improving economic conditions, and/or improved community policing, and/or harsher sentencing

---

Key date

California introduced 'three strikes and you're out': 1994

In 1998, two students shot a teacher and 12 students in Columbine High School in Colorado. What might have motivated those two students?

procedures. In 1994 California introduced 'three strikes and you're out'. This law hit three-time felony offenders with mandatory prison sentences ranging from 25 years to life. Liberals worried that one or more of those convictions could be for small-scale shoplifting or possession of drugs, but 24 other **state legislature**s followed suit.

Between 1970 and 2000, the US jail population increased fivefold (topping two million). More than 50 per cent of federal prisoners and 22 per cent of state and local prisoners during these 30 years were incarcerated because of drug-related convictions. The number of Americans in jail (around eight people per 1000 population) was by far the highest in the world.

Key term

State legislatures While Congress makes laws that apply to all US states, each state has its own legislature that makes laws on local issues, for example, crime.

(e) Winners of the culture wars

On the one hand, it could be argued that, overall, the liberals in society were winning many of the culture wars. Americans in 2000 were more tolerant of the behaviour of others, for example, homosexuals. On the other hand, it could be argued that the conservatives were winning the culture wars in the political arena, where the Republicans were doing far better than in the first three-quarters of the twentieth century.

It is of course possible that, as historian James Patterson concluded:

Key question Who had won the culture wars?

> the much discussed culture wars of the [1990s] were a little less divisive than they appeared to be, especially to polemicists like Bork, to political partisans, and to … sensation-seeking and crisis-raising profit seekers in the media.

Patterson felt that the heated debates had calmed down by 2000, that the majority of Americans were not really exercised by them and subscribed to common democratic and work ethic values.

In the early 1990s, 'grunge' music became popular, thanks to Seattle-based bands such as Nirvana (shown here performing live in 1993). Grunge music had gloomy lyrics, 'dirty' guitar, and a rebellious attitude towards capitalism and middle-class life. How much had young people changed since the 1960s 'hippie' era?

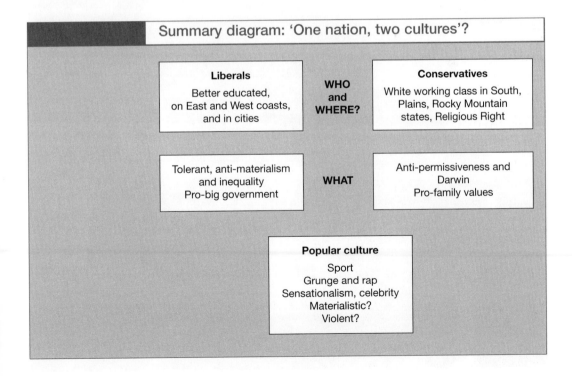

Summary diagram: 'One nation, two cultures'?

Liberals	WHO and WHERE?	Conservatives
Better educated, on East and West coasts, and in cities		White working class in South, Plains, Rocky Mountain states, Religious Right

	WHAT	
Tolerant, anti-materialism and inequality Pro-big government		Anti-permissiveness and Darwin Pro-family values

Popular culture

Sport
Grunge and rap
Sensationalism, celebrity
Materialistic?
Violent?

4 | The US Economy in 2000

(a) In decline

Some economists claimed that the United States economy was in decline. They pointed out high levels of personal debt that diverted money from more productive investment. US productivity was lower than in the 1960s, downtown areas were decayed, and unemployment was high in the **Rust Belt** and other manufacturing centres. The US had massive trade and payments deficits, and was dependent upon overseas investors. Corporate centralisation had swallowed up small companies, while huge retail chains (such as Wal-Mart) were anti-union, low payers and importing cheap goods (for example, from China) instead of buying from American manufacturers.

The marked economic inequality in 2000 owed a great deal to tax cuts that favoured the wealthy and to racial discrimination. Also, well-paid manufacturing jobs had decreased, and low-paid service sector jobs increased. Meanwhile, unions had lost members and thereby bargaining power. However, according to optimistic historian James Patterson, 'as in most times in the history of the United States, class resentments continued to be relatively muted'.

Key question
Was the USA in economic decline by the year 2000?

Rust Belt
The old manufacturing areas of the Eastern seaboard and the Midwest, where the old industries had declined and mostly disappeared.

Key term

A protest in Des Moines, Iowa, against Wal-Mart, which sold cheap goods, especially from Asia, which these protesters assert deprives Americans of jobs. Why would an American wear Wal-Mart clothes yet protest against the Wal-Mart chain?

Statistics demonstrating prosperity in 2000
Out of 107 million households: 106 million had colour TVs, VCRs and/or DVD players; 76 million had two or more TV sets; 92 million, microwave ovens; 81 million, air-conditioning; 79 million, electric or gas clothes driers; 60 million, personal computers; 51 million, access to the Internet; over 85 million, one or more vehicles. Those with medical insurance had access to ever improving medical treatment (life expectancy rose from 70.8 years in 1970 to 76.9 years in 2000).

(b) Not in decline

On the other hand, commentators who denied that the US economy was in decline also put forward some persuasive arguments. The United States was the wealthiest country in the world, producing 22 per cent of world output. Unemployment was only 4 per cent, and inflation was low. Americans in general had a very good standard of living. There were seven million fewer poor in 2000 than in 1994.

Some of the reasons why the US was so prosperous were traditional long-term causes of US wealth, such as the huge domestic market, great natural resources, the strong American work ethic, and the open, democratic, entrepreneurial culture. There were also factors specific to 2000, such as the government's fiscal discipline (Clinton ended the budget deficits), low interest rates maintained by the Federal Reserve after 1995, strong consumer confidence and spending, low oil prices and the weaker dollar (Clinton had let it drop in order to help exports).

Summary diagram: The US economy in 2000

Depressing ...
- Personal debt
- Productivity down
- Rust Belt
- Urban decay
- Trade deficit
- Balance of payments deficit
- Overseas investors
- Cheap imports

Encouraging ...
- Wealthiest nation
- Low unemployment
- Low inflation
- Consumer confidence
- Big domestic market
- National resources
- Work ethic
- No federal deficit

Key question
Was the US political system in good health in 2000?

5 | Politics in 2000

There was considerable disillusionment with politics and politicians in 2000. This was increased by the presidential election, in which many Americans felt that the rightful winner was robbed. Al Gore won more of the popular vote than George Bush Jr, and after a very close race in the electoral college, a Supreme Court decision about electoral practices in Florida gave the presidency to Bush. Democrats felt that the conservative Supreme Court had played an unconstitutional political role.

Nevertheless, Gore conceded, and proved that the US political system remained resilient, workable, and able to weather a succession of scandals and crises, even a disputed presidential election.

6 | The Thematic Approach to 1968–2001

As always, a chronological grasp of the period is essential before concentrating upon the thematic approach. The significant themes covered in this book can be followed through the following page references:

Political themes
- The power of the President – pages 54–5, 57–60, 104–6, 117–21, 132–3, 167, 170, 183–5.
- The power of the Supreme Court – pages 53, 104–6, 119, 170, 182.
- The power of Congress – pages 51–60, 82, 109, 117–21, 130, 133, 141, 164–5, 183–5.
- The relationship between the President and Congress – pages 46, 51, 60, 70–1, 80, 82, 108–10, 114–17, 130, 141, 145–6, 164–5, 167, 171–9, 192–3.
- The relationship between the President and the Supreme Court – pages 35, 53, 118, 120–1, 182.
- The relationship between the President and the press – pages 47, 51, 55, 71, 165, 177.
- The reasons for electoral outcomes – pages 15–17, 25–32, 34–46, 71, 74–7, 80–94, 101–3, 113, 145, 152–4, 161–2, 167, 180–1, 186.
- The New Right (or the Religious Right or the Christian Right) – pages 92–4, 119, 132, 146, 215–16.
- Political corruption and scandals – pages 47, 53, 69, 76, 81–2, 117–18, 178–9, 181–7, 190.
- Decreased federal government influence and expenditure – pages 59, 87–8, 106–12, 127–30, 134–5, 155, 160–1, 174.

Social themes
- Race relations and conflict – pages 3–5, 35–7, 72–4, 83–5, 119, 130–1, 147, 149, 199–201, 210–14.
- Class divisions – pages 5–8, 16, 103, 156, 220.
- Women and conflict – pages 13–14, 41–2, 72,83, 93–4, 132, 146–7, 163, 202–5, 214–15.
- Regional differences – pages 17, 19, 92, 215.
- The environment – pages 43–4, 186–6, 143, 155, 194.
- Counterculture and conflict – pages 9–12, 16–17, 38–41, 142, 217–19.
- Sport and patriotism and national identity and race – Chapter 7.

Study Guide: AS Question

In the style of Edexcel

How far did the position of black Americans in the USA improve in the years 1968–2001? (30 marks)

Exam tips

The cross-references are intended to take you straight to the material that will help you answer the question.

In order to consider 'how far' there was improvement, you will need to begin with an overview of the main problems and disadvantages faced by black Americans at the beginning of the period (pages 3–9). You can then show that some or all of these were reduced and reach an overall judgement about how much of an improvement that indicates.

To show a reduction in inequality and disadvantage you could consider:

- Evidence of the achievement of successful individuals (pages 201 and 212).
- Affirmative action in major companies and universities (page 210).
- A growing black middle class (page 210).
- Prominent office holders, e.g. Clarence Thomas's appointment as a Supreme Court justice (page 147).
- Evidence of economic gains and improvements in living conditions (page 210).
- Evidence of improvement in integration in the armed forces (page 210), government bureaucracies, police departments, etc.
- A massive increase in black elected officials in the South – but, of course, from a small beginning.

And the counter-argument:

- The Rodney King affair and the race riots (see page 149): evidence of the continuance of a divided and unequal society in the last decade of the twentieth century?
- Evidence of unequal treatment before the law – both in the justice system and by law enforcers (page 211).
- Continuing differentials in:
  - affluence (pages 210–11)
  - employment (pages 210–11)
  - life expectancy (page 211)
  - housing (pages 210–11)
  - education (pages 210–11 and 214).

Glossary

9/11 On 11 September 2002 (9/11/02), terrorists took over civilian aircraft, flying two of them into the World Trade Center in New York City. Thousands were killed.

Acculturate Adapt to, adopt and accept the dominant culture of the country.

'Acid, abortion and amnesty' In 1972, Republicans accused Democratic presidential candidate George McGovern of favouring drugs ('acid'), irresponsible sex ('abortion') and unpatriotic draft dodgers (to whom he would give 'amnesty', i.e. freedom from prosecution).

Administration When Americans talk of 'the Nixon administration', they mean the government as led by that particular President.

'A Ford, not a Lincoln' Ford was saying that he was not going to be a great President like Abraham Lincoln, playing on the public's familiarity with cars. Fords were the cars of ordinary Americans; Lincolns were expensive, prestige cars.

Affirmative action Giving economically disadvantaged African Americans extra opportunities (even if whites were better qualified) in education and employment in order to compensate for previous unfair treatment.

AIDS Acquired immunodeficiency syndrome is the result of a sexually transmitted disease. It is acquired through the exchange of bodily fluids, especially blood and semen. It strikes down the body's natural defence system, making it vulnerable to other diseases.

Alzheimer's disease A degenerative brain disease that causes dementia.

'American Way' By this, Americans meant what they perceived to be their national characteristics of democracy, equality of opportunity and hard work.

Angola When the Portuguese empire in Africa came to an end, Angola emerged as an independent nation. Ford wanted to support an anti-Soviet Angolese faction.

Antsy Uneasy, fidgety.

Aprincipled Unable to see what was acceptable and what was unacceptable behaviour.

AT&T The US equivalent of BT.

Attorney General Head of the Justice Department in the federal government.

Baby boomer An American born in the post-Second World War population boom (when the soldiers returned home).

Berlin wall The wall divided Communist East Berlin from pro-western West Berlin.

Bicentennial The USA's 200th birthday was on 4 July 1976. Americans had made their declaration of independence from Britain on 4 July 1776.

Billies Clubs used by American police.

Bipartisan When Republicans and Democrats forgo political partisanship and co-operate on an issue.

Bitburg German Chancellor Helmut Kohl asked Reagan to attend a wreath-laying ceremony at the military cemetery in Bitburg, West Germany, in May 1985. There was an outcry in the USA when it was revealed that 49 Nazis and members of Hitler's military police were buried there, but Reagan went ahead.

Black Panthers A group of militant black activists who used revolutionary rhetoric, ostentatiously carried guns, monitored police brutality and distributed free meals to the ghetto poor.

Black power A vaguely defined black movement with aims including separatism, and greater economic, political, social and legal equality for African Americans.

Blue-collar workers Manual labourers.

Brookings Institution A liberal Washington think-tank.

Busing Supreme Court rulings on integrated education meant some white children were sent (by bus) to black schools, and vice versa.

Cambodia As part of the war against Communism in Vietnam, Nixon bombed and invaded neighbouring Cambodia, through which Vietnamese Communists travelled to get to Southern Vietnam.

Camp David Presidential retreat in the rural hills of Maryland.

Canucks French-Canadians, of whom New Hampshire had a sizeable population.

Capitol Hill The location of the US Congress, the words Capitol Hill are often used as a synonym for Congress.

Caucus A political group usually sharing similar ideas.

Chicago Eight In 1969 the Nixon administration charged eight New Left leaders with conspiracy. They included Tom Hayden of SDS and Bobby Seale of the Black Panthers. Five were convicted, by an exceptionally hostile judge. Eventually their convictions were overturned on appeal.

Chicano Chicanos (also known as Latinos or Hispanic Americans) were citizens or residents of the USA. Usually Spanish speaking, they (or their ancestors) were immigrants from Latin American countries such as Mexico.

CIA The Central Intelligence Agency was set up in 1947 to monitor Communist threats early in the Cold War.

Civil rights movement The predominantly black movement for equal rights for African Americans, c1956–c68.

Coattails Americans talking of a President whose popularity helps other members of his party get elected, talk of those other members as getting in on the President's coattails.

Cold War The struggle between the capitalist USA and the Communist Soviet Union, c1947–89.

Common situs picketing When an entire construction site was picketed (that is, access was halted by union members) even though a union only had a dispute with one (or two) contractors on the site.

Communist In the Cold War the capitalist USA and the Communist Soviet Union hated and feared each other. Americans particularly disliked the Communist emphasis on economic equality.

Confederacy Pro-slavery states in the American Civil War, 1861–5.

Congress The US equivalent of Britain's Parliament. It consists of the House of Representatives and the Senate. Each US state selects two senators, and a number of congressmen proportionate to its population.

Congressional mid-term elections Some voters elect senators and representatives in presidential election years, some elect them in the middle of a President's term.

Constant dollars To make comparisons between dates more meaningful, economists factor in changes in the cost of living or the value of the currency, etc.

Constitutional amendment The USA's Founding Fathers wrote out rules by which the country was to be governed in the

Constitution. New rules or amendments can be added.

Contra rebels Opponents of the left-wing Sandinista Nicaraguan government.

The Contract with America The right-wing, 10-point governing doctrine of Newt Gingrich's Republican followers in 1995.

Counterculture An alternative lifestyle to the dominant culture; in the case of 1960s' America, the 'drop-out' mentality, as compared to the dominant, materialistic, hard-working culture of the students' parents.

Creationism A biblical account of the origins of the earth and the life that is on it.

CREEP Committee to Re-elect the President, established by the Nixon administration prior to the 1972 presidential election.

Cyprus crisis Cyprus' population was 80 per cent Greek, 20 per cent Turkish. A Greek-backed coup resulted in a Cypriot government that declared union with Greece. Turkey invaded to protect the Turkish minority.

Deep Throat The unidentified (at the time) FBI source who gave Woodward and Bernstein vital information during Watergate. In 2005, former FBI employee Mark Felt confessed to being Deep Throat.

***De facto* segregation** The segregation of blacks and whites in residential areas and some other public places in practice if not in law.

***De jure* segregation** The segregation of blacks and whites in public places by law.

Democratic Leadership Council A 1980s' association of centrist Democrats who believed the party had to move away from the left in order to be electable.

Departments of state Federal government departments such as the State Department (which deals with foreign affairs) and the Treasury.

Dissident One who disagrees with the official party line, in this case, Moscow's.

DNC Democratic National Committee, which had its headquarters in the Watergate building in Washington DC.

Dow Jones Industrial Average Stock price average compiled by Dow Jones & Co. indicating market trends in the USA.

Draft The US equivalent of British conscription; compulsory service in the nation's armed forces.

Draft dodger One who avoided being called up to fight in the Vietnam War.

Ebonics Black ghetto English.

Electoral college Under the constitution, each state's voters vote for delegates who then vote on behalf of that state in the electoral college. The number of delegates depends upon the state's population. The leading candidate in a state takes all that state's delegates. Whoever wins a majority of delegates becomes President.

Equal Employment Opportunities Commission (EEOC) A federal agency established to deal with unequal employment opportunities for ethnic minorities.

Equal Rights Amendment (ERA) Congress passed the ERA in 1972. Designed to help women and minorities in employment and education, it was never ratified by sufficient states.

Evangelical Protestantism Some would say a more fanatical and/or enthusiastic kind of Protestantism, which tended to be socially conservative, often taking the Bible very literally.

Executive and legislative branches The federal government comprises three branches: the executive (the President), the legislative (Congress) and the judicial (the Supreme Court).

Executive privilege Cold War presidents contended that in such a time of national emergency, they, as the executive branch of government, needed certain privileges, such as keeping some things secret because of the demands of national security.

FBI The Federal Bureau of Investigation was set up in 1924 to help deal with crime.

Federal agencies These include the FBI (Federal Bureau of Investigation) and the CIA (Central Intelligence Agency).

Federal government The USA is a federated state. Individual states such as California and Texas have considerable power (e.g. over transport and education). The national or federal government, based in Washington DC, consists of the President, Congress (which makes laws) and the Supreme Court (which interprets laws).

Feminists Advocates of equal political, social, economic and legal rights for women.

Flip-flop When a politician reverses a political stance.

Friendly fire When members of the armed forces are accidentally killed by their own side.

Gas-guzzling A motor vehicle using a great deal of gas (the American word for petrol).

Global warming The release of carbon dioxide into the atmosphere (mostly due to burning fossil fuels) threatened to raise the average global temperature.

GNP A country's gross national product is the aggregate value of goods and services produced in that country.

'Great Society' President Johnson said he wanted to create a US society free from the racism and poverty which were particularly prevalent in the urban ghettos.

Gubernatorial Pertaining to being a state governor in the United States.

Harlem New York City's African American ghetto.

Head Start A federal government programme to help economically disadvantaged pre-schoolers, providing educational, health, social and other services.

Helsinki Conference 1975 accord where the West recognised Soviet control of Eastern Europe in exchange for Soviet concessions on human rights.

Hippies Young people (often students) who, in the 1960s, rejected the beliefs and fashions of the older generation, and favoured free love and drugs.

HIV Human immunodeficiency virus. The virus that causes AIDS.

Homemakers Mothers who stay at home to look after their families, rather than going out to work.

House Minority Leader Leader of the political party in the minority in the House of Representatives.

HUAC The House Un-American Committee investigated suspected Communists within the USA.

Humphrey-Hawkins This bill said the federal government should be the employer of last resort during a recession. The final Act (October 1978) was a much watered-down version of the original bill.

Impeachment Under the US Constitution, Congress has the power to bring an errant President to trial, to impeach him.

Imperial presidency During the Cold War, presidential power increased so much that some commentators thought the President was becoming like an emperor – hence 'imperial'.

Impounding When the President refuses to spend money allocated by Congress.

Inauguration The President usually undergoes an elaborate inauguration ceremony on Capitol Hill, at which he is sworn into office. In the unprecedented 1974 situation, Ford was inaugurated inside the White House.

Independent counsel Also known as the special counsel; under a 1979 act, the wrongdoing of powerful figures in an administration (including the President) could be investigated by an independent counsel.

Integrated In this context, racially mixed.

Iran-Contra The 1986 scandal in which the Reagan administration covertly sold arms to Iran and diverted funds from the sale to help Contra rebels in Nicaragua.

IRS (Internal Revenue Service) US tax collection agency, which monitors taxpayers, checking whether they pay the correct sum.

JCS The Joint Chiefs of Staff were the heads of the army, navy and air force.

Junket The taking advantage of political office by accepting perks such as lavish entertainments.

Labour Blue-collar, unionised workers.

'Lame-duck' President When a President nears of the end of his second term, Congress and country, knowing that he is to lose power, look to his likely successor. Then it is hard for that President to achieve much.

Laundered money When money is to be used illegally, it is frequently laundered or 'made clean' by being put into a bank not connected with the payer. In this case, the campaign money was laundered through a Mexican bank with the aim of disguising that it came from CREEP.

Legislative docket Set of bills and proposals given by the President to Congress.

Legislature In this context, Congress, which makes laws.

Liberalism Toleration and/or approval of federal government interventionism, and 1960s' campaigners such as as feminists and civil rights activists.

Lynch In this context, unlawful killing, usually by hanging, of African Americans that was common, particularly in the South, in the late nineteenth and early twentieth centuries.

Main Street A synonym for the usually conservative, average, ordinary, small-town US resident.

Middle America A term invented by the media to describe ordinary, patriotic, middle-income Americans.

Military–industrial complex Influential figures in the armed forces and defence industry, who profited from war.

MIRANDA Supreme Court ruling that improperly obtained confessions be excluded from trials.

MLB Major League Baseball.

Moratorium In this context, suspension of normal activities to facilitate national anti-Vietnam War protests in 1969.

NAACP The National Association for the Advancement of Colored People was the oldest and most respected black civil rights movement.

NAFTA The North American Free Trade Agreement provided for the gradual elimination of tariffs and other trade barriers between the USA, Canada and Mexico.

Nannygate Two of Clinton's nominees for attorney general were forced to step down when it was revealed that one hired an illegal immigrant as a nanny and another had not paid the relevant Social Security tax.

Nation of Islam   Black separatist religion that considered all whites evil. Also known as Black Muslims.

National Convention   A few weeks before the presidential election the Republicans and Democrats both hold National Conventions in which each party selects or confirms its candidate for the presidency.

National Organisation for Women (NOW)   A pressure group for equal rights for women established in 1966.

Native American reservations   Native Americans were residents of the USA whose ancestors had inhabited the continent before the arrival of white Europeans. Whites had confined Native Americans to lands called reservations.

New American Revolution   Nixon's plan to devolve power from the federal government to state governments, to decrease bureaucracy and save money.

New Deal   Roosevelt's plan to get the USA out of the 1930s' Depression; an unprecedented programme of federal aid to those most in need.

New Economic Policy   Nixon's new policy of August 1971 froze wages and prices for 90 days. When he discovered that Lenin had had an NEP, he dumped the phrase but not the policy.

New Federalism   Nixon's plans to redirect power away from Congress and the federal bureaucracy, and back to the states and local communities, who could spend it on education and other local issues as needed.

New Left   Student group of the early 1960s, who wanted greater racial and economic equality and an end to social conformity.

New Right   This group of right-wing voters became influential in the late 1970s; their beliefs were a reaction to the counterculture of the 1960s, and included opposition to abortion, busing and Darwinism.

NFL   The National Football League.

NLF   Vietnamese Communist National Liberation Front.

NSC   The National Security Council advised the President on foreign policy.

Off-year elections   Also called congressional mid-term elections. Elections in the middle of a President's four-year term.

Panama Canal   The US built (1903–13) and ran the canal, which bisected North and South America, thereby joining the Pacific and the Atlantic. By the 1970s, some Americans thought the Canal Zone should be returned to the Panamanians.

Pentagon Papers   A collection of government documents that reflected badly on the Democratic presidents who had got the USA into Vietnam. The papers were leaked to the press by civil servant Daniel Ellsberg.

Planks   Stated policies of a candidate in an election.

Pledge of allegiance   Every morning, schoolchildren and their teachers stand before, and pledge allegiance to, the US flag.

'Plumbers'   Those on the White House staff whose job it was to halt leaks of information.

Politics of party and politics of personality   When political parties are relatively weak, they lack funding, so candidates have to raise funds for themselves. It was easier for a charismatic personality such as Reagan to raise funds when he ran for political office. Reagan represented the replacement of the politics of party with the politics of personality.

Pork-barrel politics   When a legislator will not pass legislation unless he can see benefit for his own constituents.

Poverty line   An amount set by the US government; those whose annual family income is below this are legally defined as 'poor', which is important for federal aid entitlements.

Prep school   Fee-paying school for the children of the wealthy élite.

Press the flesh   The handshaking done by US political candidates.

Primary   Before a presidential election, the Democrats and Republicans hold a kind of competition or mini-election in every state. In this competition, which is mostly called a primary, they decide which candidate they would like to represent their party in the election.

Psychobiographer   Writers of biographies who seek explanations for their subject's later actions in their youth and family background.

Quaker   A Christian group emphasising pacifism and silent meditation.

Quotas   The setting aside of a number of places for ethnic minorities or other disadvantaged groups.

Ratification   Any amendments to the US constitution have to be ratified by three-quarters of the states.

Reaganomics   Reagan's economic philosophy, which emphasised low taxes and deregulation, which it was thought would stimulate the economy.

Redneck   Poorly educated, working-class white Southerner, frequently characterised by racism and beer drinking.

Religious right   Although not all members of the New Right were religious, members of the Religious Right were usually part of the New Right.

ROE vs WADE   The Supreme Court decision legalising abortion.

Rust Belt   The old manufacturing areas of the Eastern seaboard and the Midwest, where the old industries had declined and mostly disappeared.

SALT   The Strategic Arms Limitation Treaty signed by Nixon and the Soviet leader Brezhnev in 1972.

Saturday Night Live   A popular TV programme starring comedians such as Chevy Chase.

'Saturday Night Massacre'   When Nixon sacked the Watergate special prosecutor and the attorney general resigned.

Savings-and-loan   A kind of bank.

Segregationist   Someone who believed in the separation of African Americans and white people, on the grounds of black inferiority.

Social Security   A highly valued entitlement that insured 140 million people and sent benefit cheques to around 36 million retirees, disabled workers and their families, and survivors of deceased workers. It totalled $161 billion in 1980.

Southern Strategy   Nixon's plans to win Southern voters from the Democrats.

Sovietise   Resemble the social and political structure of the USSR.

Staffers   In this context, the White House staff.

Stagflation   Slow economic growth, with high unemployment and rising prices.

State legislatures   While Congress makes laws that apply to all US states, each state has its own legislature that makes laws on local issues, for example, crime.

Status quo   The current state of affairs.

Students for a Democratic Society (SDS)   Student society established in 1960, aiming for a greater political and social freedom and equality.

Sun Belt   States in the South, Southeast and Southwest USA, with warm climates, ranging from North Carolina in the East to California in the West.

Super Tuesday   A day on which there are several primaries is known as 'Super'.

Supply-side economics   Focusing on the supply rather than the demand in an economy. In practice, this meant government should concentrate on achieving inflation-free economic growth, rather than on unemployment and providing welfare state safety nets.

Supreme Court   Rules on whether or not laws and actions are in line with the Constitution.

SUVs   Suburban utility vehicles are bulky, with around eight passenger seats and low mileage per gallon.

Swing voters   Those whose pattern of voting depends on their individual response to each issue; they are not tied to a particular party line.

Teamsters   Truck drivers.

Teflon President   When policies went wrong, the people believed Reagan was not too closely involved; the blame never stuck to him. (Teflon is a non-stick material used in saucepans, etc.)

Texaco   A US oil company.

Ticket   Party candidates nominated for President and Vice President constitute that party's 'ticket'.

Title VII   The anti-sex discrimination section of the 1964 Civil Rights Act.

Tower Commission   Reagan appointed a commission headed by Texas Republican Senator John Tower to investigate Iran-Contra. The report was published in February 1987.

Traditional Democrats   Liberals such as Senators Kennedy and McGovern still wanted massive federal intervention and expenditure to make the USA a more equal society, following in the tradition of the New Deal and Great Society.

Triangulation strategy   Clinton presented himself as a moderate, standing between the liberals and conservatives.

Trillion   One million million or a thousand billion.

Uncle Sam   A cartoon-like drawing of a distinguished looking man with the US flag on his clothing became very famous. He was taken to represent the government of the nation.

Unions   Groups of workers (for example, teamsters) organised themselves into unions in order to negotiate better pay and/or working conditions.

Voodoo economics   When Bush gave this description to Reagan's economic policies, he meant that they would need some kind of magic to work effectively.

Wall Street   The financial centre of the USA, whose big-earners traditionally vote Republican.

The Waltons   A popular, long-running (1972–81) TV series about an idealised family living through the Depression.

Watershed   In this political and social context, a turning point.

Welfare   Since Roosevelt's New Deal, the USA had a welfare safety net, which helped the very poor, sick, unemployed and elderly in varying degrees.

Welfare state   A nation in which the government ensures that, 'from the cradle to the grave', citizens are cushioned against poverty and ill-health.

Whitewater   The name by which some of the Clintons' property deals while in Arkansas were known.

Women's lib   The women's liberation movement developed in the 1960s, aiming for gender equality.

Yale   Yale and Harvard are the most prestigious universities in the USA.

Youth International Party   A radical student group that wanted to show contempt for the political system during the Democratic Party Convention at Chicago in 1968.

Index

Abortion 41, 46, 69, 83, 93–4, 112, 118, 120, 130, 132, 146–7, 153–4, 163, 170–1, 181, 216

Affirmative action 35–6, 66, 83, 93, 129–31, 146–7, 162, 180, 210

African Americans 3–8, 11, 15–17, 29–30, 32, 34–6, 38, 46, 66, 72–4, 76–7, 79, 83–5, 87–8, 91–2, 101, 118, 130–1, 135, 138, 140, 149, 154, 160–1, 168–70, 196, 198–202, 206, 208–14, 217

Agnew, Spiro 29–30, 32, 43, 52, 61, 67–8

Aid to Dependent Children (ADC) 128, 168

AIDS 119, 135, 148, 206–7

Asian Americans 131, 149, 208–9, 213

Baker, James 110, 115, 124

Baltimore 17, 29, 83

Billygate 66, 81–2, 88, 92

Black Power 5, 36, 38, 200

Blacks *see* African Americans

Blue-collar workers 16, 33–4, 46, 84, 91, 103, 123, 164

Bork, Robert 96, 117–20, 123, 131, 172, 177, 215, 218

Boston 17, 66, 73, 110

Budget (federal) 33, 42, 60, 85, 87, 96, 98, 104, 106–13, 116, 124, 126–30, 135, 141, 145–6, 155, 158–9, 164–5, 167, 170–1, 174, 176, 180–1, 185, 192, 221

Bush, George H.W. 102, 120–1, 133, Chapter 5 *passim*, 158–9, 162–3, 171, 174, 180, 194

Busing 20, 34–5, 73, 83, 93, 112, 130, 147

California 5–6, 10–11, 16–19, 22, 39, 85, 98, 100–1, 143, 152, 214, 218

Carter, James (Jimmy) 58, 66–7, 75–92, 98, 102–5, 107–11, 126, 128, 133, 135, 159, 177, 205

Catholic voters 103

Chicago 1, 2, 4, 9–12, 31–2, 42, 131, 149

Chicanos 6, *see also* Hispanic Americans and Latinos

CIA (Central Intelligence Agency) 48, 50, 53, 70–1, 77, 138

Civil rights 3–4, 12–13, 38–9, 145, 156, 176, 204–5

Clinton, Hillary 52, 154, 158, 160, 165–8, 178–9, 190

Clinton, William (Bill) 138, 152–5, Chapter 6 *passim*

Cold War 1–3, 7–8, 10, 15–16, 20, 22–4, 44–5, 71, 74, 76, 78–9, 88–9, 93, 98, 113, 121–3, 133–5, 142, 150, 155, 188, 196, 205, *see also* Vietnam War

Colson, Charles 47–51, 55, 63

Congress 20, 22–4, 36–7, 51–6, 58–60, 66–8, 70–1, 80–2, 86, 88, 90, 92, 96, 103–6, 108–12, 114–18, 120, 123, 126, 128–35, 141, 143–7, 151, 154, 158–9, 164–7, 169–77, 180–1, 183–7, 189, 191–3, 215

Contract with America 158, 174–6

Counterculture 10–12, 40–1, 46, 93, 142, *see also* Culture wars

Creationism 93, 119, 216, 219

Crime 30, 72, 91, 93, 100, 120, 140, 154, 161, 176, 198, 211, 217–18, *see also* Law and order

Culture Wars 186, 208, 215–19, *see also* Counterculture

Dean, John 20, 47–8, 51–2, 63, 76

Democratic National Convention – Chicago of 1968: 1–2

Democratic Party 3, 5, 7–12, 18, 23–4, 29–32, 34, 45–6, 49–50, 78–9, 84–8, 91–2, 103–5, 109–10, 112–14, 116, 131, 133, 141, 146, 154, 159, 164, 168, 170–1, 173, 176–7, 180–1, 184–6, 188, 190, 192–3, 221; New Democrats 160–4, 166, 180, 192–3; Old Democrats or Traditional Democrats 87, 91–2, 109, 129, 160–1, 163–4, 166–7, 169, 180

Deregulation 87, 107–8, 112, 128–9, 136, 156, 197, 204–5

Detroit 72, 86, 102, 131

Dole, Robert (Bob) 75–6, 159, 164, 166, 171, 176, 180–1

Drugs 10–11, 39–40, 46, 69, 119, 147–50, 196–200, 211, 218

Dukakis, Michael 139–40

Economy 22–3, 43, 46, 76–8, 84, 86–7, 91, 102–3, 105–9, 111, 113–14, 125–7, 135, 139, 152–3, 155, 162, 180–1, 192, 208, 220–1

Education 59, 72–4, 125, 128, 131, 143–4, 160, 192, 198–202, 204–5, 211, 214

Ehrlichman, John 20, 47–9, 52, 57, 60, 63, 67

Elections
  Congressional, 39, 70–1, 103, 109, 114,
    133, 145, 166–7, 174, 180, 183, 186
  presidential
    1968: 1–3, 5–10, 15–19, 22, 25–33
    1972: 33–46, 49–50; 1976 66, 74–7, 79
    1980: 80–94, 102–3, 176–7
    1984: 113–14; 1988 129, 138–40, 177
    1992: 138, 152–5, 158, 161–2
    1996: 158, 170–1, 180–1
    2000: 221–2
Energy crisis 66, 74, 78–80, 82, 86–8, 92, 105,
  111, 165
Environment 43–4, 46, 76–7, 79, 85–6, 91,
  107, 116, 129, 136, 138, 142–4, 155–6,
  160, 194, 217
Equal Rights Amendment (ERA) 69, 72, 83,
  93, 96, 132

FBI (Federal Bureau of Investigation) 22,
  48–50, 53, 76, 88–91
Federal government (including 'big
  government' debate) 19, 23, 26, 30, 33,
  36, 42–3, 59, 78–9, 87, 92–3, 100, 104–8,
  112, 127, 130, 134, 159, 161, 167, 170,
  174, 176, 192–3, 219
Feminism 1–2, 13–14, 17, 93, 147, 153, 156,
  160, see also 'Women's lib'
Florida 17–19, 89, 154, 163–4
Ford, Gerald 15, 21, 23, 29, 57–8, 61–3,
  66–79, 98, 101, 104–5, 108, 111, 126,
  133, 135

Georgia 17–18, 77–8
Ghettos (and urban blight) 4, 8, 16, 30, 32,
  34, 72, 77, 79, 84–5, 88, 131, 149, 163,
  168, 211
Gingrich, Newt 158, 166, 172–7, 179, 184,
  190, 193
Goldwater, Barry 25, 29, 52–3, 56, 71, 127
Gore, Al(bert) 158–9, 163, 186–7, 193–4,
  221–2
Great Society 7, 9, 26, 36, 42, 134
Gun control 164, 170–1

Haldeman, Robert (Bob) 20, 26–7, 47, 50–3,
  59, 63
Health 59, 79, 85, 87, 135, 158–9, 161, 163,
  166–7, 170, 180–1, 192; Medicaid 119,
  135, 166, 169, 221; Medicare 112, 119,
  128, 135, 164, 167
Hippies 10–11, 17, 30, 219
Hispanic Americans 6, 131, 208–14, see also
  Chicanos and Latinos
Homosexuals 17, 34, 93–4, 147, 153, 162,
  167, 177, 206–7, 218

Humphrey, Hubert 1, 9, 15, 22, 29, 31–2, 45,
  62
Hunt, E. Howard 48–50, 63

Immigrants 165, 167, 169, 208–10
Impeachment 53–6, 58, 117, 159, 176, 183–5,
  187
Inflation 32–3, 42–3, 74, 76, 86–8, 105, 111,
  127, 145, 180, 192, 221
Iran-Contra scandal 96, 98, 115–18, 123, 133,
  136
Iranian hostages 78, 81, 88, 90–2, 103

Jewish vote 90
Johnson, Lyndon 1–3, 7–9, 15, 25–6, 28,
  30–2, 38, 42, 45, 104–5

Kennedy, Edward (Ted) 45, 48–9, 62, 73, 87–9
Kennedy, Robert (Bobby) 1–2, 5–9
Kent State 12, 20, 38–9
King, Martin Luther 1–5, 8–9, 168

Latinos 149, 208–14, see also Hispanic
  Americans
Law and order 12, 30, 32, 34, 37, 46, 84,
  163–4, see also Crime
Lewinsky, Monica 152–3, 181–7, 191, 193
Liddy, Gordon 48–50, 63

Magruder, Jeb 48, 51, 63
McCarthy, Eugene 3, 5, 7–8
McCord, James 48, 50, 63
McGovern, George 20, 22, 45–6, 87, 94
Media 3, 8, 22, 25, 33, 37, 45, 47–8, 51, 55,
  58, 69, 71, 81, 93, 101, 109–10, 113–14,
  116–17, 130–1, 135, 140–2, 144, 151,
  153, 165, 171, 176–8, 183, 186, 213, 217
Medicaid and Medicare see Health
Meese, Edwin 107, 115, 120
Middle America 15–20, 29–30, 34, 39–41, 43,
  46, 92, 119
Mitchell, John 47, 49–52, 63
Moral Majority 92–3, 132, 146
Music 135, 217
Muskie, Edmund 45, 49–50

NAFTA (North American Free Trade
  Agreement) 152–3, 158–9, 164–5, 170,
  185, 192
National Organisation for Women (NOW) 13,
  118, 147, 204, 215
Native Americans 7–8, 208, 213–14
New Deal 19, 24, 26, 98, 111, 127, 133–4
New Federalism (New American Revolution)
  43, 59, 128
New Left 12, 41

New Right 92–4, 146, 153, *see also* Religious Right
New York City 11, 17, 72–3, 135, 147, 188, 217
Nixon, Richard 1–2, 9, 12, 15–19, Chapter 2 *passim*, 66–70, 75, 81, 101, 104, 108, 111, 126, 133, 135, 139, 153, 172

O'Neill, Tip 58, 80, 82, 102, 106, 109–11, 123, 128, 134, 173–4

Perot, Ross 154–5
Polls 15, 31, 36, 38, 54–6, 61, 81, 86, 88–9, 109, 113, 130, 133, 180, 183–4, 190
Protests 9–12, 15–16, 20, 26, 33–4, 38–9, 46, 54, 148

Quotas 66, 83, 145, 147

Reagan, Ronald 11, 23, 27–9, 39, 59, 66–8, 71–2, 74–8, 86–8, 91–2, Chapter 4 *passim*, 138–42, 144, 147, 149, 153–4, 161, 177, 198, 204–5
Reaganomics 106–8
Regan, Donald 115–16, 124–5
Religious Right 92–4, 112–14, 118–19, 132, 136, 140, 216, 219, *see also* New Right
Republican Party 18, 22–5, 27–8, 30, 34–5, 43, 46, 56, 58, 61, 67–8, 70–1, 74, 76–7, 90, 92, 98, 101–5, 116–17, 133, 140, 146, 153–4, 158–9, 167, 171–7, 181, 184–7, 190, 192–3, 204, 218
Riots 5, 12, 16, 26, 29–30, 32–4, 38, 54, 66, 73, 82–4, 101, 138, 148–9, 154, 198, 210
Rockefeller, Nelson 29, 68, 71, 74
ROE vs WADE 69, 93, 120, 146
Rust Belt 123, 128, 220–1

Sex 11, 31, 39, 93, 119, 136, 198, 216–17
Sexual equality 11, 13–14, 34, 41, 72
Silent majority *see* Middle America
Simpsons, The 142, 214
Snow Belt 85
Social security 85, 96, 108–9, 111–12, 128, 130, 145, 164, 167
South (and Southern Strategy) 4, 23, 29–30, 33, 35, 46, 79, 113, 154, 176, 216

Sport Chapter 7 *passim*, 217, 219; drugs 196–9; Olympics 113–14, 196, 200, 205–6; racial equality 196, 199–202; sexual equality 132, 196, 202–6
Starr, Kenneth 179, 181–7, 190
State laws 30, 78, 100, 106, 119–20, 127–8, 143, 146, 163, 170
Students 2–3, 9–12, 14–16, 37–42, 101
Sun Belt 17–19, 34, 85, 92, 216
Supply-side economics 107, 123
Supreme Court 20–1, 34–5, 42, 53, 61, 66, 72, 74, 83, 96, 117–18, 120, 130–2, 146–7, 152, 163, 170, 177, 182, 211, 215, 221

Taxation 30, 32, 36, 42, 59, 70, 74, 85, 88, 96, 98, 100–1, 106–9, 111–13, 116–17, 123, 129, 134, 145, 152–3, 156, 160–1, 164–7, 171, 176, 180, 192, 220
Terrorism 186–91, 213
Tet Offensive 1–3
Texas 11, 17–18, 24, 164, 199

Unemployment 72, 74, 83–4, 86, 88, 91–2, 103, 105, 107, 111, 127, 152, 180, 192, 210, 221
Unions 36, 46, 74, 79, 84–7, 92, 99, 103, 126, 160, 188, 209–10, 220

Vietnam War 1–3, 7–8, 10, 15–16, 23, 26–8, 31–4, 38–9, 42, 44–7, 49, 53–4, 58, 68, 70, 77, 79, 98, 104–5, 111, 135, 140, 151, 162, 176, *see also* Cold War

Wallace, George 15, 29, 33, 45
Washington DC 17, 37, 39, 50, 83, 149, 169
Watergate 20–3, 46–64, 67–8, 71, 79, 81, 98, 104–5, 111, 176
Welfare 30, 33, 35–6, 74, 77, 79, 83, 98, 100, 106, 108–9, 112, 127–8, 130, 135, 159, 161, 167–71, 174, 176, 180–1, 185, 192, 200, 210
Women 41–2, 46, 72, 77, 83, 103, 118, 132, 135, 144, 147, 152, 154–5, 181, 196, 198, 202–5, 208, 214–15, *see also* 'Women's lib' and Feminism
'Women's lib' (women's liberation movement) 13–15, 132, 144, 204